Performance

Practical examinations in speech and drama

PAUL RANGER

London New York

E. & F. N. SPON

First published in 1990 by
E. & F. N. Spon Ltd
11 New Fetter Lane, London EC4P 4EE

Published in the USA by
E. & F. N. Spon
29 West 35th Street, New York NY 10001

Typeset in 10pt Garamond
by Scarborough Typesetting Services

Printed in Great Britain by
T. J. Press (Padstow) Ltd, Padstow, Cornwall

ISBN 0 419 14460 9

British Library Cataloguing in Publication Data
Ranger, Paul
    Performance: practical examinations in speech and drama.
    1. England. Secondary schools. Curriculum subjects:
    Drama. G.C.S.E. examinations. Techniques
    I. Title
    792′.076
    ISBN 0–419–14460–9

Library of Congress Cataloging in Publication Data
Available

Contents

Acknowledgements

A book such as this depends on the help of institutions and of individuals.

I am grateful to those examining boards on which I have learnt through practical experience my craft and which have formed my attitude towards evaluating performances in speech and drama: the Associated Examining Board, the London Academy of Music and Dramatic Art, the London and East Anglian Group for the General Certificate of Secondary Education, the London College of Music, the Poetry Society and the School of Education of the University of Southampton.

I am grateful, too, to those boards which arranged for me to meet administrators and examiners: the Associated Board of the Royal Schools of Music, the Associated Examining Board, the London Academy of Music and Dramatic Art, Mountview Drama Performance Grades, the New Era Academy of Drama and Music, the Poetry Society, the Royal Academy of Music and Trinity College of Music.

Many people have contributed material and opinions which have shaped this work and I acknowledge with gratitude the contributions of the following: Kenwyn Beard, Bob Cheeseman, Irene Cockin, Greta Colson, Beryl Cook, Rosemary Costi, Tom Durham, Julia and Natalie Fellowes, Doreen Fisher, Donald Gulliver, Malcolm Higgins, Marie-Claire Hussein, Ellen Ismay, Muriel Judd, Carol Lamont, Myrtle Moss, David Owen-Bell, Kenneth Pickering, Christopher Purple, Patricia Rudd, Christine Simms, Joan Skipper, Lisa Solomons, Margaret Thomas, Brian Tilston, and Yvonne Wells.

I am further indebted to those on the above list who most generously provided hospitality as I traversed the south of England seeking information.

Paul Ranger
Oxford

1

An introduction to speech and drama examinations

1.1 THE APPEAL OF DRAMA

If a group of people connected professionally with drama was to be asked, 'Why do you give your life to drama? What do you get out of it?' the responses would be very varied. An actor might reply that he enjoyed the challenge of taking on a role, and testing that role in a particular set of circumstances evaluated by the critical eye of his audience. On the other hand a director might think of himself as an artist working in many media using performers, writers, lighting technicians and scene constructors in creating a highly complex work of art which for a couple of hours becomes a living shared experience. A playwright in the group might say that she felt impelled to explore some of the problems she encountered through her plays, and she may cite such difficult situations as parents with a disabled child or the intolerance of the police in their treatment of a family with a criminal record. Someone else in the group might have an academic interest in drama; he would discover layers of meaning beneath the surface of the play and his writings would help to give substance to an actor's interpretation of a character. So drama draws into itself people with many interests and specialisms.

This is a book primarily for students of drama, although I hope their teachers will also find it of interest. The very fact that you are reading this book indicates that you already take a serious interest in drama, and possibly you recognized yourself in the approach of the people in the group of the previous paragraph. A study of drama is a study of a living art and your vision of it will extend: gradually the incipient actor will see beyond his role to the play as a whole; the fledgling director's understanding will expand and he will see that actors are not representative characters to whom he must give moves, but people motivated by desires and thoughts; the literary scholar will want to try out her theories about a play by taking part in it as an actor so that she gains insight from her participation.

I hardly need to point out that drama is a social activity. It is impossible for a person living in complete isolation to perform, for a basic requirement is someone to perform to. Usually drama requires a group of people to make it live, for there must be other actors, as well as people with expertise in music, making costumes and sets and writing or originating ideas. We can study not only how this expertise is mastered but also the ways in which the group of experts work together and here we arrive at an important area for the purposes of this book – we can study the ways in which people reach out from their area of performance to that seemingly passive group of people interacting with them, the audience. That outreach is the subject of this book: communication through speech and drama. It encompasses communication through the written word, whether it is drama, verse or prose, as well as communication through talking and reading aloud. Drama, however, remains at its heart, for the skills we acquire through drama can be transferred to other areas of communication.

1.2 THE STUDY OF DRAMA

I've already stressed that drama means different things to different people, and as you have shown that you are interested in drama, there are a variety of ways in which you can engage in it. For some, drama will be a hobby for the evenings. You may want to join a society in your area which regularly stages plays. For others, drama will be a subject to be studied, and I've assumed that you are one of these people. I want to suggest to you two possible routes for your study. The first is to undertake a course which has a pre-set syllabus and works towards a given goal, an examination. Here are three examples of such a course:

1. If you are at school there may be an opportunity to take the General Certificate of Secondary Education in Drama and Theatre Arts. This is a flexible course composed of a number of units which include acting.
2. Also school- or college-based is the Associated Examining Board's A-level in Theatre Studies, composed of a balance of study and expression.
3. If you have completed your full-time education you can still take the A-level in Theatre Studies by enrolling as a part-time evening student at a college of further education or a technical college. The course is then specially adapted for those who can only give a limited amount of time a week to it.

The other route I want to suggest is a more flexible one. It is to study with a private teacher qualified in speech and drama. He or she will tailor-make a course for you and within this you can measure your progress by taking examinations offered by the various private boards.

Examinations play a significant part whichever route you take, for they are a component of the study method. They give you an opportunity to show your work to an examiner, who may be regarded as a member of a representative audience. He or she will evaluate your presentation and let you know, by their comments and marks, how they think your work stands at the time you appear before them. In the first route I have outlined, the examination marks the termination of the course; in the second, examinations may be seen as a series of milestones measuring your progress. These examinations can be a valuable focus for a student's work, although I believe that the study of drama must be a liberal one and the subject should in no way be constricted to last-minute cramming. I myself am an examiner for both public and private boards, and, of course, I have also taken some examinations. The purpose of this book, as its title suggests, is to relate the study of drama to examinations, and I regard them as a helpful part of the process.

1.3 DIFFERENT TYPES OF EXAMINATIONS

1.3.1 Public examinations

Let us now consider in some detail the two routes I have sketched out. The first is based on study by means of a pre-set syllabus leading to a public examination.

(a) *General Certificate of Secondary Education: Drama and Theatre Arts*

Southern Examining Group, Stag Hill House, Guildford, Surrey GU2 5XJ.

In this book I am using the Drama and Theatre Arts course and examinations of the Southern Examining Group as a model. Similar examinations are provided by GCSE boards throughout England and Wales and details of these are given in the Resources section of this chapter.

In addition to the written papers, this examination consists of a series of four components: acting, design, improvisation and dance drama; the candidate selects either one or two of these components to present at his own school to the examiner who will be one of his own teachers. Opportunity exists also for candidates to keep a written record of theatre events they have attended during the course. The course is designed to extend over two years, and is taken alongside other courses as part of the student's full-time education.

(b) *A-level: Theatre Studies*

Associated Examining Board, Stag Hill House, Guildford, Surrey GU2 5XJ.

The practical element of this examination consists of an original theatrical project evolved by a group of between five and nine candidates, and the demonstration of an individual skill which is selected from one of the following: acting, stage design, costume, lighting, sound, masks, puppets and visual images. Work is presented in theatrical conditions at the candidates' own school or college and is assessed by a visiting examiner. The full-time course normally extends over two years. This course may also be taken by candidates attending a college on a part-time basis.

1.3.2 Private examinations

The second route is by means of studying with the help of a private teacher and taking the examinations of one of the speech and drama boards. I would suggest that before you start looking at the plethora of examinations offered you find a teacher of speech and drama. It is important that the person you choose is qualified: the Society of Teachers of Speech and Drama maintains a register, regularly updated, containing the names of qualified and experienced specialists who have been elected to membership. Copies of the register may be seen in many public libraries. Membership is drawn from teachers throughout the United Kingdom and Ireland and so you should have no difficulty in finding someone living within reasonable distance of yourself. If you do experience problems though, or would like further advice, contact the secretary of the society. Details are given in the Resources section of this chapter.

Phone the teacher you have decided to approach, making an appointment to see him. During your visit explain that you wish to make a serious study of drama and that you would like to use the examinations offered by the various independent boards as part of this study. Give the teacher a clear indication of the experience you have of the subject. Remember to ask about the fees charged. If the teacher can accept you, at this stage you are under no obligation to commit yourself, and it is wise to thank him for his time and say that you will write to him later with your decision. Before doing this, think carefully whether you feel the teacher will suit your personality: this person is not only going to be a guide, he will also be a sounding board for many of your ideas and performances.

Speech, drama and examinations in allied subjects are organized by a number of boards, each of which produces a syllabus. Your teacher will enter regularly candidates for one or more of these boards. Nevertheless, it is worthwhile sending for several syllabuses so that you can decide on the examination which covers the areas in which you are interested. Below I have listed the major examining boards and given a brief summary of the examinations in performance which each offers.

(a) The Associated Board of the Royal Schools of Music, 14 Bedford Square, London WC1B 3JG

Solo speech examinations
A series of examinations beginning with a preparatory and continuing until grade 8. Diploma examinations are not offered. Early grades consist of a poem selected from a given list, prose, which may be spoken from memory or read, sight reading and a discussion. In the higher grades the candidate also gives a prepared talk and there is the additional test of a prepared reading of verse or prose, occasionally both.

Solo acting examinations

A series of examinations from grade 2 through to grade 8. Diplomas are not offered. In grades 2–7 the candidate performs an excerpt from a listed play and an excerpt from a play of his or her own choice; there is also a test of acting at sight and a discussion of the work. The format for grade 8 is different: the candidate prepares a short recital of dramatic pieces; gives a prepared talk on an aspect of theatre and one of the recital excerpts is redirected by the examiner; the work presented is discussed.

The Associated Board also offers examinations in Spoken English, English as a Second Language, Group Acting and Group Speaking.

(b) The Guildhall School of Music and Drama, Barbican, London EC2Y 8DT

Speech and drama examinations

This series of examinations extends from the preliminary to grade 8; a teachers' licentiate diploma is also offered. Junior grades consist of a dramatic or prose excerpt or a poem selected from a list of set pieces, an own choice and a discussion on the selections presented and on technical matters. At senior grades two pieces from set lists are presented; there is sight reading and a discussion on pieces, technique and literary matters. At grade 8 a written paper is set. The diploma examination consists of selections from listed prose, verse and drama, the candidate's own choice, sight reading of prose and verse and a wide ranging discussion on the selection, the psychology of teaching, correction of speech faults, on the 'more important poets and dramatists of English Literature, and particularly those of the twentieth century', and questions on 'the teaching of any subject related to Speech and Drama'; candidates are also required to give a lesson as if to a class of students, the subject of which is selected immediately prior to the examination from a list. There are also three written papers.

Solo acting examinations

A series of eight grade examinations, a certificate and a licentiate diploma in solo acting. The junior grades consist of a dramatic piece of the candidate's own choice, a prepared mime and a discussion. At the level of the senior grades the work is more focused; various authors are stipulated for an excerpt from a period play; an excerpt from a modern play is also presented; the candidate is directed by the examiner and there is a discussion of the work. At grade 8 an improvisation is given. The certificate requires the candidate to perform three excerpts from a range of verse, period and modern plays, perform an improvisation, speak two dialects and take direction from the examiner. The licentiate examination consists of an anthology programme built around a theme selected from a given list; there are tests in sight reading and dialect speaking and an opportunity to work under the direction of the examiner.

The Guildhall also offers examinations in Verse Speaking, Duo Acting, Group Acting, Group Speaking and Choral Speaking.

(c) The London Academy of Music and Dramatic Art, Tower House, 226 Cromwell Road, London SW5 0SR

Examinations in the speaking of verse and prose
A series of eight grade examinations, medals, an associate diploma and a teachers' licentiate diploma. Early grades consist of a listed poem and an own choice verse selection. Higher grades restrict the two selected items to listed pieces consisting of verse and prose and, from grade 7, a Shakespeare option; there is a sight reading test and a discussion on the pieces and technicalities. Medal candidates present a Shakespeare excerpt and a selection of prose or verse, all chosen from set lists; sight reading and a discussion are included. The associate diploma consists of a recital based on excerpts selected from a list of stipulated genres. The licentiate examination consists of a Shakespeare selection, one piece of listed verse or prose, sight reading, discussion and a talk on a technical aspect of speech and drama. The candidate writes a dissertation on an aspect of speech and drama.

Acting examinations
A series of eight grade examinations, medals, associate and licentiate diplomas. The junior grades consist of two excerpts of the candidate's own choice from two plays and the senior grades are similar in format. At medals and associate diploma levels three pieces are presented, selected from a set list of playwrights; at associate diploma level candidates are required to 'create a situation around an object or article given by the examiners at the time of the examination'; and there is a sight reading test. Candidates for the licentiate diploma present four scenes, one of which is in dialect; a wide range of choice is allowed in the pieces; an improvisation test is set and there is a sight reading test. This diploma is examined by two professional actors or directors.

LAMDA also offers examinations in Reading, Spoken English, Public Speaking, Choral Speaking, Group Acting, Group Mime and Solo Mime.

(d) The London College of Music, 47 Great Marlborough Street, London W1V 2AS

Speech and drama examinations
The range consists of three steps, eight grades, associate, licentiate and fellowship diploma examinations; there is a teachers' licentiate examination also. At the step level candidates present a piece from set lists and an own choice; questions are asked on the pieces. Early grades consist of a set piece (poetry, prose or drama), an own choice, a sight reading test and questions on theory and the pieces presented. Senior grades consist of three selected pieces, one of which is the

candidate's own choice, together with sight reading, and questions on literature, theory and the pieces presented. At grade 8 a theory paper is set. The associate examination consists of a recital of four pieces, one of which is the candidate's own choice, sight reading and questions on technique and the pieces presented. The format of the licentiate is similar. Papers are set for these two diplomas. The fellowship examination consists of a character study and a recital; no paper is set. Candidates for the licentiate teachers' examination select verse and dramatic excerpts from two set lists and present their own choice of prose; there is a sight reading test and questions are asked on teaching technique, literature and technical theory. Two written papers are also set.

The London College also holds examinations in Public Speaking.

(e) Mountview Drama Performance Grades, Ralph Richardson Memorial Studios, Kingfisher Place, Clarendon Road, London N22

Drama performance examinations

The nine grades offered by Mountview are designed to be sat by candidates in pairs; however, single candidates may enter. In the junior grades candidates present a poem and a dramatic excerpt chosen from lists, a prepared mime, and hold a conversation with the examiner on a subject of mutual interest. As the grades progress the conversation is replaced by an improvisation. From grade 6, recitals on themes replace selections from lists; an improvisation and an unseen audition piece form part of the examination. A diploma is not at present offered.

Mountview also holds grade examinations in Group Performance.

(f) The New Era Academy of Drama and Music (London) Ltd, 173B Streatham High Road, London SW16 1HJ

Speech and drama examinations

Examinations in Speech and Drama are offered at eight grade, medal, associate diploma and licentiate diploma levels. In the junior grades the candidate presents a poem from a set list, another piece of his or her own choice, and discusses the chosen pieces with the examiner. In the senior grades a dramatic selection and sight reading are added and technical matters are included in the discussion. At bronze and silver medal standard the candidate performs a poem from a set list and a scene from a pre-1920 play (bronze) or a selection from a stipulated author (silver). At the gold medal examination the candidate performs either a dramatic or a prose selection, a poem and an improvisation which may take the form of a mime; as an alternative to the improvisation a talk may be substituted; sight reading and a discussion with the examiner on the pieces and on two periods of English literature also feature. Both diplomas are geared towards teaching. At associate level the candidate performs a prose extract from a stipulated author, a poem from a set list and a poem for children; there is a sight reading test and a discussion with the examiner on the 'psychological and educational value of Speech Training and effective vocal communication'. There is also a written paper. At licentiate level the candidate performs an excerpt from a list of dramatic pieces, an own choice dramatic excerpt and a listed poem; there is sight reading and a discussion on the pieces presented, the theory of speech, the educational value of speech and drama and on English literature. Two written papers are set.

Examinations in auditions in stage technique

A series of nine grade examinations, medals and a diploma. In the junior grades the candidate is required to present two dramatic selections. For senior grades sight reading is added and for the advanced grades an excerpt from a period and a contemporary play are required, together with a sight reading test. Examinations at medal and diploma levels consist of selections from a period and a contemporary play, a dialect test, sight reading and an improvisation. Diploma candidates are required to discuss their selections in detail as well as the techniques of stage craft.

The New Era also offers examinations in Spoken English, Interview Technique, Public Speaking, Reading and Bible Reading, Choral Speaking, English as a Second Language, and Mime.

(g) The Poetry Society, 21 Earls Court Square, London SW5 9ED

Spoken poetry examinations

The examinations are offered for candidates from six years old onwards. The level of the examination is determined by the candidate's age. Candidates are 'invited' (the language of the syllabus hints that there is less formality in the Poetry Society examinations than in those of many other boards) to speak two poems from memory. There are no set lists, but the Poetry Society is able to advise candidates and teachers on suitable anthologies for children and adults. After the examination the candidate has an informal discussion with the examiner about the pieces presented.

Poetry and prose anthology examinations

The grading of the candidates is similar to that for the previous examinations but the starting age is eight. Candidates are invited to present a programme of poetry and prose on either a recognized writer or a chosen theme; notes and texts are allowed in the examination room; an informal discussion follows the examination. Senior candidates may enter for the George Rochford Porter award, presenting an anthology based on the work of one of the English Romantic poets.

Poetic form examinations
The examination in Poetic Form is for senior (fifteen to eighteen-year olds) or adult candidates, and consists of a presentation of two poems from memory varying in content and mood. The poems may represent contrasting forms or show two contrasting expressions of the same form.

Adult gold medal examination
The candidate presents, predominantly from memory, a recital programme containing at least three poems and lasting about fifteen minutes.

The Poetry Society also offers examinations in Prose Reading, Original Poetry, a Group Programme and Dramatic Verse.

(h) The Royal Academy of Music, Marylebone Road, London NW1 5HT

Licentiate teachers' examination in speech and drama
Candidates are required to present a memorized programme of poetry and drama of two selected periods; this is to include a passage of read prose; a demonstration lesson must be given to a class provided; there is a viva on the material presented, technical skills and the demonstration lesson. There are two written papers.

Licentiate performers' examination in speech and drama
The candidate is required to present from memory a programme of poetry and drama on a chosen theme; sight reading, consisting of a speech from Shakespeare and a speech from a modern play, is set, as is an improvisation in which the candidate performs the central role, a provided group taking other parts. There is no written paper.

(i) Trinity College of Music, 11–13 Mandeville Place, London W1M 6AQ

Speech and drama examinations
There is an initial and eight grade examinations; outside the United Kingdom and the Irish Republic an associate diploma examination is offered; a licentiate diploma examination for teachers and performers is also offered. The basis of the grades is a performance of two pieces (a choice of poetry, prose or drama), an improvisation, reading at sight from a prepared book, and questions on the theory of speech and the selections performed. Considerable latitude is allowed in the choice of pieces. In the senior grades an extra piece is set and the candidate is required to give an impromptu talk. From grade 5 a written paper is set. At associate level candidates perform an extract from two contrasting plays; they speak from memory a lyric poem, and either a passage of narrative verse or prose;

there is a sight reading test; an impromptu speech is given on an aspect of teaching or performance, according to one's option; questions are asked on teaching methods and materials (for those taking the examination as teachers) or on technical aspects of performance (for performers); questions are asked on the presented selection and on the literary background. There is a written paper.

For the licentiate performers' examination the candidate presents a recital of dramatic excerpts and of verse and prose; there is a test of sight reading; a discussion is held on a play of the candidate's choice from which he or she reads a selection chosen by the examiner; questions are asked on the works presented and their background and on technical and artistic aspects of performance. A written paper is set.

For the licentiate teachers' examination the candidate presents a recital of the same format as that stipulated for the performers' examination; sight reading is set and questions are asked on the presented pieces and their background, and on teaching methods, materials and philosophy relating to the candidate's special teaching interests in speech and drama. A written paper is set.

Trinity also offers examinations in Effective Speaking, Group Drama and Choral Speaking.

Although I have given a summary of the requirements of the various examinations, these are merely for your own perusal and it is imperative that you send for a copy of the syllabus of the board of your choice, addressing your request to the Examinations' Administrator. You will find that more detailed instructions and advice are given in this.

Examinations are held at the centres listed (this does not apply to the New Era Academy) and, with the exception of the Royal Academy of Music, local centres are established throughout the United Kingdom, the Irish Republic and in certain overseas areas. A number of boards hold an examination session at the end of each collegiate term. LAMDA has a wider spread of dates than many boards and the Poetry Society does not restrict its examining to certain times, but will send an examiner to a centre throughout the year.

1.4 LEVELS AND STANDARDS

You must decide at which level you will take an examination and here your teacher is the best person to guide you. Such factors as your age, ability and experience have to be taken into account. Throughout this book I am using a number of case studies, most based on my own students and examinees, although names have been altered, so that you can envisage your preparation for an examination not in terms of lists of rules, but in terms of the responses of people to challenges. Let us look at a couple of candidates who are thinking about suitable standards and levels.

Mary is a married woman in her thirties who has decided, now that her children are at school, she would like to go to speech classes on Thursday afternoons. The last examination she took was when she was in the fifth form at school, so she does lack experience in examination technique and this poses problems for her in deciding the level at which to enter. As she has had twenty lessons to date, one of the junior grades, say 3, would be a confidence booster provided that appropriate pieces were offered on the selection lists. Let us check the Trinity College speech and drama list at this grade. All of the itemized prose and the alternative drama pieces are geared towards younger candidates; however, there is latitude as any prose work and any play may be substituted for the specified excerpts. This specification is not wasted on the candidate though as it points towards the standard and kinds of literature that are expected. Similarly poetry anthologies, rather than stipulated pieces, are used for the verse selection. Such an approach by the board allows the candidate to select a couple of pieces which reflect a maturity of content and expression, allowing Mary to present her pieces without embarrassment.

Another example: Ben is twelve-years-old. In rapid succession he has taken a number of examinations, perhaps it would have been better if he had engaged in more group work, and now he wants to take the grade 5 examination of the London College. The regulations are that he has to choose one piece from the given lists of prose, poetry and drama excerpts as well as a verse or prose item of his own choice. The latter does not present any problem: he has a lively interest in Ian Fleming's novels and so chooses two paragraphs describing great carnage as an armaments factory is destroyed. The lists of set pieces contain some excerpts which are unsuitable for Ben. He has not yet the emotional capacity to speak with inner passion Ferdinand's declaration of love for Miranda in *The Tempest*, and his voice still lacks the authoritative resonance to cope with a selection from the Authorized Version of the Bible. Knowing his limitations, he chooses Jon Silkin's poem 'Caring for Animals' for it reflects his interest and he can speak it sympathetically. The poem also contrasts with the frenzied action of the prose selection. I hope that these two case studies indicate the kind of considerations you should make in assessing your suitability for a particular grade.

Here I would issue a warning: occasionally mature students attempt a diploma before taking any of the grade examinations. This is most unwise, for the candidate's lack of familiarity with the required standard, as well as a lack of experience in dealing with unknown surroundings and assessors, creates difficulties. Before sitting a diploma a student should cautiously advance by taking a couple of grade examinations. Experienced candidates taking a diploma should be aware that a divide exists in the expectations of examiners between the standard required for grade 8 and the first diploma. Don't think of the diploma merely as a further grade examination. At diploma level the examiners – usually two people make the evaluation – are looking for more than technical ability: the candidate's keen interest in a broad range of theatre and literature should be evident from the performance. A professionalism should be revealed in the strength and suitable style of the performance. Too often diploma work lacks style and for that basic reason the examiners are sadly compelled to fail the presenter. But that ought not to put you off taking a diploma! It is a reminder of the range of work and styles you must be conversant with in your preparation.

Whichever type of examination you decide to embark on, it is most important that you realize, as I've already mentioned in passing, that the study of drama should be a liberal study. Of course, teachers should ensure that this is so, but there is an onus on the student to explore beyond the immediate needs of the syllabus he is following. Be aware of the drama that is being staged in your own neighbourhood by amateurs and professionals. Look at plays on the television. Keep track of reviews in local and national newspapers. All of this is an exercise in awareness and enlarges your vision. Later, in Chapter 9, I elaborate on this in writing about the performer in training.

Once, on the way to a lecture at the Victoria and Albert Museum, I took a group of undergraduate drama students to a gallery in which several eighteenth-century room interiors had been reconstructed and furnished. The previous week the students had been working on Richard Sheridan's comedy *The School for Scandal*, set, for the most part, in London drawing rooms of the same century. A question was asked by one student: 'What relevance has this to us?' Rosemary hadn't seen any connection at all between the setting in the play and a historic example of similar rooms. A flood of questions broke from me: 'What can you learn about Georgian society from the way the furniture is arranged? How does this affect the grouping of characters on stage? How does that in turn determine the direction of conversation? How do you sit on a sofa this shape in a Georgian dress?' and so on. Don't be like Rosemary! Make connections between the world, your own experience and the texts of the novels, plays and poems you read. Widen your vision. In that way you will become a dynamic drama student possessing an awareness that will serve you in good stead at whatever level of examination you take.

1.5 RESOURCES

1.5.1 The Society of Teachers of Speech and Drama

For over eighty years the Society of Teachers of Speech and Drama has elected to membership suitably qualified and experienced teachers. The Society is able to introduce enquirers wishing to study any aspect of speech and drama to members living nearby. The registered office and address of the Secretary is: 73 Berry Hill Road, Mansfield, Nottinghamshire NG18 4RU.

The Society also invites qualified teachers of speech and drama to apply for election to membership. Full details are available from the Secretary.

A twice-yearly journal is issued by the Society, *Speech and Drama*, containing articles of interest to students taking senior grades and diplomas and to people engaged in drama teaching. A specimen copy may be obtained from the Distribution Manager, 23 High Ash Avenue, Leeds LS17 8RS.

1.5.2 Some other drama associations

The following associations may be of interest and help to candidates depending on their areas of specialized interest:

British Association for Drama Therapists, PO Box 98, Kirkbymoorside, York YO6 6EX.

College of Speech Therapists, 6 Lechmere Road, London NW2 5BU.

Dramatherapy Consultants, 6 Nelson Avenue, St Albans, Hertfordshire AL1 5RY (useful for short courses and group meetings).

National Association for the Teaching of Drama (the association usually functions at local level through the office of the County Drama Adviser from whom details may be obtained).

1.5.3 Regional Boards for the General Certificate of Secondary Education

The administration and detailed syllabus planning for all subjects, including Theatre Arts and Oral Communication, offered in the General Certificate of Secondary Education are undertaken by regional boards. The addresses of these are as follows:

London and East Anglian Group, Stewart House, 32 Russell Square, London WC1B 5DN.

Midland Examining Group, Robins Wood House, Robins Wood Road, Aspley, Nottingham NG8 3NR.

Northern Examining Group, 12 Harter Street, Manchester M1 6HL.

Southern Examining Group, Stag Hill House, Guildford, Surrey GU2 5XJ.

Welsh Joint Education Committee, 245 Western Avenue, Cardiff CF5 2YX.

2

Building the programme

2.1 THE CHOICES OFFERED IN AN EXAMINATION

A theatre director once said that preparation for a performance consisted of making decisions and solving problems, and I've found that holds true for examination preparation as much as for rehearsing a show. Once you have decided which examination board suits you and at which level to enter for an examination, you then have to make decisions about the pieces you are going to perform.

Many syllabuses print lists of pieces and you are required to make a selection of two or three. Candidates are often allowed as well to make their own choice of a piece. Let us take an example of these lists. The Guildhall School at grade 6 in Speech and Drama gives two lists: the first is a series of poems ranging from Elizabethan to contemporary and including works by John Milton, Gerard Manley Hopkins and Ruthven Todd; the second list is of excerpts from plays amongst which William Shakespeare is represented but with a refreshing emphasis on worthwhile modern writers such as Harold Pinter, Stephen Poliakoff and Willie Russell. The candidate entering for this examination has to select two pieces, one from each list for presentation. It is advantageous to know that a few boards allow a much wider choice by giving a short list of set pieces, but also letting the candidate make an own selection from nominated anthologies (in Chapter 1 we saw that Trinity College does this) whilst other boards make no specific stipulations. The Poetry Society, for example, states: 'Intermediate, Senior and Adult candidates are asked to present two *contrasting* poems from memory . . .' so in this case a very wide range of work is possible. Some candidates prefer to be directed by set lists and others are happy to read anthologies or collected works in order to make their own selection. Where this freedom of choice is given, several words of advice are necessary. Do choose a poem that is worth working on. Some poems are slight indeed, and may be little more than doggerel with a clever twist added. When I've been adjudicating at festivals I've sometimes sat through classes in which many competitors had chosen swiftly penned lines by Spike Milligan or Ogden Nash, both clever but facile writers whose work does not offer enough substance to get your verse-speaking teeth into, making the text extremely difficult to speak effectively. A poem with which you have to struggle to gain an understanding and sympathy can grow into a strong and authoritative statement especially at the senior grades.

2.2 CONTRASTING POEMS

2.2.1 Two constrasting pieces

If you have the freedom of choice such as the Poetry Society allows, choose two pieces which not only contrast with each other, but also help you to demonstrate a range of vocal and intellectual responses. One poem may be quietly lyrical, such as Robert Browning's reflective 'Home Thoughts from Abroad':

> Oh, to be in England
> Now that April's there,
> And whoever walks in England
> Sees, some morning unaware,
> That the lowest boughs and the brushwood sheaf
> Round the elm-tree bole are in tiny leaf,
> While the chaffinch sings on the orchard bough
> In England – now!

This radiates the sentiment the Romantic poets cultivated. The second stanza of the poem stresses Browning's longing for home by reiterating the images of an English spring – pear trees, hedgerows, birds and fields.

A poem of this century which contrasts strongly in content and form with the Browning is Dylan Thomas's 'Fern Hill'. Again, here is an expatriot looking at a foreign land but this time it is the country of one's own childhood seen from the standpoint of middle-age:

> . . . as I was green and carefree, famous among the barns
> About the happy yard, and singing as the farm was home,
> In the sun that is young once only,
> Time let me play and be
> Golden in the mercy of his means. . . .

Both poems are highly personal: the first is a nostalgic longing for one's homeland, whilst the second is an effusive, autobiographical outpouring. The writer himself speaks, 'as I was green and carefree', and this allows him to make the poem less of an objective description, as with the Browning, and to revel in the urgency and vigour of the lively youngster he once was. There is in this a dynamism absent from 'Home Thoughts', which energy suggests that the pace of the speaking would be faster than the speaking of the Browning, although one must still give the impression of recalling a distant country.

The form as well as the content differs. Firstly 'Fern Hill' is more expansive: there are six stanzas each similar in its pattern of long and short lines. The strong beats of the rhythm sound out more clearly. There is a greater lushness in the word choice, although Browning, in his more economical approach, is more subtle. Thomas revels in alliterative pairings such as 'clear and cold' and 'green and golden'. Certain repeated vowel sounds chime like a bell in the course of a line: 'I was grEEn and carefrEE' is one example. In all of this the speaker must rejoice as much as the poet.

We have considered the contrasts in these two poems. Before we leave them I should say again that they do have a number of points in common: both poems are about a distant experience from which one writer is separated by the sea and the other by time; each writer pictures the scenes he is recalling and for each the vision is a highly personal experience, Thomas's unequivocally autobiographical, a quality which is quietly suggested in Browning's.

2.2.2 The principles of selecting contrasting poems

From considering these two poems as possible material for a recital we can learn certain principles. As we make our selection we must consider *how* the poems contrast. The content may be totally different, with daisies in one poem and dragons in the next. The way in which the poet expresses that content may move the poem from one genre to another: a poet may look at a range of snow-capped hills and think about his response to the beauty of the scene, making a lyrical poem of this sight, or he may use this setting as the background for the activity of a gang of banditti and the shift takes us into a fragment of narrative poetry. The contrast may be in the form of the poems, with one piece, say, in sonnet form, very disciplined, compacted into fourteen lines, a regular rhyming scheme, one thought pursued throughout the piece, compared with a lively example of free verse such as D. H. Lawrence's poem 'The Snake', in which the sinuous length of the creature is suggested by the printed line stretched across the page. We must bear in mind, too, that a passage of time separating two poems helps to create a contrast. In spite of these principles we must also remember that both poems are to be spoken in one recital and so not all contrasts are suitable, and some may jar: a joke poem cannot appropriately follow a lament for a dead lover. A recital should be a unified presentation and we would do well to ensure that the poems spoken contain some common elements.

2.3 PERSONALITY AND CHOICE

We must be aware, too, of our own personality. Whether we have a completely free choice or are required to select from set lists, we shall need to take into account our own personality. 'Know thyself!' Greek sages used to say and this is essential in planning a recital. We must know our own strengths, not only immediately related to speech and drama, but in the wider spheres of life, for we need to place many of our interests and abilities at the service of performance.

2.3.1 Case study: A teenager's personality

Let us look at a candidate and see how she views herself in relation to her choice of programme. Belinda is fifteen and still manages to look like a dumpy little girl, yet she is lively and has a great sense of humour. With her, horses aren't just an interest, they are a passion and she brings to performance the great enthusiasm which she exhibits in her equestrian hobby. She knows that she is primarily an actress, happy to give herself generously to an audience, rather than a disciplined verse speaker. The recognition of this strength should help Belinda choose her pieces. Her teacher, Mrs Everett, is more knowledgeable than Belinda about the girl's limitations: that young lady is immature and it is a good job, Mrs Everett feels, that she has never pictured herself in the role of a romantic heroine, for she has neither the figure for such a part nor the voice to create such a character with credibility. In her own mind Mrs Everett has summed up her student as a 'character actress'. Belinda wants to take the bronze medal of the London Academy of Music and Dramatic Art. She has seen that this is open to people of fifteen and over. Her teacher has some reservations about her readiness for this, but has decided that if Belinda can find two pieces to suit her personality then she will prepare her for the examination. Together they look at the list of pieces: Belinda must perform one Shakespeare piece and speak either a poem or a prose extract. They decide that some of the women's speeches listed need a particular type of actress. Belinda is no Cordelia (*King Lear*) nor has she the dignity and maturity to play Helena (*All's Well that Ends Well*), however, the role of the Hostess in *Henry V* has possibilities. Here is a bustling and often cheerful woman telling of her attendance at the death of Sir John Falstaff, and although the subject is a sad one, a bawdy humour breaks through:

> . . . so a'bade me lay more clothes on his feet: I put my hand into the bed, and felt them, and they were as cold as any stone: then I felt to his knees, and so up'ard and up'ard, and all was as cold as any stone (Act 2. sc. iii).

Belinda knows she can cope with the coarseness of the woman for the dialect helps to make the bawdy an integral part of the characterization.

Belinda enjoys reading novels as well, and she feels that she would prefer to speak an excerpt from one rather than tackle a poem. However, her teacher wisely persuades her to look at several poems before she dismisses the list. 'My Busconductor' instantly appeals, but after some thought Belinda realizes that this has too many affinities with the dramatic selection: in both pieces a woman is recounting the death of a man and in both there is a bitter-sweet approach through pathos and humour; moreover, in spite of the gap of centuries between the two narrations an everyday speech register prevails in both. She jettisoned the poem and turned to two novels. One she was acquainted with from seeing *The Rocky Horror Show*, which she had enjoyed, was Mary Shelley's *Frankenstein*, but on reading it she found the language archaic and difficult to speak, although she realized that one of Mrs Everett's older students was coping with this most successfully. After careful thought Belinda decided on several paragraphs from the penultimate chapter of *Tess of the D'Urbervilles* by Thomas Hardy. The dramatic scenery – the gigantic circle of monoliths at Stonehenge – appealed to Belinda's sense of theatre, and as she read Hardy's words she felt a thrill of excitement pass down her spine:

> . . . he found that what he had come in contact with was a colossal rectangular pillar; by stretching out his left hand he could feel a similar one adjoining. At an indefinite height overhead something made the black sky blacker, which had the semblance of a vast architrave uniting the pillars horizontally.

Some weeks went by as Belinda worked on the pieces and as she became secure in them she realized that not only did they suit her personality with its attachment to characterization and dramatic situations, but they were also allowing her to show the range of her capabilities. In the extract from *Henry V* there was the need to people the stage with imagined characters, for the scene was set outside a London tavern, and that was a specific ability of Belinda's; whilst in *Tess* she was able to speak directly, in her own person, to the audience, describing as a narrator the mystery of Stonehenge. You will see from the amount of time we have spent with Belinda that I think it is fundamental to the construction of a good programme that we must search for pieces which suit our physical, vocal and intellectual strengths; they must be in accord with our maturity and they must convey the range of work we can tackle.

I'm glad that the homely Belinda didn't try to perform the listed role of Cordelia. Once I examined a candidate who presented an excerpt from the scene in which Cordelia comforted Lear at their reunion during the battles. Unfortunately she found it impossible to give any sense of scale to what was happening with the result that the scene became cosily domesticated. It was as if Lear had escaped from an uncomfortable old folks' home to Cordelia's 'semi' in the suburbs. As well as matching our temperament, pieces must be suitable for our age: I have come across some rather elderly Juliets and just as many far-too-young Lady Macbeths. If the part is not suited to our age we cannot reproduce either the passion or the experience which its portrayal requires. We must, too, in our choice make sure that we have the intellectual capacity to understand the layers of meaning contained beneath the surface of the text. In a small Yorkshire town a candidate, only eleven-years-old, presented some lines from John Milton's lament for his drowned friend, *Lycidas*. The poem was beautifully enunciated but the small girl unfortunately was unable to appreciate the many classical allusions or to understand the intellectual depth of the piece. Moreover so young a performer was not able to appreciate the dimension of tragedy in Milton's expression. All of this demonstrates that pieces must be chosen with wisdom and discernment.

2.4 FIVE MODELS

I want to pass from concentrating on the candidate and his or her abilities to considering several programmes which are suitable for different ages and levels and which contain a satisfactory combination of pieces. Our objective will be to consider why the programmes are satisfactory. These programmes are simply models; they are not linked to the particular requirements of any given board.

2.4.1 A six-year-old's choice of programme

When small children, beginners at day school as well as in speech and drama, present a programme it usually consists of two very brief poems. Often I find that the ones chosen are not linked to children's interests and experience and therefore it is difficult for them to make a personal response. The choice reflects the interest which teachers and syllabus makers feel children *ought* to have in a world of puppies, ducks and rain showers! I often have to criticize the lack of contrast between pieces: even six-year-olds are capable of a range of expressive speaking, and this can hardly be demonstrated in the limited range of poetry which is sometimes listed. The two contrasting poems I have selected in this model recital for a six-year-old are:

(a) 'Windy Nights' by Robert Louis Stevenson;
(b) 'Outdoor Song' by A. A. Milne.

Both of these poems appear in the admirable anthology *I Like This Poem* edited by Kaye Webb, who has selected poems from amongst those that children have have suggested for inclusion and grouped them together under the ages of the children.

Stevenson's 'Windy Nights' allows the speaker to draw a picture of a mysterious rider on a dark wet night:

> Whenever the moon and stars are set,
>   Whenever the wind is high,
> All night long in the dark and wet,
>   A man goes riding by.

> Late in the night when the fires are out,
> Why does he gallop and gallop about?

Other factors contribute to the poem, but they are there to assist rather than detract from the image: so there is the effect of the rhythm, suggesting the sound of the galloping hooves, and there is the repetition of the word 'whenever', which creates mystery in its lack of specific time, and there are the changes in the line lengths which engage the speaker's and the listener's attention. The poem has only two verses and the part of the skill in the speaking is to consider why the seeming mirrorings of verse in the second stanza are not in fact exact reflections.

'Outdoor Song' has a strong rhythm as well but this time the rhythm is the all-important factor. Milne helps the speaker by putting into capitals some of the rhythmic key words. He also helps the speaker to find the rhythm in the pattern of words on the page:

> The more it
> GOES – tiddely-pom
> On
> Snowing.

There are four lines here, not two, or even one as speakers sometimes suggest, and only in learning to speak four lines will the performer discover Milne's rhythm. This poem contrasts well with the first because of its sense of fun and humour and with its difference in shape and rhythm. A small girl is quoted in the anthology saying, 'I especially like the "tiddely-poms" which make me laugh'.

We don't always appreciate how mature in response small children can be. In the anthology many six- and seven-year-olds selected the witches' spell from *Macbeth*, 'Double, double, toil and trouble' as a poem they liked, and the thoughts of Marie Harbour reveal her own insight into the meaning and technicalities of the piece which she expresses in her own terms: at first she likens 'fire burn and cauldron bubble' to a volcano, then she goes on to consider the impact of sounds:

> The second 'fire burn and cauldron bubble' is the volcano erupting again. 'Double, double' sounds like my soup boiling. 'Snake, bake' sounds like the fat in the frying pan spitting. 'Frog, dog' sounds like Mummy's cake ingredients going thud in the bowl. 'String, wing' is the cooking starting to hum. The rhyming words sound like the cooking gaining energy. I think that everything the witches put in makes the spell stronger.

2.4.2 An eleven-year-old's choice of programme

In suggesting an anthology for an eleven-year-old boy I had this maturity of insight of some young verse speakers in mind. As before, the recital consists of two poems which are:

(a) 'Consider the Snail' by Thom Gunn;
(b) 'Windy Boy in a Windswept Tree' by Geoffrey Summerfield.

Both of these are, in a sense, nature poems, yet a far cry from the children's painting-book world of nature. Thom Gunn isolates the snail and his natural world, peering at both with the interest of a detailed recorder:

> The snail pushes through a green
> night, for the grass is heavy
> with water and meets over
> the bright path he makes, where rain
> has darkened the earth's dark.

Deliberately the word sweeps are long although, contradictorily, the lines are short, giving a slow but lightly stressed rhythm to the poem. Here, technically, is plenty to work on, especially when the young speaker arrives at the point of appreciating the idea of the harmonization of snail progress with snail passion:

> . . . I would never have
> imagined the slow passion
> to that deliberate progress.

Geoffrey Summerfield's poem explores the kind of kinship with nature that a tree-climbing boy possesses once the wind starts to hurl through an arc the branch to which he clings:

> The branch swayed, swerved,
> Swept and whipped, up,
> Down, right to left,
> Then leapt to the right again,
> As if to hurl him down
> To smash to smithereens
> On the knife-edge grass . . .

Alliteration, mounting pace and intensity and variations in line length are challenges waiting to be explored in the speaking, as well as the boy's ambivalent attitude towards the dangers of the tree and his own safety. But above all there is the speaker's response to this situation and the possibility of relating it to a personal experience of similar adventures.

2.4.3 A teenage girl's choice of programme

The next model envisages a fifteen-year-old girl who is to present a recital made up of a poem and an excerpt from a play:

(a) 'Ian, Dead of Polio' by Elizabeth Bartlett;
(b) A speech of Teresa from scene 1 of *Tuesday's Child* by Terry Johnson and Kate Lock.

'Rather static' is probably your response on reading the pieces, but I have in mind a performer who is shyly aware of her adolescence. Pieces for her must be selected with sympathy and they can also help the teenager to come to terms with the process of growing up. The theme is 'Death and Life'. 'Ian', the title is the name of a dead child, reflects the first element. Its last few lines let us know that this is a mystery poem although there is no need for an artificial questioning style ('upward inflection here') for Elizabeth Bartlett writes all of her poems, however complicated their ideas, in an everyday idiom following natural speech rhythms:

> This was an ordinary child who fled
> From the semi-detached houses,
> And television at five,
> Who died, either in the sterile darkness of the ward,
> At the age of six, or on the road to Leeds, cardboard
> Boxes heaped on the worn back seat, at the age of sixty
> Half in a ditch and smelling of whisky.

In *Tuesday's Child* Teresa, a teenager living in a small Irish town, claims that she has miraculously become a virgin mother. In the excerpt she is kneeling in the confessional talking to Father Doyle about the moment of conception; this she does in a spirit of rapturous happiness, avoiding any lushness in the description:

> . . . he smiles at me. And all the tumble in my mind and all the heat in my body sort of got mixed up together, and that smile seemed to reach down inside me and turn me inside out.

The bubbling effusions of the girl make a pleasing contrast with the quiet reflective nature of the poem, and yet this contrast is kept within bounds so that the change from one piece to another does not jar.

2.4.4 A young woman's choice of programme

Let us look next at a model suitable for a young woman performer aged eighteen, giving a grade recital made up of poetry, prose and a dramatic excerpt. The order is:

(a) An excerpt describing Louis XIV's queen, Marie-Therese of Spain, taken from *The Sun King* by Nancy Mitford;
(b) 'To a Friend with a Religious Vocation' by Elizabeth Jennings;
(c) A speech of Lady Randolph from *Douglas* by John Home.

The three pieces contrast strongly and demand a range of responses from the performer; they are chosen to reveal the ability of a more-than-competent speaker.

There is a homogeneity about the excerpts as each reveals a woman making a response to a situation. They are chosen too as they allow the performer visual variety in her presentation. The anthology could be entitled 'Three Women'.

The first piece from *The Sun King* paints a picture of Marie-Therese of Spain written in Nancy Mitford's inimitably tart style. There is a distancing from the subject in her barbed selectivity:

> . . . she had the mentality of a child, liked to play with little dogs and half-mad dwarfs and never learnt to speak French properly.

One notices the formality of the sentences for they are carefully balanced and this becomes pronounced in her binary structures:

> In spite of a pretty face she was not attractive: she had short legs and black teeth from eating too much chocolate and garlic.

This distancing and formality are pointers to the stance that a performer could adopt: it may be formal, standing and almost demonstrating the objectively observed queen. Once a suitable stance has been decided, the correct tone of voice often follows naturally. In this one would expect an element of satirical comment accompanied by precision in the use of pointing and emphasis. Mitford's style suggests that an audience is being addressed.

Elizabeth Jennings's poem 'To a Friend with a Religious Vocation' is very different in tone. The 'I' of the poem, which is not necessarily the poet herself, is ostensibly writing to a friend:

> Thinking of your vocation, I am filled
> With thoughts of my own lack of one.

Yet this conversation is so quiet, so ruminative, so caught up in the speaker's observations about her own life, that it is as much a voicing aloud of personal indecisions and resolutions as a true dialogue with the recipient. This suggests that the performer could recite the poem with a quiet, interior sincerity, taking the piece slowly and reflecting on the various problems of vocation and authorship that are raised. In turn this suggests that the speaker could sit down, a physical help in gaining the self-contained tone of the poem. A set of sequential ideas is traced painfully but bravely and this demands great concentration from the speaker:

> Your vows enfold you, I must make my own;
> Now this, now that, each one empirical.
> My poems move from feelings not yet known,
> And when the poem is written I can feel
> A flash, a moment's peace.

The curtain will be drawn across your grille.
My silences are always enemies.

The third of the three pieces comes from John Home's play *Douglas* in which Lady Randolph is the tragic heroine. To impersonate her demands a bold style of acting and a wide-ranging, powerful voice, able to rely on the strong rhythms with which Home underpins the dialogue. The pacing across the stage, the dramatic gestures and the declamation create a strong contrast aurally and visually from the performance of the two previous pieces and demonstrate the range of work the candidate can capably present. A detailed description of another candidate performing an extract from this eighteenth-century tragedy is given in Section 5.2.3.

2.4.5 A licentiate candidate's choice of programme

The final model is built on a diploma examination and in this I have assumed that the syllabus for the licentiate allows some freedom of choice, stipulating either one or two contrasting selections of dramatic text together with some prose and poetry. I have assumed, too, that it is desirable to have a theme running through the pieces and that the candidate will introduce this and provide a brief linking commentary. The following pieces constitute the fifteen-minute programme:

(a) The words of William Shakespeare in scene 3 of *Bingo* by Edward Bond;
(b) 'Still Falls the Rain' by Edith Sitwell;
(c) The words of Lear in act 4, scene 6 of *King Lear* by William Shakespeare;
(d) A selection from Chapter 17 of *Elizabeth and Essex* by Lytton Strachey.

The title of the recital is taken from a phrase spoken by Lear, 'The creature run from the cur', a reference to the reaction of sufferers to despotic regimes whatever the period of their establishment. The imagery binds the anthology together, an image such as the stricken Gloriana lying on cushions with her finger in her mouth which questions the nature of authority; authority is undermined, too, in Shakespeare's image of the beadle lusting after the whipped whore, and there is the telling image of the blinded bear, the typification of all suffering, used by both Sitwell and Bond.

There is an obvious contrast in the two dramatic pieces, although both centre on Shakespeare. In Bond's play we see Shakespeare as a man in late middle age, near to his death, aware in his plays of inhumanity in the world and yet, as Bond points out, benefiting from a Goneril-society with its 'prisons, workhouses, whipping, starvation, mutilation, pulpit hysteria and all the rest of it'. Many of the words that Bond's Shakespeare speaks are the voiced memories of an old man. Shakespeare's Lear is very different. He is out in the storm, his madness emphasized by the garlands he has strewn over himself, accompanied by the blind Gloucester and Edgar, feigning imbecility, with whom Lear has a violent conversation indulging in play-acting, and finding a culmination in the reiterated cry of 'Kill!' as he imagines himself wreaking a horrible revenge on the families of his two daughters Regan and Goneril.

Years ago I heard Edith Sitwell chanting her poem 'Still Falls the Rain'; now whilst the author's rendering may colour the interpretation and help the candidate to realize the importance of its musical quality found in the strong rhythm and the vowel lengths, the individual speaker's interpretation should not be a copy of the poet's for the candidate must discover their own way of conveying the meaning. Sitwell felt deeply the pain of humanity and expressed herself through a series of historical and biblical vignettes, the Potter's Field bought with the betrayal money Judas had gained, the cross on Calvary and scenes from Elizabethan blood sports. One's vocal delivery of this quiet yet dynamic poem will contrast with the analytical, weary voice of Shakespeare in Bond's play.

Yet a further vocal register is introduced in Lytton Strachey's prose as he eagerly tears away the semblance of royalty from Elizabeth I.

2.4.6 Editing the text

The preparation of this last recital introduces the subject of editing the text. The poem can be taken in its entirety, that is no problem, and the prose only needs to be excerpted from the seventeenth chapter of Strachey's book. The dramatic pieces require detailed editing, however. A solo performer can only effectively play one character and although he has to 'people' his stage he must not allow other characters to intrude. For example, it is rarely satisfactory for the recitalist to 'listen' to the unspoken words of imagined characters: this strains credibility and causes a hiatus. Therefore it seems best to cut out the words and interjections of characters other than the principal one the recitalist is portraying. Sometimes the dialogue following a cut needs sensitive editing: further cutting may be necessary or a name may have to be substituted for a pronoun; cross references to material in cut speeches also have to be edited out, but obviously the words of the playwright must be respected and altered as little as possible. I am reminded of syllabuses in operation some thirty years ago in which a dramatic piece would frequently be set containing a conversation between two characters and the recitalist was expected to realize both. Fortunately this is no longer expected and the technique of dual presentation has been relegated to the acts of a few comedians.

2.5 AN ANALYSIS OF A RECITAL PROGRAMME

I would like to move away from generalized models and look at an example of a recital which was given by Tom Durham, an actor and an examiner for the

Poetry Society, at one of the Society's day conferences, making a brief analysis of what was a most satisfying aesthetic experience. A Lincolnshire widower, George Rochford Porter, left a bequest to the Society in 1985, expressing a wish that recitalists should be encouraged to study the work of Burns, Cowper, Keats, Tennyson, and Wordsworth. Accordingly an examination was set up in which the candidate builds a recital around the work of one of these poets, linking the pieces with commentary and possibly some illuminating prose. Tom Durham's recital was given as a model for this award and he based it on the writings of Alfred Lord Tennyson.

A quotation from 'The Two Voices' took us directly into the performance:

> 'Tis life whereof our nerves are scant,
> Of life, not death, for which we pant,
> More life, and fuller, than I want.

A few introductory sentences led into the last section of 'The Lady of Shalott' and then the listeners were prepared for cantos 55 and 56 of 'In Memoriam'. A lyric from 'Maud', 'Birds in the high Hall-garden' followed. There were fleeting references after this to 'The Northern Farmer' and 'The Charge of the Light Brigade' and finally the recital was brought to a close with 'Vastness'.

Tom gave me some illuminating comments on the thinking that lay behind his selection, for after all there is a formidable corpus of work from which to choose, and he spoke of his objectives in arranging the selection in the order I have outlined. Obviously the opening lines of the recital were used as a 'scene setter', introducing ideas that were going to be picked up later. 'The Lady of Shalott' which followed the introductory remarks is a minutely detailed story but it is more than this for the poem gives us psychological insights into the poet who saw himself doomed if he left the realm of his imagination for the 'real' world. Tennyson, however, did not live only in a past of castles and maidens, he was also a man of his times: he wrestled with religious doubt, with the intellectual challenge of the theory of evolution and with the pain of the death of his close friend Arthur Hallam, the subject of 'In Memoriam'. Just as his friendship with Hallam had been cut short by death so his love for Rosa Baring was blocked by differences in class and a lack of money, and in the lyric from 'Maud' a very disturbed person can be glimpsed, morbid and unbalanced. The snatches from 'The Northern Farmer' and 'The Charge of the Light Brigade' show something of the range – humour, fun and sheer excitement – of Tennyson's work opening out the subject matter as the end of the recital is approached. There is a hint of resurrection in the last poem, 'Vastness', which speaks of Tennyson's faith in the power of human and divine love reaching beyond the constraints of his material existence.

Much thought and careful planning had been poured into this recital and, whilst I cannot, with the limitations of print, do proper justice to it, at least the programme and the description of Tom's determining principles will help you to grasp what is involved in presenting a recital of this complexity. Whatever the examination, do make your selection of pieces with great care as this is crucial to your success. Prepare extra pieces which may also be suitable and be prepared to cast aside your first choices if you feel that others are more appropriate to the recital or better suited to yourself.

2.6 RESOURCES

2.6.1 Bibliographical details of books mentioned in the text

Bond, E. (1974) *Bingo*, Eyre Methuen, London.

Booth, M. (1965) *Eighteenth Century Tragedy*, Oxford University Press, London (contains the text of *Douglas* by John Home).

Hardy, T. (ed. S. Elledge) (1980) *Tess of the D'Urbervilles*, W. W. Norton, London.

Johnson, T. and Lock, K. (1987) *Tuesday's Child*, Methuen's New Theatre-scripts, London.

Mitford, N. (1983) *The Sun King*, Michael Joseph, London.

Shakespeare, W. (ed. K. Muir) (1964) *King Lear*, Methuen, London.

Shakespeare, W. (ed. J. H. Walter) (1969) *Henry V*, Methuen, London.

Shelley, M. (ed. J. Kinsley and M. K. Joseph) (1980) *Frankenstein*, Oxford University Press, Oxford.

Strachey, L. (1971) *Elizabeth and Essex*, Penguin Books, Harmondsworth.

Tennyson, A. Lord (ed. W. E. Williams) (1985) *Poems*, Penguin Books, Harmondsworth.

2.6.2 Sources of the poems cited

Bartlett, E., 'Ian, Dead of Polio' in Bartlett, E. (1979) *A Lifetime of Dying*, Harry Chambers, Liskeard, Cornwall.

Browning, R., 'Home thoughts from Abroad' in Browning, R. (ed. I. Jack) (1970) *Poetical Works*, Oxford University Press, Oxford.

Gunn, T., 'Consider the Snail' in Copeman, C. and Gibson, J. (1969) *As Large as Alone*, Macmillan Educational, London and Basingstoke.

Jennings, E., 'To a Friend with a Religious Vocation' in Penguin Modern Poets (1962) *Lawrence Durrell, Elizabeth Jennings, R. S. Thomas*, Penguin Books, Harmondsworth.

Lawrence, D. H., 'The Snake' in Lawrence, D. H. (ed. V. de S. Pinto and F. W. Roberts) (1981) *Complete Poems*, Penguin Books, Harmondsworth.

McGough, R., 'My Busconductor' in Penguin Modern Poets (1967) *The Mersey Sound*, Penguin Books, Harmondsworth.

Milton, J., 'Lycidas' in Milton, J. (ed. B. A. Wright) (1980) *Poems*, Dent, London.

Sitwell, E., 'Still Falls the Rain' in Sitwell, E. (1982) *Collected Poems*, Macmillan, London.

Summerfield, G., 'Windy Boy in a Windswept Tree': see Copeman and Gibson (1969) above.

Thomas, D., 'Fern Hill' in Thomas, D. (1984) *Collected Poems*, Dent, London.

2.6.3 Secondary works on some of the texts mentioned

Barber, C. (1980) *York Notes: King Henry V*, Longman, London.

Draper, R. P. (1975) *Thomas Hardy: the Tragic Novels*, Macmillan, London.

Ferris, P. (1978) *Dylan Thomas*, Penguin Books, Harmondsworth.

Grindley, R. E. (1972) *Browning*, Routledge and Kegan Paul, London.

Meyers, J. (ed.) (1987) *The Legacy of D. H. Lawrence*, Macmillan, London (ch. 3).

Muir, K. (1986) *Masterstudies: King Lear*, Penguin Books, Harmondsworth.

Pitt, V. (1962) *Tennyson Laureate*, Barrie and Rockcliffe, London.

Sinfield, A. (1986) *Alfred Tennyson*, Blackwell, Oxford.

Thomas, D. (1978) *A Child's Christmas in Wales*, Dent, London.

Turner, P. (1976) *Tennyson*, Routledge and Kegan Paul, London.

2.6.4 Books on planning recitals

Hartly Hodder, E. (1986) *Words, Words, Words*, Guildford School of Music and Drama, London.

Mulcahy, B. (1969) *To Speak True*, Pergamon Press, Oxford.

2.6.5 A selection of anthologies

Brownjohn, A. (1969) *First I Say This*, Hutchinson Educational, London (poems especially suitable for speaking aloud).

Copeman, C. and Gibson, J. (1969) *As Large as Alone*, Macmillan Educational, London and Basingstoke.

Gollancz, V. (1950) *A Year of Grace*, Victor Gollancz, London (contains many suitable prose excerpts for senior performers).

Guildhall School of Music and Drama (1987) *Nineteenth Anthology of Poetry,*

Prose and Play Scenes, Guildhall School of Music and Drama (a full range of material).

Harvey, A. (1987) *In Time of War*, Blackie, Glasgow.

Harvey, A. (1985) *Poets in Hand*, Puffin Books, Harmondsworth.

Hayward, J. (1956) *The Penguin Book of English Verse*, Penguin Books, Harmondsworth.

Huth, A. (1987) *Island of the Children*, Orchard Books, London (suitable for junior performers).

Ireson, B. (1977) *Rhyme Time*, Beaver Books, Hamlyn Publishing Group, London (suitable for junior performers).

LAMDA Anthology of Verse and Prose (1988) vol. xii, Max Reinhardt, London (a range of verse and prose for all ages and abilities).

Mathias, B. (1987) *The Hippo Book of Funny Verse*, Scholastic Publications, London (suitable for junior performers).

Morpurgo, M. and Simmons, C. (1974) *Living Poets*, John Murray, London.

Norwich, J. (1980) *Christmas Crackers*, Penguin Books, Harmondsworth (a selection of highly unusual prose excerpts).

Reeves, J. (1955) *The Merry-Go-Round*, Penguin Books, Harmondsworth (a good selection of very simple poems in the early sections of this).

Rumble, A. (ed.) (1983) *Have You Heard the Sun Singing?*, Bell and Hyman, London.

Silkin, J. (1960) *Living Voices*, Vista Books, London.

Turnbull, M. (1981) *Verse for the Eighties*, Society of Teachers of Speech and Drama, London (contains sections of verse written for speaking aloud).

Webb, K. (1979) *I Like This Poem*, Puffin Books, Harmondsworth.

Words on Water (1987), Puffin Books, Harmondsworth (winners of the *Observer* competition for young poets).

Young Words (1985) (ed. M. Mackenzie), Macmillan, London (winners of the W. H. Smith competition for young poets).

2.6.6 Spoken word recordings

Argo Treasury of Victorian Poetry, 419 009–4.

Carroll, J. (ed.) *Birds, Beasts and Flowers*, NIMBUS 4112.

English Romantic Poetry, 3005.

Handbook for Witches – Stories and Poems for Hallowe'en, 1497.

Jennings, E., *Harvest and Conservation*, 414 772–4.

Jupiter Anthology of 20th Century English Poetry, OOA8.

Man be My Metaphor – A Celebration of Dylan Thomas, TTC PSO3.

Stevenson, R. L., *A Child's Garden of Verses*, COL2009.

A useful guide to spoken word recordings is: Seeley, R., *Gramophone Spoken Word and Miscellaneous Catalogue*, General Gramophone Publications Ltd. (published annually).

3

In rehearsal :
Verse speaking

3.1 ENJOYMENT AND COMMUNICATION THROUGH POETRY

In this chapter I shall take several well-known poems and encourage you to consider how you would prepare to speak these in an examination. This is closely focused work and demands that I deal with each poem in some detail. Don't think of the points we are to consider as sets of rules to follow slavishly. My suggestions are to be treated flexibly. Their purpose is to help you: to help you to enjoy the meaning, form and tone of the poem and to help you communicate to your listeners your enjoyment and understanding of the poet's intention in writing. Try not to think of your preparation as being 'in order to pass the examination'; it has a broader purpose, which might be summed up as true enjoyment and effective communication. Eventually I hope that your communication will be more than effective; inspired would be the goal to aim for.

3.2 POETRY FOR BEGINNERS

I'm not going to give a detailed analysis of a poem suitable for very young children to speak. Sufficient to say that an examiner looks for obvious enjoyment in the speaking which is more important than the mastery of a few technical points. He hopes, too, that he may hear an emotive response to the poem, such as an overt expression of sympathy with the subject or the ability to convey an atmosphere. The possibility of this depends on two factors. Firstly the speaker must understand the meaning of the poem and what it is the poet is saying. A surprising number of small children have but hazy ideas about this and sometimes no notion of the meaning of individual words in the vocabulary. Secondly the speaker must give a shape to the piece in the speaking and this depends on their response to the content and the pattern of the verse. In the previous chapter we considered several pieces which six-years-old enjoyed and there I gave brief notes on preparatory work.

   The besetting sin of very young performers is the rapidity with which they tend to speak their poems; children need help in using the rhythm and diction as a guide to the pace of the verse. This speeding up often happens only in the examination room once the candidate realizes he or she is face to face with a stranger and for this reason some boards encourage examiners to make friends with the candidate on their arrival in the room so that the speaker can communicate through the recital. Examiners, too, often make a pause between the two poems by sitting the candidate down for a breather and asking one or two informal questions about the performer's response to the piece before the second is undertaken. Teachers can also help their candidates by bringing in a friend shortly before the examination to hear the pieces. This gives the young person an opportunity to perform to someone other than teacher or parents and it takes the edge off the strangeness of performing to an unknown examiner.

3.3 FOCUS ON FOUR POEMS

3.3.1 'The Wife of Usher's Well'

The first poem I shall give detailed attention to is a Scottish ballad, 'The Wife of Usher's Well':

> There lived a wife at Usher's Well,
>   And a wealthy wife was she;
> She had three stout and stalwart sons,
>   And sent them o'er the sea.
>
> They had not been a week from her,
>   A week but barely one,
> When word came to the mother herself,
>   That her three sons were gone.
>
> They had not been a week from her,
>   A week but barely three,
> When word came to the mother herself,
>   That her sons she'd never see.
>
> 'I wish the wind may never cease,
>   Nor fishes in the flood,
> Till my three sons come home to me,
>   In earthly flesh and blood!'
>
> It fell about the Martinmas,
>   When nights are long and dark,
> The mother's three sons they all came home,
>   And their hats were of birch bark.
>
> It neither grew in marsh or trench
>   Nor yet in any ditch;

But at the gates of Paradise
    That birch grew fair and rich.

'Blow up the fire, my maidens!
    Bring water from the well!
For all my house shall feast this night,
    Since my three sons are well.'

And she has made to them a bed,
    She's made it large and wide;
And she's taken her mantle about her,
    Sat down at the bed-side.

Up then crew the red, red cock,
    And up and crew the gray;
The eldest to the youngest said,
    ''Tis time we were away.'

The cock he had not crowed but once,
    And clapped his wings at dawn,
When the youngest to the eldest said,
    'Brother, we must be gone.

'The cock doth crow, the light doth grow,
    The channelling worm doth chide;
If we be missed out of our place,
    A sore pain we must abide.'

'Lie still, lie still, but a little wee while,
    Lie still but if we may,
If our mother should miss us when she wakes,
    She will go mad ere day.'

'Fare ye well, my mother dear!
    Farewell to barn and byre!
And fare ye well, the bonny lass,
    That kindles my mother's fire.'

Jamie is eleven and he has decided he will make this poem his own choice in an examination. He has chosen the piece as he lives in Edinburgh and he enjoys links with Scotland's past. As spirits and the supernatural are much to his taste, he likes the mystery in the story.

Some time before he started to work on this poem his teacher had taught him that any narrative poem needs to be spoken with a degree of rapidity; one cannot dwell too long on the details or the listener's interest in the overall tale wanes. Although there is a punctuation mark at the end of each line, these clarify the sense, contributing little to the speaking for separate ideas are clearly confined to each line. There was not, therefore, the need to make a deliberate break at the end stops. When Jamie brought pace to the verse speaking the rhythm started to make itself clear. A strong metrical beat ran through the couplets so that the second line of each completed the rhythm of the first:

> And SHE has MADE to THEM a BED,
> She's MADE it LARGE and WIDE.

He noted that there were four stresses in the first line of each couplet and only three in the second, realizing that this rhythm helped to push the speaking forward. He also discovered that when he spoke some of the longer lines, such as

> The MOTHer's three SONS they ALL came HOME

extra unstressed syllables were there which gave a pleasing variety to his speaking. It felt good that the rhythm was helping him to gain a suitable pace for the narration. Repetitions of words and phrases, too, helped to give urgency to his speaking. The rhyming scheme was a further help to Jamie: in each stanza the second and fourth lines clearly rhymed. At first he stressed the rhyming words until his teacher pointed out that this wasn't necessary. Occasionally a word within the line rhymed:

> The cock doth CROW, the light doth GROW

and this helps to make explicit the haste of the ghostly brothers as they made their dawn get-away from the cottage. As well as the internal and end rhymes, repeated words and sounds help to hold the stanzas together. Firstly the repeated words:

> LIE still, LIE still, but a little wee while,
> LIE still but if we may.

And secondly, in the same couplet there was the repetition of the 'l' sound as well as the repeated 'w' of the first line.

Now it may seem strange that we have spoken about Jamie's discoveries relating to the pace, the rhythm and the rhymes in the ballad before we have talked about the story line. However, poems are more than stories, even a narrative poem, and it is wise, as Jamie discovered, to allow the meaning of the story to become clear to you as you work on the piece. This is especially true of ballads as there are several layers of meaning to explore. It would be too easy for Jamie to fix a simplified narrative line in his head and not progress beyond that. It took him a little while, for example, to appreciate the strength of the image of the 'channelling worm'.

Changes of mood and changes of voice run through the ballad. It is these that give the poem variety and interest. Soon Jamie was boldly declaiming the first verse, switching to sorrow in the next two and gaining an atmosphere suggestive of the long dark nights mentioned in the fifth verse as he described the return of the three lost voyagers which intensified as he allowed his hearers to fathom for themselves that this homecoming was no ordinary one. These rapidly and economically expressed changes of mood are like a series of filters which colour the speaking accordingly, sometimes matter-of-fact, sometimes sorrowful and often mysterious.

The direct speech in the ballad brought its own challenges. 'However skilful you are at creating voices,' Jamie's teacher told him, 'they must all be in keeping with the ballad as a whole and they mustn't hold up the story.' He thought carefully, about the voices of the various characters. There was the bitterness of the mother in her first speech in which there is a highly significant line:

> In earthly flesh and blood.

She is giving the listener a contrary hint that the sons' appearance certainly would not be in that form. In contrast her later words to the servants are commanding and energetic. Towards the end of the poem there is the conversation between the eldest and the youngest sons. Jamie realized that without necessarily acting he had to differentiate between each voice through the degree of character he gave it.

Jamie talked with his teacher about the visual presentation of this narrative poem. This genre demands a vibrancy of speech so strong that sometimes it bursts out of the confines of standing or sitting still and needs gestures and movements. There is a passage of time between the fourth and fifth verses which, without a change of posture, may escape the attention of the listener, so Jamie began the poem standing, which felt appropriate for the early scene-setting verses, and after the fourth he introduced a slight break in the narration as he made his way to a chair placed to one side of the performance area. He stood by this until the line

> Sat down at the bedside

a natural indication that he should be seated and then he was suitably placed for the conversation between the two brothers. He found it helpful to adopt a slight change of eye focus as each brother began to speak his lines. This younger performer had enough nous to know that the kind of moves we have been thinking about could easily be artificial and awkward. Jamie's success lay in his ability to make each appear to arise spontaneously out of the demands of the text.

Of course Jamie's teacher wasn't going to limit his appreciation of poetry by working on only one ballad with him; this seemed an excellent opportunity to get the young speaker tackling several other ballads such as 'Sir Patrick Spens' and 'Lord Randal' so that intuitively he began to appreciate the characteristics of ballads and so formulate his own ideas about them instead of learning a set list of their properties. She introduced him, too, to several other types of narrative poem outside this genre such as 'The Pied Piper' by Robert Browning and Edward Lear's 'The Owl and the Pussy Cat' which he dramatized and recorded with the help of some of his friends. The ballad was a wise choice for the examination. It did not make great technical demands: the short lines presented no breathing problems nor were there complications with pauses beyond the basics of maintaining shape and sense. Eleven is an age when powers of invention are strongly developed and this helped the young verse speaker to cope with the characterization needed. Jamie's ability and the choice of poem were a happy marriage.

3.3.2 'Tarantella' by Hilaire Belloc

The second poem is 'Tarantella' by Hilaire Belloc which I am assuming a fourteen-year-old candidate will speak.

> Do you remember an Inn,
> Miranda?
> Do you remember an Inn?
> And the tedding and the spreading
> Of the straw for bedding,
> And the fleas that tease in the High Pyrenees,
> And the wine that tasted of the tar,
> And the cheers and the jeers of the young muleteers
> (Under the vine of the dark verandah)?
> Do you remember an Inn, Miranda,
> Do you remember an Inn?
> And the cheers and the jeers of the young muleteers
> Who hadn't got a penny,
> And who weren't paying any,
> And the hammer at the doors and the Din?
> And the Hip! Hop! Hap!
> Of the clap
> Of the hands to the twirl and the swirl
> Of the girl gone chancing,
> Glancing,
> Dancing,
> Backing and advancing,
> Snapping of the clapper to the spin
> Out and in –
> And the Ting, Tong, Tang of the Guitar!
> Do you remember an Inn,
> Miranda?
> Do you remember an Inn?
> Never more;
> Miranda,
> Never more.
> Only the high peaks hoar:

> And Aragon a torrent at the door.
> No sound
> In the walls of the Hall where falls
> The tread
> Of the feet of the dead to the ground.
> No sound:
> But the boom
> Of the far Waterfall like Doom.

The first question that probably comes to mind is, 'What is a tarantella?'; after that you probably want to know who Miranda is and then you might get round to thinking about Hilaire Belloc who wrote the poem. Italy is the habitat of a large venomous spider called a tarantula. For a long time it was thought that a man bitten by one of these would start to perform the dance of a maniac as his nerves became highly strung by the poison. This is a useful snippet of knowledge as it leads us to see that the rhythm of this poem is a dance rhythm. Possibly in performance the rhythm is as important as the words. 'Who is Miranda?' you ask. A. N. Wilson, Belloc's biographer, has suggested that the name stems from a diplomat in London, the Duke of Miranda, and so we can picture him as the virile travelling companion of the poet. 'Tarantella' was first published in 1923, a fact which helps us to savour the period of the writing and it would be a good idea to fill in your own background to the piece, discovering some of the important events in England at that time and looking briefly at several other poems of the period. This poem, the work of a seasoned traveller, celebrates some of the excitement that 'twenties travellers experienced as they made their ways on foot and by train over Europe before the days of package holidays, stopping at such inns in the mountains as that described in the text, often 'detestable', the description is Belloc's, because of their lack of cleanliness and comfort.

At this point it is a good idea to jot down some of your initial responses on reading the poem. In the margin of my own anthology I have scribbled, 'Rhythm, fun, adventure'. Keep this first response in front of you, even if you have to revise it as you work on the poem. It will eventually help you perform the piece with freshness and spontaneity.

The poem suggests that the writer and the duke are reminiscing about their travels which seem to have been highly enjoyable, hardships and all, and then comes a change of tone for Miranda has died; it is with his spirit the writer is conversing as he realizes that the travelling days are done. This content is held within a structure, the form. Although this poem is conceived as a single block, the repeated question.

> Do you remember an Inn, Miranda,
> Do you remember an Inn?

creates a number of divisions. Some line-end words rhyme in couplets, such as 'spreading' and 'bedding', or 'doom' and 'boom', but the poet employs no regular rhyme scheme and in the middle of the piece where the lines are scaled down to a single word, one rhyme occurs four times:

> Of the girls gone chancing,
> Glancing,
> Dancing,
> Backing and advancing . . .

This has the effect of speeding the pace, a point to remember in the speaking.

Let us turn to the rhythm. Read the first three lines aloud, sensing where the stresses occur:

> Do YOU remember an INN,
> Miranda?
> Do YOU remember an INN?

Sometimes internal rhymes accentuate the rhythm:

> And the FLEAS that TEASE in the HIGH PyrenEES . . .

Most of the longer lines contain four beats. Sometimes this changes to three:

> SNAPping of the CLAPper to the SPIN

and later, within the lament:

> In the WALLS of the HALLS where FALLS . . .

This, strangely, has two opposing effects. In the first line quoted the change to three stresses accentuates the rising pace, but where Belloc uses single syllable words to express his desolation, as in the latter quotation above, the three stresses slow the pace of the line. When you are working on the rhythm, try to feel it within yourself and avoid the temptation to cover your text with markings. If you have difficulty with the rhythm, try saying the poem aloud, tapping softly on a tambour on the stresses.

From these simple pointers we can make some observations about the changing pace of the verse when spoken. The poem starts with a repeated question resembling the opening gambit of a conversation and from that point the pace starts to increase. According to one's interpretation the questions could make a break in the pace which could then intensify until the single word lines

> Glancing,
> Dancing,

are reached. The plosive consonants in

> And the Ting, Tong, Tang of the Guitar!

suggest that this line could mark the start of a rapid deceleration. The tone of regret that the joys of travel are in the past demands, of course, deliberate and solemn speaking.

> . . . In the walls of the Halls where falls . . .

is a particularly noteworthy line. The long vowel 'aw' in its reiterations becomes a mournful bell tolling, reinforced by the single syllable of each word which gives weight to the speaking. This use of single syllable words is continued, with the same effect, through the next four lines. The long 'oo' of 'boom' and 'Doom', similarly slows down the pace of the final couplet. Without giving the vowel disproportionate play, you need to relish the speaking of it.

In writing about this poem I've stated that each speaker must give his own interpretation of it. This is an important point which needs elaboration. There is no 'correct' interpretation of a poem and certainly we should not attempt to reproduce another speaker's method of delivery; we each have our own representation. There are very few rules in poetry speaking. Instead of applying a set of commandments we have to use our own intelligence and discernment and this places a great responsibility on us. That is one of the reasons why I recommend that you should look at a number of related poems alongside your examination choice for this helps to sharpen discernment. There are two questions which help us: 'What is the poet's intention in writing this piece?' and 'How can I best convey this to the listener?' In looking at the background to this poem we have been exploring Belloc's intention. We bring life to that intention by deciding on such matters as the tone, the shape and the pace of the verse and we convey the intention of the poet to the listener with our enjoyment, our involvement and our technical expertise. Technical expertise on its own, especially if it does not really belong to the speaker, is of little value.

We must not allow the pace with which we speak 'Tarantella' to obscure the shape of the poem. As we speak it the listener should be able to gain an understanding of what the text looks like on the page. Pauses, the thrust of our delivery and our vocal inflections all help to make the pattern clear. Let us look at several places in the poem as examples. The question marks at the end of the repeated query 'Do you remember . . .' imply there is going to be a pause after each, so that the sets of questions sectionalize the verse. Within these sections further questions occur making minor breaks in the delivery, a moment in which the listener can picture the inn and its frequenters. Strong rhymes and rhythms in the first two-thirds of the poem suggest to me that there is no need to make any kind of break at the end of unstopped lines for the shape of the verse is easily discernible. At the point where the pace of the poem changes there is a group of unpunctuated lines:

> No sound
> In the walls of the Halls where falls
> The tread
> Of the feet of the dead to the ground
> No sound.

A suspensary pause is needed at the end of each line in this section or the listener could fail to appreciate that the very short lines exist.

I want to go on to think very briefly about the dynamics and the word quality. 'Dynamics' refers to the variations in volume and intensity of our speaking and any decisions about dynamics must take into account the meaning of the verse. We have spoken of the poem as a dance and this implies that the volume of the speech may be louder than if the poem were just a description of a mountain tavern. Alongside this we must bear in mind that the rapid changes of subject suggest that the dynamics must also change with rapidity. But towards the end of the poem the rhythm changes from a dance to a lament: the sad impression of 'We'll go no more a-roving' coupled with the eerie sounds of the footsteps of the dead implies that this section is muted in performance.

Lively verse speakers enjoy the feel of sounds released from their mouths. Lines in the first part of the poem are peppered with plosives such as

<blockquote>AnD the TeDDing and the sPreaDing</blockquote>

which require accurate tongue action. I like to imagine that the plosives represent the background music of castanets and plucked guitar strings. Short vowels also give sharpness to the sounds as in

<blockquote>SnApping of the clApper to the spIn.</blockquote>

The vowel quality alters in the latter section as sounds become lengthy and gray in tone colour:

<blockquote>But the bOOm
Of the fAR waterFALL like DOOm.</blockquote>

As you work on the poem you will discover further instances of Belloc's skilful merging of sound and sense. A word of caution is necessary here. Whilst you must be aware of these tactile values of sound you must not overplay them for their own sake or your work will become self-indulgent. Balance is important. This is yet another instance of the discernment you must employ in verse speaking.

'Which posture best serves the presentation of this piece?' For an energetic poem such as 'Tarantella' you would wish to stand alert ready to gesture or move if the mood and content suggested that this was appropriate. I once saw a candidate stand with one foot raised on a box as he spoke this piece, a stance which suited his interpretation. Another candidate had a tambourine with which she established a rhythm before her speaking started. That was fine. Later a difficulty occurred when voice and tambourine were used together as the sound of the instrument hindered the speaking and I realized it would have been better if she had punctuated the speaking with this rather than trying to use it as an accompaniment. Unless the syllabus disallows them, any such devices can be an effective part of your recital. In fairness I must point out though that a candidate would not normally be given credit for an experiment which landed him in difficulties and that is a reflection of the harsh judgment of any audience watching a presentation: either an interpretation is a success or it fails; there are no half measures.

3.3.3 Sonnet CXXX by William Shakespeare

The next poem I would like to look at is a sonnet, number 130, by William Shakespeare and I will think about this piece in relation to a male candidate preparing to take a licentiate examination.

> My Mistres eyes are nothing like the Sunne,
> Currall is farre more red, than her lips red,
> If snow be white, why then her brests are dun:
> If haires be wiers, black wiers grow on her head:
> I have seene Roses damaskt, red and white,
> But no such Roses see I in her cheekes,
> And in some perfumes is there more delight,
> Than in the breath that from my Mistres reekes.
> I love to heare her speake, yet well I know,
> That Musicke hath a farre more pleasing sound:
> I graunt I never saw a goddesse goe,
> My Mistres when shee walkes treads on the ground.
> > And yet by heaven I thinke my love as rare,
> > As any she beli'd with false compare.

This is a strange sonnet and capable of more than one interpretation. The conventional beauty of Shakespeare's day was a pale-skinned woman with red-gold hair, a reflection of the idealized portraits of Queen Elizabeth I, and in contrast the subject of this sonnet has black hair and grey-brown skin. Shakespeare is writing about no conventional beauty. One reading of the lines might indicate that the poem is a cynical jest, in which Shakespeare reverses all of the accepted notions of beauty; however, further study may indicate that the poet's passion for his mistress runs so deep that all conventional notions of human beauty or all literary exaggerations and idealizations of fairness are cast aside in this declaration of true love. I have already mentioned that the 'I' of any poem is not always the writer and that warning is applicable here; nor must the black-haired lady of this sonnet necessarily be equated with the Dark Lady who appears in other poems for this mistress may be a fictional concept to pair with the 'I' character. I have presented various contradictory ideas to you and if you are to speak this sonnet with conviction you must come to a justifiable decision about your own understanding of the identity of the writer, his mistress and their feelings for each other.

Sonnets have several different forms; Sonnet CXXX is an English or Shakespearean sonnet. The rhyming scheme indicates that it is sectionalized into three groups of four lines or quatrains, and a final couplet. Within each quatrain alternate lines rhyme and these rhymes are strongly made. The change from this alternation to a couplet at the end of the poem offers the poet an opportunity to make a summation of his previous points or even to introduce an unexpected element into his poem. Within the confines of this form Shakespeare expresses himself with economic skill. In the first four lines he contradicts our ideas about idealized beauty using each line to describe a different attribute of his mistress. By the third and fourth lines, each opening with a conditional 'If', we begin to suspect that the writer may be purposefully adopting a cynical attitude. The next two quatrains proceed at a more leisurely pace, for two lines are expended in considering each aspect of the mistress which lessens the sting of the unfavourable comparisons. At this point it is opportune to explain that 'reekes', which today has a pejorative meaning, in Shakespeare's day simply meant 'exhales'. The writer's conclusion on the reality of his love for his mistress fits neatly into the couplet and the conclusive nature of this is stressed by the oath 'by heaven' accompanying the declaration: in the light of this couplet a speaker may feel it necessary to revise any earlier suspicions he may have had about the tone of the poem.

Sonnet speaking is a difficult art for there is great compression in the writing. Here, however, Shakespeare's listing format does make for a more immediate comprehension and so the slow pace with which many of his sonnets must be spoken for the sake of unravelling the thread of meaning is not in this case encumbent on the performer. Nevertheless, the speaker must be clear about the lines he sees as the climax of the poem and drive his speaking towards them; I see the climax as the final couplet.

David is a young man preparing to speak this sonnet as part of his recital for a licentiate diploma. He has carefully considered the various readings that can be made of the piece and he has opted for one which is, in part, cynical. However, he feels that in spite of the humorously expressed recognition of the so-called 'defects' of the mistress, in the final analysis the poet's love for her is genuine: she is no conventional beauty but she has positive qualities of her own. It could be, David feels, too easy to milk a quick laugh from the contradictory antitheses and the pointing required to do this would hold up the speaking of the piece. David recognizes though that the antitheses are important for they stress the formality of the construction: either by an 'if' clause or by a statement Shakespeare postulates what constitutes conventional beauty and follows this by a 'knock down' statement about the graces of his own mistress. This formality must leave its mark on David's own performance: the sonnet is a formal statement and if David presented it as anything else he would be untrue to the form.

David is fortunate in his teacher. She has worked with him on principles relating to the text and together they have discussed the subtext or meaning beneath the surface from which point she has decided she must leave many of the practical decisions about speaking the poem to David. Indeed, his voice and his brain working in conjunction will make many of these decisions subconsciously. As he is about to speak he does not say to himself, 'I am to make a formal statement; what pitch, inflections and volume shall I use?' because, given a real understanding of the poem, his voice will respond instinctively to his needs. The work will then be vibrant and spontaneity will ensure that it is dynamic and fresh in the presentation. This is an important point: at the time of the examination you must trust your instantaneous reaction to the text you have mastered, for only then will you gain the immediacy to make a genuine communication with your audience. Each time you speak a poem feel the words welling through your body and mind in a reliving of its sentiments.

I am not discounting technical work but the place for this is in the early stages of rehearsal. Once the technical aspects have been mastered you must then forget them, as David did, and allow spontaneity to take over. So often candidates feel that once the technical approach has been mastered the poem is ready for recitation. Not so, for the candidate's mind is too wrapped up in problems of breathing, rhythm and modulation to focus on communication. Alongside the work on Sonnet 130 David tackled several of Shakespeare's other sonnets and later in this chapter I shall write of his discoveries about one of these. At this point, however, I want to share with you some notes on the technical work which David tackled in the early stages of his preparation and we shall consider this under the key headings of rhythm, pauses and phrasing, and breathing.

(a) Rhythm

The rhythm is the pulse which runs through a poem. Rhythm is not confined to poetry; it is a part of our everyday life. As you walk along the street your bodily movement, putting one foot in front of the other, introduces a rhythm to the rest of your body. Often your breathing, especially if it is slow and relaxed, introduces a rhythm to your system which permeates even to your mind. Shakespeare wrote his sonnets in iambic pentameters; in other words there are five stresses within each line. A combination of sense and patterning determines where these occur. The rhythm often helps us discover the sense, although there can be ambiguities. Let us take one of the 'if' lines:

If snow be white, why then her brests are dun.

Now if we think of the beat occurring regularly through the line, we get a purely factual statement about the object of the poet's gaze:

If SNOW be WHITE, why THEN her BRESTS are DUN.

However, if the speaker wishes to criticize the mistress because she lacks ideal beauty, he tends to stress both the conditional and 'her' with the result that the pattern is changed:

> IF snow be WHITE, why THEN HER brests are DUN.

Some may disagree but it seems to me that one can make a legitimate choice between either way of speaking the line. Other ambiguities occur. An instance is the later line:

> My Mistres when shee walkes treads on the ground.

A regular scanning will leave some unimportant words stressed:

> My MIStres WHEN shee WALKS treads ON the GROUND.

This is, literally, pedestrian although it can be claimed in this context that is just what Shakespeare is after; we find that the line moves more easily if in the latter half of the line the stress is reversed:

> My Mistres when shee walks, TREADS on the GROUND.

The effect of this is that, with the stress on 'treads' we get a clearer impression of the mistress and the measure of her stride. There are metaphysical implications too about Shakespeare's regard for a woman with her feet on the ground. A secondary effect is that the line gains in pace. A similar reversal may be intended by Shakespeare at the beginning of the line, giving us the freedom of:

> MY Mistres WHEN shee WALKS, TREADS on the GROUND.

I labour this because I'm trying to show you that in his sonnets Shakespeare does not use a mechanically repetitive metre and it is up to you to discover which words he wishes to be stressed in each line. As you speak the poem don't, except in special cases, accentuate the stressed word vocally, simply feel the rhythm in your body and, as you concentrate on the meaning, this will influence your speaking.

Whilst we are thinking about feeling the rhythm there is a further aspect you should be aware of. Each line contains a caesural pause. In the line we have just been considering this occurs at the asterisk:

> My Mistres when shee walks, * treads on the ground.

Each of the other lines contains such a pause:

> My Mistres eyes * are nothing like the Sunne,

and so on. The term 'caesural pause' is misleading for if you make a full break in the middle of each line your speaking becomes monotonously regular. We simply feel the pause rather than deliberately break unless, of course, sense and punctuation tell us otherwise:

> I love to heare her speake, * yet well I know . . .

The summary of these two paragraphs is simply that our appreciation of the subtle changes of rhythm running through Shakespeare's sonnets brings variety to our speaking. Listen to the waves of the sea breaking on the beach at night. There may be a regular repetition but within this are an infinite number of variations. So too with the rhythm of sonnet speaking.

(b) Phrasing and pauses

There are other kinds of pause and their use determines the phrasing, the grouping together of clusters of words so that the ideas they convey are made clear. When I spoke of the caesural pause I implied that usually we take each line, if it is end-stopped, as a single sweep of sound. In that way we begin to ensure that linear rhythm is preserved. Occasionally I have heard a speaker, in his endeavours to convey the impression that words are spoken from his heart, fragment the line, so that the second line of the sonnet would contain the following pauses:

> Currall * is farre more red * than * her lips * red . . .

Piecemeal speaking of this sort destroys the rhythm. When there is a punctuation mark in the middle of a line, this may imply a more definite pause than a caesural, but do avoid a complete break in the line which tends to give the impression that it has snapped in two. This is yet another area in which the speaker has to experiment using his teacher as an amalgam of listener, critic and coach.

Of course, if there is no punctuation at the end of a line then we must make sure that the sense continues until the complete idea is expressed, as in:

> And in some perfumes is there more delight
> Than in the breath that from my Mistres reekes.

An unpunctuated line such as this is referred to as 'enjambed'. In order to convey to the listener that this is two lines of poetry and not one single line grown to an unwieldy length, the speaker needs to employ a suspensive pause at the end of the first line on the second syllable of 'delight'. He will simply hold on to this syllable slightly and then make up the time with an extra drive on the speaking at the beginning of the next line, 'Than in the breath. . . .' As with all technical expedients this can easily become a mannered trick and the speaker must use judgment in deciding how best to time his delivery of the unpunctuated line.

Often Shakespeare uses a word at the end of a line on which the speaker needs to dwell in order to savour its meaning. The final couplet is a good example:

> And yet by heaven I thinke my love as rare,
> As any she beli'd with false compare.

The important word 'rare' is not only one to be savoured, it must also be emphasized in order to make clear the unique qualities of the mistress, and its position at the end of an unstopped line helps you as you pause slightly on the word itself. This last couplet of the sonnet, because it contains the principal idea in the poem, needs to be spoken at a slower rate than the rest of the piece in order to indicate summation and finality.

(c) Breathing

'Where do I take a breath?' is a question one asks in the early days of working on a piece. In this particular sonnet the breathing should present the competent candidate with few problems as sense clusters are contained within either one or two lines. Full stops and semi-colons are indications of breathing spaces. Needless to say, any inhalations must be silent and unobtrusive and in the section on breathing in Chapter 9 advice is given on the process of breathing and the economical use of breath. Sufficient here to say that as Shakespeare often puts his most important words or ideas at the end of a line or couplet we must ensure that we have enough breath to work towards that point and to give the final word the required weight of emphasis. It is a common fault for a speaker not to project towards the end of the line when part of his mind switches to the next set of ideas. Concentrate on the speaking of the moment and deliberately work towards the key word.

Projection is reliant on breathing and a proficient candidate will not find this a problem. The degree of projection required for sonnet speaking is, however, a matter for debate. Probably your first response is that the sonnet is a personal, lyrical poem and therefore you should be reserved in the force of your expression. However, the formal structure of the poem and the dynamism of the argument can easily be lost if too muted an interpretation is given. One year I heard a trio of actors speak several of Shakespeare's sonnets at the annual commemoration service in Southwark Cathedral and although the two male speakers used a microphone their meditative approach seemed to leave the message unspoken; then Dame Peggy Ashcroft made her way to the podium and the words of 'Shall I compare thee to a summer's day?' rang through the gothic arcades with assurance and strength. Here was an articulated passion, almost dramatic in its intensity, which worked perfectly for that form in that place.

May I repeat that the technical work we have been considering must be mastered in the early days of working on a poem. Once thoroughly digested it can then be forgotten so that in performance you concentrate on transmitting the ideas and emotions of the verse. Your sincerity is of great importance. A firm technique will not rob you of sincerity, it will free you so that you can release the sonnet as a living reality.

3.3.4 Sonnet XXIX by William Shakespeare

Before I began to write about the technical aspects of sonnet speaking I mentioned that David was not going to work solely on Sonnet CXXX; as a contrast he felt that he would like to study several others. I would like to look briefly at one of these, Sonnet XXIX, so that we can see David's response to a text in a slightly different format.

> When in disgrace with Fortune and mens eyes,
> I all alone beweepe my out-cast state,
> And trouble deafe heaven with my bootlesse cries,
> And looke upon myselfe and curse my fate,
> Wishing me like to one more rich in hope,
> Featur'd like him, like him with friends possest,
> Desiring this mans art, and that mans skope,
> With what I most injoy contented least,
> Yet in these thoughts my selfe almost despising,
> Haplye I thinke on thee, and then my state,
> (Like to the Larke at breake of day arising)
> From sullen earth sings himns at Heavens gate,
> > For thy sweet love remember'd such welth brings,
> > That then I skorne to change my state with Kings.

Shakespeare this time isn't writing a mere description; the subject matter is more complex. It is a poem addressed to 'the Friend', the subject of a group of sonnets, possibly Shakespeare's patron, the Earl of Southampton, a young, cultured and attractive nobleman. Before the poem can be spoken with conviction the performer must know instinctively if he is identifying the 'I' of the sonnet with Shakespeare himself. For his part David felt he could make that identification: he thought of the actor–playwright losing contentment in his practice of the theatre and wishing that he had been born into the wider world of the nobility, but then calling to mind his patron, a thought which fills him with joy and contentment. In its tone this sonnet is far more personal than the former for here the writer passes through a slough of despair hoping for an impossible change in his social status. It contains not only darkness, though, but the dawning of joy and in the image of the soaring lark Shakespeare paints a glorious picture of a rise in spirits.

In Sonnet 130 we saw that antithesis can be a useful device and it occurs here too but this time the contrasts are ones of social standing. The shape of the poem determines the expression of these sentiments through antithesis. The content is neatly expressed in the two parts of the sonnet, the octet and the sestet: the first eight lines are an articulation of despair and the remaining six are an affirmation of hope. As before, the final couplet sums up the poet's feelings; it completes the antithesis, for the first line told of the poet's lack of fortune, whereas in the last line Shakespeare spurns the state of kings.

'How,' you ask, 'does this become more than an academic exercise in poetic form? How does it affect one's speaking of this sonnet?' Firstly, the information will determine the tone of your speaking: it is addressed to a patron of whom the writer is genuinely fond. This recipient is not evident in the first eight lines but the second half of the poem becomes a direct address to the patron. Additionally a complete range of emotion is expressed from self-pity to joy. This is a journey the speaker must make, changing in tone and address with subtlety once the conjunction 'yet' is reached.

We have spent a long time in thinking about sonnet speaking. It is a highly sophisticated art form but it is also an excellent training ground for the verse speaker, as in performance it helps him to find his way through a maze of related ideas expressed in the tightest of structures. If a performer can successfully cope with this, then other verse forms will be open to him.

3.3.5 A summary

Before we leave these key texts some kind of recapitulation in an itemized form of the process the candidates went through may be helpful. Although for clarity these remarks are stated as imperatives, don't think of them as a set of rules to which you must adhere:

(a) Read the poem through several times and jot down your initial responses to it;
(b) Look carefully at the title and the content and research any names, words or ideas that are new to you; gradually come to terms with the meaning of the poem;
(c) Undertake some research on the poet and the circumstances in which he lived or still lives; discover the circumstances in which the poem you are studying was written;
(d) Discover the intention of the poet in writing this piece; think about the tone of the poem;
(e) Work on the technical aspects: structure, rhyming scheme and divisions, rhythms, the fusion of content and form, pace, word quality, dynamics;
(f) Beware of the technical demands the poem makes on you as a speaker;
(g) Think about the visual presentation of the piece;
(h) Put technical matters behind you and make the poem a living reality; go back to your initial impressions and try to feel in human and personal terms the principal thrust of the poem; how can you release this?

Be flexible. Gradually come to terms with a way of grappling with a poem which makes it truly your own work. Remember to use your teacher as a sounding board for your interpretation.

3.4 SOME MISCONCEPTIONS ABOUT VERSE SPEAKING

At this juncture it might be helpful to consider several misconceptions about verse speaking in examinations. The first is that verse should be spoken in a special 'poetry speaking voice'. This entails an over-reverent tone, unnatural dwelling on vowel sounds and the candidate attempting to iron out of the voice any trace of regional dialect by adopting a pseudo 'BBC voice', choosing to imitate one now out-dated. This makes the interesting qualities of a candidate's speech disappear. As I've examined people who have mistakenly put on this voice I've been amazed when we arrived at the sight reading and the answers to questions at the life and enthusiasm which is heard once this falseness is discarded. Your own voice is the voice which is to speak the poetry if it is to represent your interpretation of it.

Another misconception is that all poetry is to be spoken standing and often this stance is an artificial one. 'Why did you stand to speak the poem?' I've sometimes enquired. 'I wouldn't be able to breathe if I didn't' is often the amazing answer I receive. Some poems such as reflective, lyrical verse, gain by being spoken by a seated performer as this helps to give the impression that the sentiments expressed are quietly recalled and dwelt on. So don't get into a rut in your presentation of verse. Poets experiment in speaking their work. Edith Sitwell, for example, projected the words of 'Façade' through a megaphone whilst an orchestra played William Walton's music. Feel free to experiment; the only proviso is that you must remain true to the intentions of the poet.

A further misconception occurs about the way in which verse speaking is assessed. A small boy once missed out a stanza of a three verse poem and anxiously asked the examiner of he would lose a third of the marks. No – examiners don't measure poetry speaking by the yard. There are many other qualities beyond the recitation of the words which are looked for and these are discussed in the next section.

3.5 THE EXAMINER'S EXPECTATIONS

I have asked a number of examiners representing different boards what they were hoping to find in the candidate's performance of verse speaking. The responses I received are summarized here. Sometimes the answers I was provided with covered all levels of work, at other times examiners differentiated between junior and senior grades. The Guildhall School defines grades 1–4A as 'junior' and those above as 'senior' – a useful guide.

(a) The Associated Board

The representative of the Associated Board, when listening to a young performer, looks for someone who obviously enjoys speaking poetry and is able to share both the poetry and the enjoyment. In older candidates technical accomplishment helps to convey the initial enthusiasm and a personal technique gives the senior candidate confidence in his work. At the senior levels the examiner looks for performance quality, taking into account the skills required to convey the wholeness of poetry to a listener. However, it is emphasized that communication is of greater importance than sheer technical proficiency. One's technical training must be totally absorbed: it is preferable for a candidate's technique to be underplayed than to be obtrusive. The two highest grades demand fluency in a range of styles if the pieces are to be presented adequately.

(b) LAMDA

The LAMDA examiner looks for expressive speaking of poetry revealing an understanding of the content and a sympathy with it. The expectations of the examiner are clearly stated in the syllabus:

> Interpretation means the extent to which the feeling, mood and changing thought of the writer has been understood and communicated. In verse it includes a true feeling for the rhythm and the sound pattern of the words as a means of expression as well as a complete understanding of what is spoken.

(c) Mountview

The Mountview representative stressed the need to enjoy verse speaking; language must be coloured and alive. Candidates at the higher grades study the background to the poetry they present and appreciate the style in which it demands to be spoken.

(d) New Era

There must be a 'ring of truth' in the speaking of the poetry which gives the work credibility. The candidate must demonstrate an ability to share the work. A sense of rhythm is most important. Regional accents are acceptable as long as the vowels are not distorted, for the tune and rhythm of regional speech add colour and richness to the recital. That said, it is stressed that there is a need for clarity and audibility. Sensitivity to the poetry is important. The candidate needs an effortlessly produced voice in order to convey the shape and music of the verse. Senior candidates are expected to possess technical competence but this must be mastered and then 'forgotten' so that it does not obtrude during the performance.

(e) The Poetry Society

The Poetry Society examiner expects the poem to be a shared experience with its message coming across clearly. The words of the syllabus offer an amplification on this point:

> Teachers should encourage candidates to give an uninhibited truthful interpretation of the chosen piece, reflecting the writer's intention. In other words, little credit will be given for a beautifully articulated poem if it is spoken without conviction.

The examiner wants to be sure that the candidate appreciates the form of the poem and the literary period in which it was written. His expectations about the senior candidate's technical powers are that the speaker must be proficient in breathing and in the placing of the voice, releasing it from the front of the mouth; the speaker must be able, too, to give the listener the shape of the poem and it is important that the candidate has a wide vocal range at his or her disposal. John Loveday's admirably clear introduction to the Poetry Society's syllabus offers a helpful gloss on these comments:

> Though an examiner's attention will be, essentially, upon the quality of the spoken presentation, in all sections the candidate will be expected to have an appropriate knowledge of the texts presented. This requirement emphasizes the need for the speaking of poetry . . . to be an intelligent and sensitive engagement with the mind of the writer and no mere exercise in elocution. It should be noted that there is no bias against regional accents; there might, indeed, be occasion for accents appropriate to particular texts to be favoured.

(f) Royal Academy

The expectation of the Royal Academy's examiner is that the candidate should present poetry with understanding and integrity. He or she must interpret the intentions of the poet, and technically must be aware of the rhythms of English speech used in the poem and be able to realize the verse form in the speaking.

(g) Trinity College

Trinity College expects young candidates to show an understanding and an imaginative interpretation of the verse. Prior to grade 3 technical expertise is not expected but careful phrasing is looked for. Senior candidates are expected to offer an interpretation which is imaginative but also true to the text.

3.6 TECHNIQUE AND VERSE SPEAKING

I would like to turn to a controversial and somewhat vexed subject, the candidate's demonstration of the technique of speech applied to verse speaking.

Rarely are clear and precise statements on this given by boards and one has to glean remarks on technique from a number of places in the syllabus such as those sections headed 'Questions' or 'Discussion' whilst at other times they appear in a preamble to the examinations. Later, in Section 9.3, I give a summary of the various boards' expectations of the technical knowledge and accomplishment of candidates. Most boards accept the premise that technical knowledge must be demonstrated in the pieces so a careful look at these requirements is necessary. You must then relate the requirements to your speaking of the poetry selection. It has to be admitted there is a wide range of expectations about technical accomplishment. Amongst the various examining boards there is little agreement on what constitutes the fundamentals of the technique of verse speaking and what are the finishing graces. Thus whilst some boards concentrate on the candidate – the posture, relaxation and ability to breathe and project, others concentrate on the technicalities of transmitting the text.

My own response to this dichotomy is that candidates need progressively to establish their own technique. It is only when the performer has tackled a wide range of verse speaking that he is ready to recognize his own limitations and discover ways of gaining release from them. As I examine I am conscious that much technical training has not brought this release; instead it has imposed its own thraldom. Small children are adepts at spotting the irrelevant and leaving it alone. Colleagues tell me that in preparing children younger than twelve-years-old their pupils have little inclination to study theory and its pursual often degenerates into mere 'knowledge' learned by rote. It certainly does not become an aid to transmitting the text.

There is also a danger that when a technique is overlaid, whether assimilated or not, it only 'works' when the performer speaks the verse of the past. What of contemporary verse and its demands? Technique quickly becomes a petrification of a once acceptable way of speaking poetry, often to large audiences in spacious buildings. Nowadays poetry is intimately shared in club rooms or small arts centres, and where there is a need to expand the presentation then microphones can more easily help the speaker than elaborate breathing systems, some of which stem back directly to the Kemble era. Unfortunately the use of the microphone is a technique we neglect in teaching verse speaking. There is room to discover the technique which is required today for poetry speaking rather than in adopting uncritically techniques of the past which now serve neither the poetry of the past nor of the present. In this area boards must look to the future.

Remember the old adage, 'Don't let your technique show!' Master technical matters so thoroughly that in speaking a poem they will look after themselves whilst you concentrate on sharing the meaning of the piece.

3.7 RESOURCES

3.7.1 Bibliographical details of poems referred to in the text

Anon., 'The Wife of Usher's Well' in Untermeyer L. (ed.) (1933) *The Albatross Book of Verse*, Collins, London and Glasgow.

Belloc, H., 'Tarantella' in Webb, K. (ed.) (1979) *I Like This Poem*, Puffin Books, Harmondsworth.

Shakespeare, W., Sonnets 29 and 130 in Burton, W. (ed.) (1964) *William Shakespeare: The Sonnets*, New English Library, Signet Classics, London.

Sitwell, E., 'Façade' in Sitwell, E. (1950) *Façade and Other Poems*, Duckworth, London.

3.7.2 General works on poetry and prosody

Blackburn, T. (ed.) (1966) *Presenting Poetry*, Methuen, London.

Brewer, R. F. (1962) *The Art of Versification and the Technicalities of Poetry*, John Gaunt, London and Edinburgh.

Fraser, G. S. (1970) *Metre, Rhyme and Free Verse*, Methuen, London.

Hamer, E. (1930) *The Metres of English Today*, Methuen, London.

Hughes, T. (1967) *Poetry in the Making*, Faber and Faber, London.

Reeves, J. (1979) *Understanding Poetry*, Heinemann Educational, London.

Roberts, P. (1986) *How Poetry Works*, Penguin Books, Harmondsworth.

Spender, S. (1955) *The Making of a Poem*, Hamish, London.

Untermeyer, L. (ed.) (1961) *Collins Albatross Book of Verse*, Collins, London and Glasgow (this contains a helpful appendix on poetic form).

Williams, J. (1985) *Reading Poetry*, Edward Arnold, London.

3.7.3 The ballad

Bratton, J. S. (1975) *The Victorian Popular Ballad*, Macmillan, London and Basingstoke.

Graves, R. (ed.) (1967) *English and Scottish Ballads*, Heinemann Educational, London.

Hodgart, M. (ed.) (1982) *The Faber Book of Ballads*, Faber and Faber, London.

Reeves, J. (1976) *The Writer's Approach to the Ballad*, Harrap, London.

3.7.4 The sonnet

Burton, W. (1964) *William Shakespeare: The Sonnets*, New English Library, Signet Classics, London.

Cruttwell, B. (1966) *The English Sonnet*, Longman, London.
Fuller, J. (1972) *The Sonnet*, Methuen, London.
Lever, J. W. (1968) *The Elizabethan Love Sonnet*, Methuen, London.
Nye, R. (ed.) (1976) *A Book of Sonnets*, Faber and Faber, London.

3.7.5 On verse speaking

Bruford, R. (1963) *Speech and Drama*, Methuen, London (ch. 8).
Crump, G. (1964) *Speaking Poetry*, Dobson Books, London.
Mulcahy, B. (1988) *How to Speak a Poem*, Autolycus Press, London.
Thurburn, G. (1939) *Voice and Speech*, James Nisbet, London (ch. 7).

3.7.6 Background reading

Pearson, J. (1980) *Façades. Edith, Osbert and Sacheverell Sitwell*, Fontana, London.
Rowse, A. L. (1973) *Shakespeare the Man*, Book Club Associates, London.
Sitwell, E. (1972) *A Poet's Notebook*, Greenwood Press, London.
Wilson, A. N. (1984) *Hilaire Belloc*, Hamish Hamilton, London.

3.7.7 The Poetry Society

The Poetry Society (21 Earls Court Square, London SW5 9DE) exists to promote poetry and poets. It does this through its spoken poetry and prose examinations, through the Poets in Schools Scheme, through many lectures and public recitals held at the headquarters, through writing courses and competitions, and through its occasional children's events. The Poetry Society Bookshop situated on the ground floor of the headquarters is well stocked and worth a visit; it can supply books by post.

4

In rehearsal :
Speaking the prose selection

4.1 PROSE EXCERPTS

Selections of prose excerpts appear in the lists for most grade examinations and often a prose selection is required at diploma level as well. In this chapter I've chosen several different kinds of prose writing so that we may consider our responses to the text and the preparation that is required. A couple of the selections are excerpted from novels, one for a children's and the other for an adult readership; two non-fiction excerpts are included and finally some verses from the Authorized Version of the Bible. As before, we eavesdrop on a couple of candidates preparing their pieces. For the most part I have used easily available texts so that the excerpts represent the kind of pieces set by examining bodies.

4.2 EXCERPTS FROM NOVELS

4.2.1 *The Wind in the Willows* by Kenneth Grahame

Tracey, aged nine, is working on an excerpt from *The Wind in the Willows* by Kenneth Grahame:

> 'Hullo, mother!' said the engine-driver, 'what's the trouble? You don't look particularly cheerful.' 'O, sir!' said Toad, crying afresh, 'I am a poor unhappy washerwoman, and I've lost all my money, and can't pay for a ticket, and I *must* get home tonight somehow, and whatever I am to do I don't know. O dear, O dear!'
>
> 'That's a bad business, indeed,' said the engine-driver reflectively. 'Lost your money – and can't get home – and got some kids, too, waiting for you, I dare say?'
>
> 'Any amount of 'em,' sobbed Toad. 'And they'll be hungry – and playing with matches – and upsetting lamps, the little innocents! – and quarrelling, and going on generally. O dear, O dear!'
>
> 'Well, I'll tell you what I'll do,' said the good engine-driver. 'You're a

washerwoman to your trade, says you. Very well, that's that. And I'm an engine-driver, as you well may see, and there's no denying it's terribly dirty work. Uses up a power of shirts, it does, till my missus is fair tired of washing of 'em. If you'll wash a few shirts for me when you get home, and send 'em along, I'll give you a ride on my engine. It's against the Company's regulations, but we're not so very particular in these out-of-the-way parts.'

The Toad's misery turned into rapture as he eagerly scrambled up into the cab of the engine. Of course, he had never washed a shirt in his life, and couldn't if he tried and, anyhow, he wasn't going to begin; but he thought: 'When I get safely home to Toad Hall, and have money again, and pockets to put it in, I will send the engine-driver enough to pay for quite a quantity of washing, and that will be the same thing, or better.'

In the examination which Tracey is taking the candidate is allowed to select any excerpt from the set book to a time limit of three minutes. Tracey read the whole of *The Wind in the Willows* finding several of the chapters difficult and slow but there was enough action in the story to entertain her. She latched on to the character of Mr Toad and eagerly awaited each of his appearances in the story. From Ernest Shepard's illustrations she gained a clear impression of what he looked like and as his outrageous exploits landed him in deeper troubles she was able to visualize these frenetic scenes. She was a little surprised to find herself actually liking Toad in spite of his boastfulness, and that, she surmised, was one of the reasons why she chose this particular excerpt, for in it Toad appeared at his most vulnerable. He had recently escaped from prison, where he had been held for joy-riding in a stolen car, by disguising himself as a washerwoman, a get-up that appealed to his flamboyant imagination. Wanting to make his way home to Toad Hall, he discovered that he had no money and, in his state of consternation, was noticed by a kindly engine-driver.

Tracey read over the excerpt that she had chosen several times. It seemed about the right length but for the time being she kept an open mind on where exactly to finish the speaking. Her teacher, Mrs Knibbs, suggested she began by thinking about the two characters in this excerpt: she could visualize them and by moving around Mrs Knibbs' studio as each of them in turn she tried out their ways of walking, their gestures and the angle at which they looked at each other. All of this, Mrs Knibbs felt, would eventually help Tracey to discover the voices of the two conversationalists. There was no point in arriving at a set voice for each too soon; 'funny voices' restrict the range of speaking and hinder a real expression of the emotions of the characters. Instead they began to think about the number of voices that lay implicit in the text. There was, first of all, the voice of the narrator, a business-like voice, not too caught up in the emotions of the piece but giving the gist of the action to the listener and explaining things such as Toad's ignorance of the practicalities of washing. The narrator's voice, Mrs Knibbs suggested, needs pace in order to hold the interest. Next they thought about the engine-driver. His burliness was touched on just before the selected piece and after it his individuality and strong principles became evident; these traits gave one or two hints about the nature of his speaking. In the excerpt itself he is presented as a thoughtful person, suggestive of vocal warmth. There was a danger that Tracey would make herself hoarse as she tried to discover the speaking voice but by tackling all of the early work very quietly she gained authority as well as ease. Her teacher helped Tracey to use her resonators to the full rather than strain to attain a gruff, deep voice. The ways of doing this are explained in Chapter 9. Toad was a complicated figure to represent for he possessed two voices, the falsetto of the washerwoman and, towards the end of the extract, the confident, braggart voice of the creature himself.

As Mrs Knibbs worked with Tracey she knew that, with a young performer, there were a number of specific objectives to achieve. The telling of this part of the novel had to be fun: Tracey must enjoy the work arising out of the story and be happy in sharing the piece with the examiner. The most direct way to obtain this sense of fun was to aim at spontaneity in the conversation. In spite of the character voices the speaking, too, had to be clear. It was important that Tracey could see the point of some of Kenneth Grahame's rather literary jokes peppered throughout the conversation. Let us take two of these. The first is just a verbal remark:

> 'And they'll be hungry – and playing with matches –
> and upsetting lamps, the little innocents! . . .'

A good example of irony. Mrs Knibbs brought this to Tracey's attention: those who play with matches and upset lamps are hardly innocent. Understanding the point of the remark Tracey's absorption in the character enabled her to make the point economically in the speaking far more effectively than would a more technical introduction to variations of tone, pitch and pace. When Tracey reaches senior grades, then will be the time for her to analyse the way in which she conveys the layers of meaning which lie beneath the text. The second of Grahame's literary jokes is in the double antithetical contrast he makes between Toad and the engine-driver, 'You're a washerwoman. . . . And I'm and engine-driver. . . .' There is an obvious superiority in one of the roles: the engine-driver will employ the washerwoman to launder his shirts. Moments later, however, the roles are reversed as Toad thinks of the donation he will make the engine-driver. By playing a game in which Mrs Knibbs and her pupil traced 'who's up and who's down?' in the telling of the story, Grahame's satire on status became evident. Although this runs through the excerpt the point must not be unduly stressed or the quiet humour with which Grahame invests it will be lost.

In preparing this piece, then, Mrs Knibbs has concentrated on conversation and tone. The latter is a very difficult subject for a young performer to comprehend but by working instinctively and intelligently the speaker can be most expressive in this area. It would be too easy if Mrs Knibbs had merely selected key words for emphasis for then the speaking inevitably becomes mechanical. If a candidate can't at first appreciate a point the author is making, it is necessary for the teacher to take indirect steps: perhaps a parallel situation can be set up in relation to the child's own experience which can eventually be expressed in their own terms so that these can be compared with the text. It is not suitable to annotate the text with stress marks, rising inflections and pauses. I have even seen at the moment of a dramatic pause in a prose excerpt the scribbled note, 'Count to three'! During any pause the candidate must concentrate on the meaning being transmitted and not on such dubious devices.

4.2.2 *The Bell* by Iris Murdoch

The other fictional excerpt I have selected, a piece suitable for senior candidates, is from Iris Murdoch's book *The Bell*. Its plot is complicated but there are two interwoven strands easily extrapolated. In the opening sentences of the novel the reader is introduced to the first of these:

> Dora Greenfield left her husband because she was afraid of him. She decided six months later to return to him for the same reason.

There is an exploration throughout the novel of Dora's strange relationship with Paul, the man she fears. The story of the day by day affairs of a small lay community forms the second strand and it is with this community that the couple become involved. The excerpt is taken from the final chapter of the novel and in it is signalled the end of Dora's and Paul's relationship.

> The station was just outside the village on the Imber side. A lane with high overgrown hedges wound away across the fields, and the footpath to Imber left it a quarter of a mile further on. Dora wondered whether to cross the line and go into the village. But there was no point in it, since the pubs would not be open yet. She turned into the dark tunnel of the lane. The sound of the train and the car had died away. A murmur accompanied her steps, which must come from a tiny stream invisible in the ditch. She walked on, her hands in her pockets.
>
> Her hand encountered the envelope which Paul had given her. She drew it out fearfully. It would have to be something unpleasant. She opened it.
>
> It contained two brief letters, both written by herself. The first one, which she saw dated from the early days of their engagement, read as follows:
>
> > Dear *dear* Paul, it was so wonderful last night and such absolute pain to leave you. I lay awake fretting for you. I can't wait for

tonight, so am dropping this in at the library. It's agony to go
away from you, and so wonderful to think that soon soon we
shall be much more together. Wanting to be with you always,
dearest Paul, ever ever ever your loving Dora.

Dora perused this missive, and then looked at the other one, which read
as follows:

> Paul, I can't go on. It's been so awful lately, and awful for you
> too, I know. So I'm leaving – leaving you. I can't stay, and you
> know all the reasons why. I know I'm a wretch and it's all my
> fault, but I can't stand it and I can't stay. Forgive this scrappy
> note. When you get it I'll be finally gone. Don't try to get me
> back and don't bother about the things I've left. I've taken what
> I need. Dora.
>
> P.S. I'll write again later, but I won't have anything else to say
> than this.

This was the note Dora had left at Knightsbridge on the day she de-
parted. Shaken, she reread both letters. She folded them up and walked
on. So Paul carried them always in his wallet and wanted to have them
back to go on carrying them. So much the worse for Paul. Dora tore the
letters into small fragments and strewed them along the hedge.

Two letters from Dora to Paul are entries into time past, the first bringing to
light the passionate emotions of a love now dead and the second, nearer to the
present, expressing a kind of annihilation. As I read this extract I am struck by
the decisions I must make about my performance. I must decide, first of all, on
the tone. A weary sadness envelops the situation, it even permeates the landscape, greying in the autumn light of a late afternoon. My tone must reflect that
sadness and yet there must be variations in it for living speech cannot exist as an
expression of a single emotion. Neither of the letters is written in Iris Murdoch's own style, both are a pastiche. So it is the letters which are going to offer
some variety of tone. A longing passion prompts the writing of the first and this
must be conveyed in the speaker's voice; yet at the same time the passion is
tempered by Dora's present sadness. Times past and present meet and so too do
the emotions engendered at each of these times. Cold despair is the keynote of
the second letter. An inevitable finality, the parting described at the beginning
of the novel brought full circle, must govern the speaking of the content of the
second letter which, from the trick of pairing to give emphasis, I realize is
Dora's style:

> . . . I can't stand it and I can't stay . . .
> Don't try to get me back and don't bother about the
> things I've left . . .

Something of Dora's mannerisms must come into the speaking but here I must tread warily for merely to act the part would transpose the speaking into the wrong key.

As I reread aloud the passage, thinking about tone, I become conscious of the importance that Murdoch attaches to pauses. A mannerism of hers is to reduplicate words as she does with 'the station' at and after the end of the first sentence. This demands a complete break on the punctuation mark. So too with the end of the first letter in its repeated 'ever'.

The punctuation marks, the short sentences, the reduplications, all help a speaker to discover the rate at which a passage is to be spoken. Content-wise the writing is descriptive; there is a lull in the nvoel as the emotions of meeting and parting are reflected on; the setting, the exterior of the railway station from which Paul has just left by train, is an appropriate place for these considerations. Descriptive prose seems to require less dynamism than narrative. At this stage I begin to see how tone and pace coalesce. There is the sadness we have spoken of, the ruminative description of the countryside and, with the help of the two letters, a pondering on the past. However, as a speaker I cannot allow the pace to be constant. Occasional phrases are of lesser importance: 'there was no point in it' (the reason is given, which requires the stronger emphasis); 'I can't wait for tonight', a reduplication of the structure of the previous statement and the emotional meaning, although reinforced by repetition, is much the same as in the previous sentence. These instances can be multiplied. As such phrases are of lesser importance I can use the actor's technique of 'throwing away' the words, lightly passing over them on a dynamic level different from that I use in speaking the more important surrounding sentences and phrases. The letters, too, will encourage variations in pace. I could try to reinforce the finality of the separation by gradually increasing the pace as I make the speaking more deliberate, but this must be within the limitations of the overall rate I have adopted.

I need to discover the climax of the passage. The emotional cross-threads complicate the issue, and other people's choice of the climactic moment may differ from mine. One brief sentence, the penultimate, struck me as highly significant:

So much the worse for Paul.

In its brevity this sums up the complete fracture of the relationship. As in a line of poetry much feeling is compressed into the six monosyllabic words: they speak of finality. The difficulty faces me: 'How do I give this interpretration to a listener?' I find in playing a recording that I have made of the passage that I became very separated from Dora in the sentences that follow the text of the second letter. A matter-of-fact tone gave a commentary on Dora's actions and thoughts. And then, as if I had suddenly entered into Dora's emotional orbit, realizing the energy with which her decision had been made, I spoke the climactic six words with slow force. Murdoch's writing resembles Richard Sheridan's here in spite of the time gap. Often, when moved by emotion, he couched his prose in iambic feet; here, too, there are three feet with three stresses and the weight in the force of my speaking falls on the strong beat. This determination carries through into the last sentence.

The reading must be prefaced by a carefully prepared but brief introduction. My intention must be to ensure that the examiner understands what has led to the first sentence of the excerpt so I must succinctly speak of the theme of the damaged relationship running through the book. Iris Murdoch's writing is colourful enough to convey the atmosphere of the moment so I needn't worry about that. I would choose to say a word, however, about the village of Imber with its rustic peace and turmoil of relationships contrasting with Knightsbridge, swamped in traffic noise yet emotionally tranquil. There would be no need to speak about the bell of the title or of the community for neither directly affects this excerpt. Hopefully these themes, fundamental to the novel, could be introduced in a discussion of the pieces.

I would choose to speak these paragraphs seated, appearing more relaxed so that I could draw the listener into the reflective pace at which I wanted to take the first half of the selection, the watercolour in words of a rural setting on an autumn afternoon. My introduction could then, by way of contrast, be spoken standing slightly to one side of the performance area so that I could 'walk into' the piece and its setting. Some speakers, of course, would feel far happier sitting for the introduction as they would then be ready to launch into the piece. Sometimes my students ask me whether they should learn by rote the introduction and any other links. If this helps in maintaining succinctness, then do but you must speak them with spontaneity or they are in danger of becoming extra pieces in the recital, however brief. Preferably several key words may be learnt in advance and the candidate left to trust his in-built brain and speech links to build sentences around these words.

There must be a fluidity in my performance. I don't want to pre-set each turn of my body and know in advance the directions in which I will focus my eyes as the speaking progresses. However, I should be aware of how I must convey the substance of certain parts of the speaking through my body language as much as though my voice. I will position my chair to one side of the performance area so that I can regard the examiner as one member of a larger audience. Much of the piece could be spoken to an audience other than the examiner. There are, however, a couple of sentences after Dora discovers Paul's envelope which I would choose to speak directly to the examiner for I wish to emphasize their importance:

She drew it out fearfully. It would have to be something unpleasant.

The text of the two letters, I think, demands some rearrangement of posture. I wouldn't want to act the role of the writer but the way in which I sit should convey something of the joy and despair of each letter's sentiments: for the first letter, for example, I could experiment sitting in an open, confident manner changing this to a more withdrawn posture later with a shift in eye focus. In writing down my intentions it is very easy to give the wrong impression. Everything that I have described must take place so easily that the audience does not register consciously that these minor physical changes have occurred.

4.2.3 Setting the excerpt in the context of the novel

Several words of advice, additional to those I have given on prose excerpts in the previous paragraphs, are needed relating to the section of the examination in which questions are asked on the pieces. First and foremost, do read the complete novel or story from which the selection is taken. This applies to small children as much as to any other candidate and if the complete book is not easily comprehensible to a youngster, then another selection should be chosen. Spoken word tapes of novels are available and, provided there is no abridgment, listening to one of these may be a suitable alternative to reading the text. The candidate must be aware of the way in which the chosen extracted selection fits into the novel as a whole. A possible approach by the examiner might be to ask a junior performer who had spoken a couple of paragraphs from one of Michael Bond's books about Paddington Bear, 'What different kinds of trouble does Paddington get into?' Or a question might throw the responsibility for appreciation back on to the candidate: 'What makes Paddington a lovable bear?' With senior candidates the examiner might well be interested in the development of a character who is mentioned in the excerpt or with the outcome of a particular incident mentioned. The novel could be approached in general terms: 'Why do you like . . .?' or 'Why did you choose . . .?', and from the answer the examiner judges how to focus his next question. Sometimes questions might be on a moral level. I've asked candidates who have presented excerpts from Roald Dahl's book *The Twits*, 'How can such a nasty pair of individuals be interesting?' One might enquire, too, whether a candidate had read any other books by Dahl and invite comparisons of incidents and characters. With the older candidate the examiner sometimes wants to see if the candidate is aware of the literary and social context of the chosen novel: sometimes candidates have described the workhouse depicted in *Oliver Twist* without realizing that they are confronted by historical primary source material. It is not unreasonable for the examiner to assume that older candidates will have briefly researched this phenomenon and compared their findings with Dickens's experience. Adults working at diploma level sometimes forget that it is important to see the novel from which they have made their selection against its literary background: for example, with Jane Austen's *Northanger Abbey* it is important to appreciate the contemporary vogue of Gothic horror stories. Here, as with all senior grades and diplomas, it is necessary to be aware of the reasons for the author's acceptance as a person of literary merit.

So often when I've asked candidates to give me some information on, say, Laurence Sterne, they merely repeat the dates of his birth and death. In themselves these have no value. Instead candidates need to be aware of the range of his work and his strange experimentation with the structure and content of the novel in *Tristram Shandy*. Some kind of appraisal of his literary worth should also be made. It is important that teachers devote time in their lessons to holding a discussion with their students on the background to the pieces, for this helps the candidates to sort out their ideas and to articulate them. Occasionally I meet a candidate who had made ample written notes on some of the points I have mentioned but was quite unable to make the transition from the private page to the more public discussion. If we see the speaking of prose as the sharing of ideas, we must view as equally important this sharing of literature.

4.2.4 Characterization

A problem which often bedevils speakers is whether to give characterization to direct speech. Although we saw earlier in this chapter that Tracey opted to do so, it certainly wasn't a mandatory part of the exercise. The performer must use her discernment. Younger candidates often find the direct speech a welcome point of fun in which they can 'act' with their voices and this is often acceptable, especially as children tend to be unselfconscious about this. However, where the text of an adult novel is shot through with gobbets of conversation one needs to be wary. The speaker's primary purpose is to tell a story through the narrative; this can easily be forgotten if the narration gets bogged down under a welter of over-elaborate characterizations. For many pieces all that is required is a suggestion of the person speaking by hinting at one of the vocal characteristics.

4.2.5 Selecting the excerpt

Sometimes the onus is on the candidate to select a passage from a book and the problem is at which point to end the excerpt. Occasionally I find the chosen ending is indecisive. Aim to end as an incident closes or when a character makes a particularly telling point or at a moment of suspense. In your speaking, of course, your decreasing rate and falling inflection will signal to the listener that you are finishing. Don't let go of the prose speaking too rapidly. Think about it quietly for a couple of moments after the last word. If there is a stipulated time limit, do stick to it.

4.3 NON-FICTIONAL PROSE

It is time to look at couple of examples of non-fictional prose writing and here I have chosen a letter, slightly edited in the version give here, written by Horace Walpole, and an essay by Gilbert Keith Chesterton.

4.3.1 A letter from Horace Walpole

This is a letter from Horace Walpole, Earl of Orford, to Sir Horace Mann, the British envoy at Florence.

Arlington Street,
March 11, 1750
'Portents and prodigies are grown so frequent,
That they have lost their name.'

My text is not literally true; but as far as earthquakes go towards lowering the price of wonderful commodities, to be sure we are overstocked. We have had a second, much more violent than the first; and you must not be surprised if by next post you hear of a burning mountain sprung up in Smithfield. In the night between Wednesday and Thursday last (exactly a month since the first shock) the earth had a shivering fit between one and two; but so slight that, if no more had followed, I don't believe it would have been noticed. I had been awake, and had scarce dozed again – on a sudden I felt my bolster lift up my head; I thought somebody was getting from under my bed, but soon found it was a strong earthquake, that lasted near half a minute, with a violent vibration and great roaring. I rang my bell; my servant came in, frightened out of his senses: in an instant we heard all the windows in the neighbourhood flung up. I got up and found people running into the streets, but saw no mischief done: there has been some; two old houses flung down, several chimneys and much chinaware. The bells rung in several houses. Several people are going out of town, for it has nowhere reached ten miles from London: they say, they are not frightened, but that it is such fine weather, 'Lord! one can't help going into the country'. A parson, who came into White's the morning of earthquake the first, and heard bets laid on whether it was an earthquake or the blowing up of powder mills, went away exceedingly scandalized, and said, 'I protest, they are such an impious set of people, that I believe that if the last trumpet was to sound, they would bet puppet-show against Judgment'. If we get any nearer to the torrid zone, I shall pique myself on sending you a present of cedrati and orange-flower water: I am already planning a *terreno* for Strawberry Hill.

Phillip is seventeen and is preparing to present this piece at a grade 8 examination. He is a punctilious fellow and without prompting from his teacher he has read a number of Walpole's letters using the index to the multi-volume edition to help him select topics of interest. Living in Richmond he first became interested in Walpole when he cycled past his strange castle, Strawberry Hill at Twickenham, and was later fascinated to find in the local paper a photograph of an oil painting of this eighteenth-century arbiter of taste: a small neat man with powdered wig, impeccably dressed in embroidered frock-coat, dove-grey trousers met at knee level by white stockings and block-heeled buckle shoes. It was this picture that gave Phillip the clearest insight into Walpole's writings for his style seemed to mirror the image of the man, a neat style in which carefully balanced sentences did not blot out the humanity of the author but through which he shot his arrows of wit.

Once Phillip had understood that Smithfield was a meat-market on the edge of the City of London and that White's was a club to which cultured gentry repaired he felt that there were no further difficulties in comprehending the content. His next job was to check his own initial impressions of Walpole's style with the selected letter. This reinforced his opinion that Walpole wrote in balanced sentences, for many of them were in binary form with each of the two sections separated by a semi-colon. Often, as in the second sentence, the first half is a simple statement of fact leading on to either a conjecture or a development arising from the factual statement. At once Phillip had an insight into the way in which his speaking must develop in order to match this patterning. A further pointer towards the speaking required was Phillip's recognition that Walpole enjoyed listing one activity after another. This is most in evidence in the sentence beginning 'I got up . . .' with its description of citizens in panic, damage in general, toppled houses, crashed chimneys and stacks of broken china. Obviously such listings would help Phillip to gain impetus as he described the scenes. It was with surprise that he noticed that the second word of the letter was 'text'. The epistle to Mann is in the form of a sermon: the description of the earthquake is not really addressed to the single recipient of this letter but rather to a gathered audience, and the oratorical devices we have just considered, the formal structure and the listing process, are to be seen in that light.

This analysis of the style was not a dry business and Phillip soon realized that Walpole was a wit whose barbs were in evidence even in this short excerpt. At times the humour was grotesque as when Walpole felt his bed rise and surmised that an intruder was hiding beneath it; at other times it could revel in the *bons mots* of others as when Walpole repeated verbatim the parson's remarks. In this dangerous situation Walpole doesn't hesitate to level his sarcasm against those who attempt to leave London in the studied deceit that they wished to enjoy the fine weather in the country. Walpole was, Phillip decided, an observer of life rather than a total participant and thinking of this he began to arrive at the tone in which the passage should be spoken: it must be objective and distanced; he must speak as a highly interested onlooker, someone who is ready to use circum-stances to make play with the thrust of his ready wit. Walpole was not a man to report events as they occurred; he would select from life, elaborating and even inventing where necessary in order to make his point. This discovery, too, affected the tone: the manner of conveying the information was as important as the information itself. Walpole, Phillip knew, could be charged with self-consciousness in his writing.

As Phillip made his discoveries about the tone of the letter he became conscious of the shape. The epistle consists of more than a simple description. It begins with a quotation – unusual – and the first sentence serves as a preamble to whet the reader's appetite. Then the reader is introduced to the earthquakes. Phillip decided that the news of the exodus from the danger area was the climax of the letter and the gossip about the parson a coda, or afterthought, so his speaking would work towards news of the country-bound travellers. He felt that a judicious increase of pace from Walpole's realization of the first earthquake until he arrived at the climax would help to convey this shape.

Walpole's mannered prose style requires mannered speaking but this must be neither an affectation nor done at the expense of communciation. Often a single word or phrase needs to be isolated for emphasis, a technique known as pointing, but this must be undertaken with some delicacy. To allow one's technique to be obtrusive would condemn one as a 'wit-wanton' in the eighteenth century. Let us take a couple of examples of pointing. In the first Walpole makes it plain by his punctuation where an expectant pause (marked *) is to occur:

> I had been awake, and had scarcely dozed again – *
> on a sudden I felt my bolster lift up my head.

Phillip had to learn that his concentration must focus on the pause and during it he was to will the attention of the listener to anticipate what was to follow. Pauses without concentration reduce speech to sogginess. When he broke the pause by speaking the second half of the sentence, Phillip had to get a move on until he arrived at the all-important words, 'lift up my head'. These were then spoken so crisply that they became stressed. In some of the longer sentences where punctuation was no guide thought had to be given to the words which required emphasis. In the direct speech of the parson it seemed to Phillip that 'impious' was an important word, at least in the cleric's estimation, and that in order to make his antithesis effective two opposing ideas were to be expressed in 'puppet-show' and 'Judgement', each of which had to be spoken with weight. There are, of course, other examples of words which benefit from pointing in the letter.

As Phillip rehearsed the letter aloud he realized that many of the sentences required to be spoken on a single breath: much eighteenth-century writing makes this demand on a speaker. In order to be fit for this challenge, Phillip worked carefully on his breathing, gradually extending the length of phrase which he could speak on a controlled outgoing breath. He worked on some of the exercises suggested in Chapter 9.

In the reference library Phillip consulted illustrated volumes of eighteenth-century portraits. He was eager to look at portraits of seated gentlemen of this period for he felt that the selection was best spoken as if Walpole was sitting reading aloud the letter, a preferable ploy to impersonating the recipient. In paintings by Francis Hayman and Arthur Devis he found gentlemen seated in upright positions, head erect, legs either crossed to show a well-shaped calf or splayed out to create a careful balance with one hand on the thigh whilst the other arm rested on the side table, a relaxed hand hanging over the top. A portrait by Devis of Henry Fiennes Clinton, Earl of Lincoln, provided just the hint of studied informality Phillip was looking for. As the letter continued Phillip could shift his position and address the small coffee-house group he envisaged as his audience in a more intimate tone.

There were a couple of minor points for the candidate to sort out. 'Ought I to give this letter a formal introduction?' Phillip asked, but eventually he abandoned this and announced 'A letter of Horace Walpole', for in speaking the address and the date his listener was given enough information to cue him in to the circumstances. Whilst he was not going to wear a costume, Phillip realized that if he dressed with some formality and wore a tie and jacket, this would help to convey the preciseness of the character.

4.3.2 An essay by Gilbert Keith Chesterton

To contrast with Walpole's prose I have selected an essay by Gilbert Keith Chesterton, a description of a sketching outing to the Sussex downs.

> As I sat scrawling these silly figures on the brown paper, it began to dawn on me, to my great disgust, that I had left one chalk, and that a most exquisite and essential chalk, behind. I searched all my pockets, but I could not find any white chalk. . . .
>
> I sat on the hill in a sort of despair. There was no town nearer than Chichester at which it was even remotely probable that there would be such a thing as an artist's colourman. And yet, without white, my absurd little pictures would be as pointless as the world would be if there were no good people in it. I stared stupidly round, racking my brain for expedients. Then I suddenly stood up and roared with laughter, again and again, so that the cows stared at me and called a committee.
>
> Imagine a man in the Sahara regretting that he had no sand for his hour-glass. Imagine a gentleman in mid-ocean wishing that he had brought some salt water with him for his chemical experiments. I was sitting on an immense warehouse of white chalk. The landscape was made entirely out of white chalk. White chalk was piled mere miles until it met the sky. I stooped and broke a piece off the rock I sat on: it did not mark so well as the shop chalks do; but it gave the effect. And I stood there in a

trance of pleasure, realizing that this Southern England is not only a grand peninsular, and a tradition and a civilization; it is something even more admirable. It is a piece of chalk.

Chesterton was a large, avuncular figure, noisy and gregarious, producing a vast literary output of essays, novels, religious works and magazine articles. Something of the sheer exuberance of the man comes across in this selection. Earlier paragraphs in the essay describe his liking for using coloured chalks on brown paper in order to draw not actual objects but their 'souls', unhindered by the need for close representation. It was at this point that he realized he had not brought any white chalk with him.

I'd like you to consider the following questions and see to what extent your own responses to Chesterton's essay match mine:

(a) Is the gender of the performer important?
(b) What age would this excerpt be suitable for?
(c) What is the tone of the piece?
(d) At what rate would you speak it?
(e) How would you present Chesterton's essay to your audience?

When you read my responses to these questions, if they differ from your own try to see why and try to decide whether your answer is merely an alternative or whether you should re-examine the question.

(a) It seems to me that Chesterton, although he is writing of a personal experience, is very much aware that he is writing an essay and that, in common with many essays, it doesn't matter at all whether a male or female candidate speaks the piece. An essay is really a ramble through a number of ideas clustering around a theme; the section printed here is the conclusion in which the focus is solely on Chesterton's use of the artist's improvised chalk.

(b) This piece, I feel, is suitable for a wide age range. An intelligent teenager from thirteen upwards would be capable of making an interesting presentation of the essay. I don't feel that there is an upper age limit.

(c) I think you can almost 'see' Chesterton in his prose. It suggests an ebullient person, overflowing with ideas, a mind capable of making far-ranging connections, and a man with a great enthusiasm for the countryside, especially that of Sussex. Ideas come tumbling out and although Chesterton is careful always to write with clarity you never know where he is going to take you next: in this piece he unexpectedly introduces us to travellers in the Sahara and mid-ocean voyagers. Reiteration reinforces some of his ideas: look at the number of sentences containing the phrase 'white chalk' once he starts to make his discovery. In the expression of his ideas he is never afraid to lay bare his own response and feelings in such phrases as 'I stared stupidly around . . .' and 'I stood there in a trance of pleasure . . .'. Chesterton's own love of words can be seen in his descriptions (the downs as an 'immense warehouse' of white chalk), in his use of original similes ('. . . as the world would be if there were no good people in it'), his equally original use of metaphor ('the cows . . . called a committee') and his way of building up a description like a tower of bricks (southern England is 'a grand peninsular, and a tradition and a civilization'). He is a man scattering words broadcast but they all take root.

(d) When you consider speaking this essay, you must obviously convey to your listeners many of the points I have jotted down in the previous paragraph. Chesterton's enthusiasm must become your enthusiasm. Unlike Walpole, Chesterton is never self-conscious and finicky about expression and therefore native enthusiasm can carry you along much of the way with this piece. You don't need to draw attention to any of Chesterton's stylistic devices: there is no need to point them up. This means that your rate of speaking must be rapid enough to convey your enthusiasm. Obviously the first three or four sentences are plain statements of regret and you make these in the way you would make any other such statement; but then the enthusiasm builds and so does the pace as you speak again and again of the white chalk. The pace helps with the identification of the climax, which for me came with the sentence, 'The landscape was made entirely out of white chalk', but a friend put it at the previous sentence. It is the repetitious nature of the prose which allows different people to opt for a different apex in the speaking. Again one can use pace in order to lead up to the last sentence of the excerpt, a joke sentence, a slang expression not used as often now as in Chesterton's day; nevertheless it needs to be spoken with firm deliberateness.

(e) Of the various pieces we have looked at in this chapter, this is the one which, I feel, has least need of meticulous preparation. If you can recapture Chesterton's zest for living, then you are well on the way towards presenting his words with spirit and assurance.

4.4 BIBLICAL PROSE

4.4.1 Saint Mark's Gospel, Chapter 16

The last selection in this chapter consists of a passage from the Authorized Version of the Bible which would be suitable for a teenager to present. Saint Mark's gospel is a biography with a purpose, to show that Jesus is the Messiah. The verses from it given here are the first eight of the final chapter. Jesus had been nailed to the cross on which he died; his body had been taken down and buried in a garden tomb; over the entrance to this a large stone had been rolled in order to prevent anyone entering.

1. And when the sabbath was past, Mary Magdalene, and Mary the mother of James, and Salome, brought spices, that they might come and anoint him.
2. And very early on the first day of the week, they come to the tomb when the sun was risen.
3. And they were saying among themselves, Who shall roll us away the stone from the door of the tomb?
4. And, looking up, they see that the stone is rolled back; for it was exceeding great.
5. And entering into the tomb, they saw a young man sitting on the right side, arrayed in a white robe; and they were amazed.
6. And he said unto them, Be not amazed: ye seek Jesus the Nazarene, which hath been crucified: he is risen; he is not here: behold, the place where they laid him!
7. But go, tell his disciples and Peter, He goeth before you into Galilee: there shall ye see him, as he said unto you.
8. And they went out, and fled from the tomb; for trembling and astonishment had come upon them: and they said nothing to any one; for they were afraid.

Before we think of the piece as a whole I would like to take you through each of the verses and consider carefully the meaning. By doing this I hope that we shall discover something of the atmosphere Mark was intent on creating and which you, as a speaker, must convey to your listeners.

1. Here we are introduced to three women, Mary Magdalene, another Mary and Salome. It is necessary that you draw the attention of the listener carefully to these three names for the people are key figures in the story. To clarify it would be acceptable to substitute 'Jesus' for 'him' in this verse.
2. In Israel dawn arrives quickly, suddenly flooding the countryside with light; this story is bathed in a mysterious new light. In your speaking you must give the sense of newness to listeners.
3. Mark does not present the women's problems as a series of questions in the way they must have asked them but he simply puts the challenge into one general question. Therefore this query must not be over-inflected as if it occurred in everyday speech.
5. By 'a young man' Mark means an angelic visitor so the speaker's voice must reflect the wonder an onlooker feels in the presence of this messenger.
6–7. The resurrection message is couched in two phrases: 'He has risen . . .' and '. . . he is going before you to Galilee'. Here is a joyful proclamation which obviously affects the telling of the story.
8. The reactions of the women are those used by biblical writers to describe an encounter with God, amazement, fear and awe. These emotions must guide the speaking of the last verse of the excerpt. This is the final verse of St Mark's gospel for the remaining verses printed in the Bible were added later.

Therefore the resurrection message has to be conveyed totally by the time this verse is reached.Conclusiveness is needed as the last words are spoken; this is not just the end of an excerpt.

In reading from the Authorized Version a number of problems become apparent. The first is the language. This translation of the Bible was made during the reign of James I and its language is the same language employed by Jacobean tragic playwrights, vibrant, formal and dignified. Generally it should be spoken slowly with a realization of the grandeur of its phrases and a recognition of some of its characteristics. Thus in this passage we can note the use of paradox in verse 6:

> '. . . you seek Jesus of Nazareth who was crucified.
> He has risen . . .'

Quite often actions are presented in pairs:

> . . . they went out and fled from the tomb

a device of which the speaker must be aware so that he can balance one action against the other. A further problem, in part arising from the archaic language, is that many people have heard an over-reverent, monotonous 'Bible-reading voice' especially in evidence at cathedral evensong. As with any other passage of prose the speaker has to discover the vibrancy of the message and then convey this with dynamic skill. Don't be afraid, for example, to let the angelic proclamation ring out, and to balance this give the response of the women a full measure of wonder. The third problem to which I'd draw your attention is that the Bible has become well-known, especially in church-attending circles. This familiarity makes your task more difficult for you have to bring newness to the speaking and this resurrection story must have all the freshness of that daybreak in the garden of the tomb. To convey this you must make the story new to yourself.

'How do I introduce the reading?' There are no prescribed ways of doing this. You may give the excerpt a simple title which will serve as an introduction, such as 'Saint Mark's account of the first Easter morning'. You may find it helpful to bear in mind a couple of the ways the reading is introduced in church. The simplest form would be 'A reading from Saint Mark's gospel' or a more formal introduction would be to announce, 'The first verse of the sixteenth chapter of the gospel according to Saint Mark'. The formality of the latter helps the listener to attune to the sonorous language which is to follow.

4.4.2 Translations of the Bible

In addition to the Authorized Version other translations of the Bible exist and as you may be allowed to make a choice from one of these I would like to look at three further versions thinking of their suitability for reading aloud.

Under the auspices of the Roman Catholic church the Jerusalem Bible has been produced. The version is in a lively, modern English. In the story we have been looking at something of the mystery of the occasion is lost in the angel's words, 'There is no need for alarm' and in the women's reaction, 'they were frightened out of their wits', although we have to remember that the style of Mark is unadorned, written with an urgent brevity which is apparent in the Jerusalem translation.

The New English Bible is more formal than the Jerusalem and its sentence structure tends to be more complicated. Its translators strove to 'use the English of the present day . . . the natural vocabulary, constructions and rhythms of contemporary speech'. In this I think they have been more successful than their brief might have allowed, for there are very few jarring phrases couched in transient English. If we use the same two fragments as a test case we find the introductory words of the angel as 'Fear nothing' – nebulous but dignified, and the women's reaction is described: '. . . they went out, and ran from the tomb, besides themselves with terror'.

The United Bible Societies produced the Good News Bible, again in everyday English. Tactfully, versions for American use and British use were made. The latter has crisp short sentences which when read aloud can sound staccato but as long as this is realized the speaker can compensate. The women are described as being 'alarmed' when they first confront the angel and the same word is picked up in his command, 'Don't be alarmed', a repetition which does not sound well. At the end of the story the women run from the tomb 'distressed and terrified', a good enough description in itself, but does it convey the awe experienced in an encounter with one of the mighty acts of God?

4.5 A SUMMARY OF THE ADVICE ON SPEAKING PROSE

We have covered much ground in looking at the five examples of prose for speaking aloud. It would be helpful if I made a brief summary of the more important recommendations:

(a) See the excerpt chosen in the context of the rest of the work;
(b) Be well informed about the author, his times and literary background, his style, his themes and his intentions in writing;
(c) As with poetry consider carefully the tone of the writing, the style, the vocabulary, the characterization and the descriptive writing;
(d) Consider how this is to be interpreted in terms of intention, pace, shape, tone, characterization, impersonation, gesture, etc. Ask: 'What basis for communication with my audience does this writing demand?'

4.6 RESOURCES

4.6.1 Bibliographical details of works mentioned in the text

Allen, B. (1987) *Francis Hayman*, Yale University Press, New Haven.

Austen, J. (ed. A. H. Ehrenpreis) (1972) *Northanger Abbey*, Penguin Books, Harmondsworth.

Bible, The (1982) *Authorized Version*, Collins, London.

Bible, The (1976) *Good News Bible*, British and Foreign Society, London.

Bible, The (1966) *Jerusalem Bible*, Darton, Longman and Todd, London.

Bible, The (1975) *New English Bible*, British and Foreign Bible Society, London.

Bond, M. (1972) *Paddington Helps Out*, Collins, London.

Chesterton, G. K. (ed. M. Smith) (1984) *The Spirit of Christmas: Stories, Poems and Essays*, Xanadu Publications, London.

Dahl, R. (1982) *The Twits*, Penguin Books, Harmondsworth.

Dickens, C. (ed. J. Kennett) (1980) *Oliver Twist*, Blackie and Son, Glasgow.

Grahame, K. (ed. P. Green) (1983) *The Wind in the Willows*, Oxford University Press, Oxford.

Murdoch, I. (1958) *The Bell*, Chatto and Windus, London.

Sartin, S. (1983) *Polite Society by Arthur Devis, 1712–1787*, Harris Museum and Art Gallery, Preston.

Sterne, L. (ed. H. Anderson) (1980) *Tristram Shandy*, W. W. Norton, London.

Walpole, H. (ed. W. S. Lewis) (1937–83) *Horace Walpole's Correspondence*, Oxford University Press, London and Oxford.

4.6.2 Books on places and writers

As with the excerpt from Chesterton's essays, it is often interesting to connect locations with writers. The following literary guides to places and writers will help to do this.

Drabble, M. (1979) *A Writer's Britain*, Thames and Hudson, London.

Eagle, D. and Carnell, H. (1977) *The Oxford Literary Guide to the British Isles*, Oxford University Press, Oxford.

Morley, F. (1980) *Literary Britain*, Hutchinson, London.

Weinreb, B. and Hibbert, C. (1983) *The London Encyclopaedia*, Book Club Associates, London.

In addition to the books mentioned, many literary trails are produced in pamphlet or broadsheet form. A good example is Blackwell's *Literary Heritage Trails* published in conjunction with the English Tourist Board and dealing with Oxford, Oxfordshire, the Thames Valley and the Great Ouse areas.

4.6.3 Background reading

Barclay, W. (1978) *Communicating the Gospel*, St Andrew's Press, Edinburgh.

Chesterton, G. K. (ed. M. J. Parry) (1975) *Father Brown Detective Stories*, Macmillan Educational, London.

Ffinch, M. (1988) *G. K. Chesterton. A Biography*, Weidenfeld and Nicolson, London.

Green, P. (1982) *The World of 'Beyond the Wild Wood'*, West and Bower, Exeter (on Kenneth Grahame).

Smith, W. (1967) *Horace Walpole: Writer, Politician and Connoisseur*, Yale University Press, New Haven.

5

In rehearsal :
The period play

5.1 THE CHALLENGES OF SOLO DRAMATIC WORK

All of the boards offer the opportunity to perform a dramatic excerpt in the course of their examinations; quite often plays of the past are either specifically instanced or the work of a given playwright, such as William Shakespeare, is stipulated. Where the choice is left to the discretion of the candidate, it is worth remembering that period plays can be most effective vehicles for demonstrating your ability in performance. In this chapter I would like to consider the classical Greek theatre, the Elizabethan theatre and the Georgian theatre, choosing a play of each era as a key text from which I use an excerpt to demonstrate the technique of solo performance. This demands a very different approach to the staging from that using a full cast in a theatrical setting. In a solo recital you have not only to convey to your audience your own role but also such other characters as might be on stage, the setting, your costume and your relationship to the audience. This places considerable demands on you as an actor. There is some advice covering the three key texts I would wish briefly to give you. Let me present this as a set of imperatives:

(a) Know your words with absolute certainty;
(b) Know your role;
(c) Know the costume your role dictates you should wear;
(d) Know your relationship with the audience;
(e) Know the limitations of your acting area.

A few words on each of these principles will, I hope, help you to see why they are important:

(a) A total security in the knowledge of the text will be the biggest confidence-booster you can get. There are various methods of learning your lines. For some of your preparatory period rest content to learn them through the process of rehearsal, allowing the emotions and thoughts beneath the words, as well as the lines themselves, to permeate you. Try to understand what motivates the character you are playing so that speech, gesture and

movement spring from an inner compulsion. As the time for the performance nears check that the words are so much part of you that you can say
them in the face of any distraction: try, for example, turning on the radio and
with the volume high speak your lines at the rate they will be spoken in
performance. This sounds strange, but many candidates discover, too late,
that whilst they are performing in an examination distractions can occur. I
have found these more pronounced than distractions on the stage.

(b) 'Know who you are!' may sound somewhat obvious advice but it is
surprising how many candidates have not thought carefully about the
character they are portraying in relation to other characters and within the
context of the play. Books of audition pieces in which excerpts from plays
appear are of dubious value for you need to look at the development of your
character within the progress of the play, gathering all the facts and reported
opinions about the character into a dossier from which you study how to
present a rounded person to your audience. In subsequent discussion the
examiner will be keen to hear about your response to this character and how
you prepared the role for performance: without a knowledge of the complete
play your answers would be thin indeed.

(c) Think carefully about the costume of the character. Several boards allow
suggestions of costume such as scarves, gloves and hats to be worn: these
tokens can be helpful to candidates provided they have been used in
rehearsal. Practice skirts are nearly always allowed. You will need to make a
detailed study of the costume your character is wearing and think about the
way this influences your movement and gestures. Candidates who live in
London are fortunate enough to be able to visit the excellent costume court
of the Victoria and Albert Museum at South Kensington where examples
from Elizabethan times to the present day are on show. Similarly there is a
museum of costume in Bath and many provincial museums have at least a few
examples. For those who cannot find such exhibits plates in books can be
informative. James Laver and Doreen Yarwood have each produced
scholarly works, *Costume and Fashion: A Concise History* and *Outline of
English Costume*. Your purpose in looking at costumes is to imagine yourself
wearing one appropriate to your character so that you gain the feel of it and
understand how it will affect your stance and walk. In this context
anthologies of paintings of various periods are useful for posture and the
spatial relationship between one person and another is instantly observable.
When I've directed classes for repertory companies on eighteenth-century
movement and manners I have arrived with armfuls of pictures of people on
horseback, sitting at table, performing various indoor and outdoor tasks,
standing and talking, shopping at London markets, so that actors may get an
impression of characters and their 'shaping' through costume. Don't forget
(many do!) that underwear is an important constituent of costume.
Eighteenth-century ladies, for example, were so tightly constricted by stays

and corsets that these gave erectness to their carriage and ensured that when they sat down they glided with a straight back to the seat of the sofa. Wear suitable shoes for the period and avoid performing without footwear, a passing fashion in which some candidates indulge.

(d) Dependent on the shape of the interior of the theatre and on the text of his play, the actor's relationship with the audience has varied over the centuries. For example, in the plays of the late seventeenth century actors often addressed the audience directly in set speeches at the end of scenes, and even in the course of a scene one-line asides were made to the audience stressing its complicity in the action. However, in the early decades of the twentieth century realism in scenic design helped to fix the notion that the stage was a room of a house of which the fourth wall, the opening of the proscenium arch, had been removed and that the audience was a body of eavesdroppers on the action. Hence there was virtually no reference to the audience at this period. All performers need to be aware of the audience–actor relationship for although there will be only one or two examiners watching the performance they are a token audience.

(e) In your mind's eye you must know the limits of your stage and convey these clearly through your acting to the examiners. No examiner wants you performing on top of him, so leave an area – a no-man's land – between yourself and him. Envisage clearly the front line of your stage and don't play beyond that. If the examination room allows, make your neutral area six feet in depth. Be aware of the upper limit of your stage: this will not necessarily be the back wall of the room for the simple reason that, with only one performer, the stage has to be scaled down so that you do not become lost. If you don't work within a limited acting area, but insist on a stage as large as that of Drury Lane, you will find yourself rushing about making extraordinarily lengthy moves, to no good effect. In defining your stage be aware, too, of its shape at the time at which the dramatic excerpt was written: for example, in classical Greece the stage or *proskenion* tended to be a long narrow shape far removed from the audience, whereas in Elizabethan times the stage consisted of a large bare platform thrust into the midst of the audience. Generally you are welcome to present your dramatic selection either as if you are performing in the original theatrical conditions or you may adapt the staging for your own purposes.

In planning your staging you should bear in mind that some of the theatrical devices of full-scale performance cannot effectively be communicated by you because of the limitations of solo performance. At times I have been left unclear about what was happening within the acting area: this might have stemmed from the fact that the candidate had introduced too many imaginary properties or peopled the stage with too many imaginary characters. I have seen chairs dotted over the performance area and been told that these represented people, perhaps the ballroom dancers in *Lady*

Windermere's Fan or the king's troops preparing for the battle of Agincourt in *Henry V*. Sometimes a candidate has placed an empty chair on stage imagining that the person with whom he was conversing sat there. Unfortunately in all of these instances empty chairs remained as empty chairs to me. It is much better to work solely at creating the reality of the characters through the strength of your imagination, the direction of your speaking and by your eye focus; by your artistry and technique you must cause other characters to stand, move about the stage and leave the scene.

In previous chapters I wrote of the need to choose your pieces with care and to ensure that you know your limitations and strengths. This applies to dramatic pieces also. An obvious limitation is one of gender. If a playwright creates a male character, then it should be played by a man; similarly with women's roles. I am uneasy when I watch gender transference on stage. Several academies, however, do not share my dis-ease. The LAMDA syllabus in the introduction to the Junior Acting examinations states that parts written for boys may be played by girls but at the Senior Acting level it is stipulated, 'Male characters must not be played by women (and vice versa)' and the Poetry Society in a note on its examination in Dramatic Verse advises:

> Since 'boy-players' are part of the English theatrical tradition and 'girl-players' part of the English educational tradition, examiners are prepared to accept performances by speakers of opposite sex to that of their chosen roles

The performer's physical appearance is a further limitation. It is obvious that the performer should conform more or less to the character in age: a person in her late thirties cannot effectively play Juliet. An exception to this may be made in character parts. On stage it is acceptable for a thirty-year-old actor to turn himself into a seventy-year-old through his acting technique aided perhaps by his make-up and costume. There are, too, various conventions which must be kept in mind. To return to Juliet, romantic imagination has pictured her as a mere slip of a girl. A heavily-built fifteen-year-old may find herself working against the audience's acceptances if she undertakes the part and examiners are, to some extent, audience representatives. I once saw a painfully thin candidate tackling the role of Falstaff. Certainly he was trying to 'think big' and on the stage, with the help of a padded costume, he might have been acceptable, but in the solo performance I found my belief in his characterization severely strained. Don't despair about these limitations, for if tackled positively they help you to eliminate unsuitable roles so that you are left with those you can undertake to advantage.

The final point that I would like to make is that the dramatic selection must be *acted*. From time to time I am presented with a bland recitation of words – and that is all. That won't do! The sentiments expressed must stem from one's heart with such intensity that the character and his emotions live through the performer; this strength of feeling prompts the speaking and impels gesture and movement.

5.2 KEY TEXTS

5.2.1 *The Eumenides* by Aeschylus

The first of the key excerpts is from *The Eumenides*, one of the plays in the trilogy *The Oresteia*, written by Aeschylus in 458 BC and translated here by Robert Fagles. The person speaking is Pythia, the priestess, at the Temple of Apollo, Delphi. She has just entered the shrine to consult the oracle and discovered there the Furies, strange creatures who exert revenge. Orestes, who in an earlier play in the trilogy avenged his father's death by killing his mother, has found refuge in the temple where he has been pursued by the Furies.

> Where are the Greeks among you? Draw your lots and enter.
> It is the custom here. I will tell the future
> only as the god will lead the way.

She goes through the doors and reappears in a moment, shaken, thrown to her knees by some terrific force.

> Terrors –
> terrors to tell, terrors all can see! –
> they send me reeling back from Apollo's house.
> The strength drains, it's very hard to stand,
> crawling on all fours, no spring in the legs . . .
> an old woman, gripped by fear, is nothing,
> a child, nothing more.

Struggling to her feet, trying to compose herself.

> I'm on my way to the vault,
> It's green with wreaths, and there at the Navelstone
> I see a man – an abomination to god –
> he holds the seat where suppliants sit for purging;
> his hands dripping blood, and his sword just drawn,
> and he holds a branch (it must have topped an olive)
> wreathed with a fine tuft of wool, all piety,
> fleece gleaming white. So far it's clear, I tell you.
> But there in a ring around the man, an amazing company –
> women, sleeping, nestling against the benches . . .
> women? No,
> Gorgons I'd call them; but then with Gorgons

you'd see the grim, inhuman . . .
      I saw a picture
years ago, the creatures tearing the feast
away from Phineus –
     These have no wings,
I looked. But black they are, and so repulsive.
Their heavy, rasping breathing makes me cringe.
And their eyes ooze a discharge, sickening,
and what they wear – to flaunt *that* at the gods,
the idols, sacrilege! even in the homes of men.
The tribe that produced the brood I never saw,
or a plot of ground to boast it nursed their kind
without some tears, some pain for all its labour.

Now for the outcome. This is his concern,
Apollo the master of this house, the mighty power.
Healer, prophet, diviner of signs, he purges
the halls of others – He must purge his own.

She leaves.

(a) *The original performance conditions*

I would like to think about the theatrical setting in which each of the key texts was originally staged. My notes are necessarily brief and hopefully you will want to amplify your knowledge by looking at some of the books I have suggested in the Resources section at the end of this chapter.

At Epidauros the greater part of a classical Greek theatre still stands and my remarks on Greek theatrical conditions are based on that. The acting area consisted of a platform, the *proskenion*, slightly under one hundred feet wide and about twelve feet in depth; at either end of this was a ramp by means of which some of the characters made their exits. The number of characters on the stage at any one time was usually limited to three and so no great depth was required. In front of the stage was a vast circular flat area, three or four feet below the level of the stage, the *orchestra*, in the middle of which was an altar dedicated to Dionysos, the god of new birth. Within this area the chorus performed. To the rear of the *proskenion* was a large wooden flat-roofed two-storey building entered by means of three double doors, the *skene*. At the selected part of the play the area in front of the *skene* is the forecourt to the Temple of Apollo and the interior of the *skene* represents the shrine. Apart from Pythia there are no other performers either on the *proskenion* or in the *orchestra*. When Pythia enters the temple she does so through the central doors, emerging the same way. At either side of the *proskenion* is the *parados* or exit route and when, at the end of the scene, Pythia leaves the stage she does so by walking down the ramp and along the *parados*. Entrances and exits were lengthy, ceremonial affairs often accompanied by music. The audience, a mass of twenty thousand spectators, was seated in a semi-circular auditorium on rows of rising steps; the greater part of the audience was raised above the level of the actor so that projection was not only outwards but upwards. The acoustics at Epidauros are superb and a whisper on stage can be heard at the rear of the auditorium.

In the classical Greek theatre all of the performers were male so that Pythia would be played by a man. Most noteworthy, he would wear a large mask completely enveloping his head. A larger-than-life face would be sculpted on the front of this in cork or thin strips of wood. This device made evident to the furthermost members of the audience which character was on stage, and it must be remembered that some of the audience were as much as two hundred and twenty feet distant from the acting area. Costumes were simple: Pythia would be clothed in a full-length loose robe either white, to signify her role as a virgin priestess, or brightly coloured, gathered round her waist by a girdle. The robe would have long sleeves to hide the over-muscular arms of the actor. Sandals were probably worn.

Two factors governed the acting style. Firstly the size of the theatre demanded a performance that was clear with actions magnified. When the actor spoke he possibly struck a pose which altered with each change of emotion. Secondly the mask demanded projected, rhetorical speaking. Obviously no facial expressions could be seen with the result that the remainder of the actor's body had to register his emotions. Vase paintings show that the actor's arms and hands were most expressive in achieving this. To some measure your own performance ought to reflect this style of presentation.

(b) Study and interpretation

In order to help you with your own preparation of a selection from a Greek tragedy we shall watch a candidate, Dione, working with her teacher, Mrs Barrett, on the key text. Dione is seventeen and she is entering for a grade 8 examination. Her preparation for the A-level examination Greek Literature in Translation had whetted her appetite for classical drama and she is delighted that this grade gives her the opportunity to work intensively on one character in a play. Dione's first task is to come to terms with the meaning of the text. Her researches reveal to her that at the time Aeschylus was writing the priestess at the Temple of Apollo was ordered to be at least fifty-years-old; some were far in excess of this. In this excerpt she is the only person on the stage, so her question, 'Where are the Greeks among you?' is addressed to the auditorium and is a means of linking the audience with the stage. The Greeks would have been a group of suppliants visiting Apollo's temple. The priestess goes into the temple, pauses there a moment and then reappears so visibly shaken by what she has witnessed that the shock brings her to her knees leaving her only able to crawl; her speech too is affected as she repeats the word 'terror'. After several lines she attempts to compose herself and finds the strength to rise so that she can tell directly to the audience what she has seen. Orestes was seated at the stone which marks the navel of the earth, in one hand the bloody sword, the symbol of matricide, and in the other the signs of the suppliant. Near him were the Furies, monstrously ugly women: Pythia falters as she tries to describe them. She compares them to gorgons, monsters with snaky hair and great spat-out lips but that isn't sufficiently horrible, so she goes on to compare them with winged harpies, another group of women demons, who snatched the food of King Phineus away from him. However, these comparisons can only inadequately describe the horror of the Furies. She goes on to give a factual description of their appearance. Pythia finishes her speech by pointing out that Apollo, the god who cures individuals and dynasties of foulness, must purge his temple of the presence of the Furies. She then makes her way from the stage to be seen no more in the play.

After looking at the excerpt a number of times Dione set it within the context of the play, noting how the roles of Orestes, Apollo and the Furies developed. She learnt more about Pythia by consulting a classical encyclopaedia and undertook further research about the Greek theatre. She looked too for pictures of extant masks used in tragedy.

By this time she felt ready to rehearse the piece. From the start she had to decide whether to wear a mask. The syllabus she consulted allowed props to be used – but was a mask a prop? Mrs Barrett phoned the examination secretary who pointed out that as the use of a mask was not specifically disallowed Dione could feel free to wear one in the recital. However, if her voice became muffled by it, then it would be only right that the examiner's mark reflected a lack of vocal clarity. Dione was a practical person and she produced a three dimensional papier-maché face to which she fitted a hood, covering this with grey horse hair. At the first wearing it became obvious that Dione would have to rehearse with the mask in order to get used to this unfamiliar style of acting.

Dione wanted most of her lines to be spoken as she stood at the centre of the acting area directly to the audience which she imagined encircled her. She was keen to give the impression she was performing to a vast crowd of which the examiner was a part, sitting at the front of the central block of seats. She had decided that the climax of the speech was the priestess's description of the Furies, and she would perform this in a widespread attitude which would allow her, in her shocked state, to declaim the lines forcibly. She then went on to build up the surrounding parts of her performance.

Had you been able to see Dione in rehearsal several days before the examination you would have discovered that her performance had acquired shape. Before putting her mask on she introduced the piece explaining in a couple of sentences the function of the priestess. She then walked to the rear of the acting area and with her back to the audience, she placed the mask on her head. Her black practice skirt was the only other concession to costume. Slowly she turned to face the audience and then, equally slowly, she moved to the centre, indicating in her walk the age of the character which she had decided should be seventy, old enough to give her a wealth of wisdom and experience which was most necessary in this piece. Then she asked the initial question. On her sentence, 'I will tell the future . . .' she made her way upstage to the imagined temple doors, miming her passage over the threshold and then, with her back to the audience, she imagined as strongly as she was able that she was confronted by the Furies. Clutching her breast, for the shock had caused chest pains, she staggered back to the central area and fell to her knees whilst speaking: 'The strength drains . . .'. There was no break in the speaking as she tried to compose herself and gain enough energy to stand. As she described the vision of Orestes at the navelstone she circled the remembered object gazing at the fugitive. When she told of the Furies the sheer terror of that encounter was relived: Pythia staggered from one point to another as she encountered in her memory gorgon and harpy and then, gaining in grandeur and sureness, she stood again at the centre of the performance space and delivered the nine horrific descriptive lines. There was a pause in the speaking as Pythia walked upstage to the temple where she spoke her final four lines. In complete silence Pythia slowly, brokenly walked to the corner of the acting area facing away from the audience and waited in momentary repose. With no sense of rush she quietly took the mask from her head, laid it on the floor against the wall and made her way to the side of the stage ready to announce her next piece.

In this practice run you would not have seen the difficulties Dione encountered earlier. The technique of the mask posed problems, although to her surprise Dione found it offered her chances of freedom which she had not suspected. The collapse of her legs, that time of shock which reduced her to a child-like crawl, was a difficult action to achieve, for tragic dignity had to be maintained and yet terror must be evident. By practising the fall in slow motion, and in performance keeping a tight control on the speed of the collapse, an eerie effect was obtained. The reiterated use of the word 'terror' suggested that a total release of sound was required, splendid in an amphitheatre but not suited to a performance in an examination room, so here there had to be some holding back of the sound and in compensation an increase of tension. Dione found the ending of the piece difficult to time with sensitivity: she had to establish in her mind that there must be no rush simply because the text had been spoken; silence still had to be used as a performance adjunct.

In dealing with this performance of an excerpt from the theatre of over two thousand years ago I've stressed that you need to have a clear picture of the conditions in which plays of the past were acted, not merely as academic knowledge, but so that the conventions may guide you in developing the necessary style. It so happened that Myrtle, another of Mrs Barrett's students, decided to work on the same excerpt but to replan it for presentation in modern studio conditions. In order to rescale the work she found that it was still necessary to study the original conditions and to make sure that she maintained the spirit of classical tragedy which can easily be lost. In watching small-scale productions of Greek tragedies in a studio in Oxford I have noticed how very easy it is to mislay that extra dimension, the feeling of destiny, the knowledge that the gods were involved in human downfall and so, with that loss, to reduce tragedy to the level of a sad story.

5.2.2 *Hamlet* by William Shakespeare

The next excerpt is taken from William Shakespeare's *Hamlet*, Act 1, scene 2. It is a speech of King Claudius to Hamlet:

> 'Tis sweet and commendable in your nature, Hamlet,
> To give these mourning duties to your father.
> But you must know your father lost a father;
> That father lost, lost his; and the survivor bound
> In filial obligation for some term
> To do obsequious sorrow. But to persever
> In obstinate condolement is a course
> Of impious stubborness; 'tis unmanly grief.
> It shows a will most incorrect to heaven,
> A heart unfortified, a mind impatient,
> An understanding simple and unschooled.
> For what we know must be, and is as common
> As any the most vulgar thing to sense,
> Why should we, in our peevish opposition,
> Take it to heart? Fie! 'Tis a fault to heaven,
> A fault against the dead, a fault to nature,
> To reason most absurd, whose common theme
> Is death of fathers, and who still hath cried,
> From the first corse till he that died today,
> 'This must be so.' We pray you, throw to earth
> This unprevailing woe and think of us
> As of a father. For let the world take note,
> You are the most immediate to our throne,
> And with no less nobility of love
> Than that which dearest father bears his son
> Do I impart toward you. For your intent
> In going back to school in Wittenberg,
> It is most retrograde to our desire,
> And we beseech you, bend you to remain
> Here, in the cheer and comfort of our eye,
> Our chiefest courtier, cousin, and our son.

(a) The original performance conditions

As before I would like to think about the original performance conditions of the play. The first Globe playhouse was built by the Lord Chamberlain's Men in 1599 and situated on Bankside, a riverside area to the south-west of London Bridge. It was polygonal in shape measuring about one hundred feet in diameter. Beyond that we know little for certain and in order to gain a workable knowledge of the interior we have to make some deductions based on the next theatre built on that site in 1613. A large bare stage jutted into the auditorium, with an acting area of roughly thirty feet in depth and forty-three feet in width. At the rear was the tiring house and the backstage. Entrances situated on either side of the tiring house were the actors' principal means of getting on and off the stage. Above the entrances, for the length of much of the tiring house, ran a gallery. It has been conjectured that the height of the stage was in the region of six feet.

The audience was divided into those 'penny stinkards' who stood at ground level throughout the performance looking up at the stage, and the people sitting in the two or three galleries which ran round the inside edge of the building. The first of these galleries was possibly at the same height as the stage and linked, as were the galleries above it, with the tiring house.

Reconstructions by such scholars as Walter Hodges give detailed refinements to this bland sketch. For our purposes we are interested in the size of the stage on which the actors performed and in their relationship with the audience. A couple of further points are worth considering for they implicitly affect acting style. The central part of the theatre and the foremost part of the stage were open to the sky, whilst the rear of the stage was covered by a roof supported on pillars; the galleries too were covered. This meant that the weather could affect performances. Additionally the noise of Bankside infiltrated into the theatre as the plays were performed in the afternoons, a busy part of the working day. There would have been, too, some movement from the people surrounding the stage. Actors had to overcome these distractions and noises by adopting a well-projected style of speaking, perhaps at the expense of subtlety. The rate at which the text was spoken must have been considerable if the play really was, as the Prologue to *Romeo and Juliet* states, performed in two hours.

An Elizabethan actor was highly aware of his audience for its members sat grouped around him and others pressed against the front of the stage at his feet; all were highly evident in the daylight. Sometimes the text was addressed to characters on stage but on occasions Shakespeare draws the attention of his audience to the fact that it is watching a play by employing metaphors based on the theatre. Hamlet does this in speaking to Rosencrantz and Guildenstern. Suddenly we are no more in a room in Elsinore when he points out the 'excellent canopy' over the stage with its underside adorned with a gilded carving of the sun. In conversation, too, Shakespeare sometimes explores the strangeness of the concept that a common player may undertake the roles of aristocrats and kings.

The pretence that we are at the court of Elsinore is broken when an actor, remaining in role, speaks directly to the audience, a device sometimes given to a single character at the end of a scene. An example occurs at the end of this key scene: Hamlet is left alone on stage to share with the audience his unease that his father's spirit is roaming restlessly.

(b) Study and interpretation

Let me introduce you to Gerard. He is entering soon for his gold medal examination. A stocky rugby-playing enthusiast, twenty-years-old, with much experience of acting in his home-town Shakespeare company, Gerard has decided that his physique well fits the part of Claudius whom he sees as a man achieving his own ends through bullying. That over-simplified response Gerard has to check by tracing the progress of Claudius through the play. Act 1, scene 2 is the first scene in which Claudius appears: he speaks a highly formal rhetorical language and adopts a kindly but reserved approach to his nephew; we might approve of such a figure at first sight. Later in the scene Hamlet presents us with his own impression of his uncle, 'no more like my father Than I to Heracles'. This is the start of the reordering of our vision of the king. We become aware of the true state of affairs when Hamlet's father's ghost describes the way in which he was poisoned by his brother, so that Claudius, an 'adulterate beast', might marry Gertrude. This was a crime of lust for both power and a woman. The next time the audience sees Claudius the spectators view him in a new light; he is a schemer plotting with Rosencrantz and Guildenstern. With the arrival of the players Hamlet has the means to stage a replay of the murder so that he may watch the reaction of Claudius; he has, still, some scruples lest he has been deceived, for the spectre, whom Hamlet assumes to be his father, could be an evil spirit. The plotting of Claudius runs parallel to that of Hamlet as the king determines to send his nephew to England. When the players perform 'The Murder of Gonzago' Claudius recognizes his own guilt and calls for lights, not only to illuminate the Great Hall but also to allay the guilt which is creeping over him. When next we see Claudius he is alone, confronted by his crime: 'O my offence is rank . . .', he cries, trying to earn forgiveness from God through prayer. To date, the guilt of Claudius, his machinations and his inability to receive forgiveness have been uncovered.

Gerard has to decide how much of the complexity of the King's character – he is much more than a bully, Gerard has decided – can be introduced into the excerpt he is to perform. He decides that the king's apparent care of Hamlet must occasionally reveal a sharp edge, that, for example, Claudius's injunction to 'think of us As of a father' must be tinged with irony. As he studied the text Gerard was interested in Hamlet's relations with his uncle for these would affect the way in which Claudius addressed the young man. By the time Claudius has betrayed his guilt to the court Hamlet has a deep loathing of him: he always speaks of him as a man, neither as a king nor as a stepfather. He determines that the time at which he will exact revenge will be a time when Claudius is drunk or in a rage, or engaged in incestuous sexual relations with Gertrude, so that his soul will be 'as damned and black As hell whereto it goes'. Hamlet's feeling for Claudius is one of deep hatred, putting Claudius on the defensive. Something of this could be shown in the speech Gerard is to perform. It was in Claudius as a schemer that Gerard was most interested: he had listened to a radio talk in which it was suggested that Claudius was modelled on the ideal Renaissance ruler which Machiavelli drew in his treatise *The Prince*, so Gerard tried to clarify in his mind what was the real tone of that book: was it a satire or a serious study of politics?

Having considered how he may present Claudius as a rounded character, more sophisticated and interesting than his previous concept of the royal bully, Gerard looked in detail at the text, attempting to appreciate fully the thoughts and passions that lay beneath each sentence spoken by the king. The speech is highly formal in tone, the royal 'we' is used, in vocabulary and in construction. It begins with a proposition, that it is a duty to mourn a father, but, says Claudius putting a counter-argument, it is lacking in respect to prolong grief beyond the time propriety demands. He points to the round of life and death and the inevitability of each father's death: the adjectives he uses are gifts to the performer: 'obstinate condolment' (sorrow) and 'impious [disrespectful] stubborness'. This mourning, claims Claudius, shows that Hamlet is 'unfortified', 'impatient', 'simple' and 'unschooled'. How little Claudius knows of Hamlet in spite of his protestations of kinship, for none of these words can be applied to the prince who painstakingly tracks down his father's murderer, and who has been schooled not only at the University of Wittenburg but has also learnt from hard experience. Confronted by the cycle of life and death the listener realizes that here is one of the themes, that of mutability, running through the play. Therefore the actor must bring this into prominence in the given speech.

In the nature of a proclamation, 'For let the world take note . . .', Claudius changes from personal, moral matters to politics. He announces that Hamlet is nearest in succession to the throne. It is noteworthy that when old King Hamlet died his son was not crowned in his place. Hamlet is in a position, should he wish, to arouse a faction against the usurper and Claudius determinedly attempts to win the allegiance of his nephew, choosing his words with care. For this reason Claudius is anxious that Hamlet does not return to university in Germany but remains in Denmark under surveillance. The final line of the extract reinforces Claudius's assumed regard for Hamlet.

Shakespeare gives us insights into the workings of a person's mind – the subtext of the play – through the images he uses, but Gerard noticed that there were few of these in the speech. The image-less, formal language spoken by Claudius acts as an opaque screen to the real thoughts in his head. However, Gerard noted the structuring of the language. The king had a habit of stressing ideas by repeating phrases: thus there were the mutability phrases lengthily expressed, and the reiteration of an imperfection in Hamlet by restating it in terms of his will, heart and understanding. This is the pompous, mindless side of Claudius.

At first Gerard worked on the speaking alone, leaving this to prompt him to later moves. He realized that if he was to master the rhetoric he would have to take care that the capacity and control of his breath ensured projection to the conclusion of each statement. If an urgent argument was to be presented, inhalations could not be taken on the punctuation pauses or its impetus would be lost. Thus, near the beginning of the speech, the urgency of the passage beginning 'But you must know . . .' until 'To do obsequious sorrow' requires it to be spoken on a single breath. So, too, the impatience with Hamlet's defects – 'It shows a will most incorrect. . . . An understanding simple and unskilled' – did not allow for a pause between each itemization, for Claudius's criticism was unified. Impatience and urgency, too, prevented a pause after the rhetorical question, for Hamlet must have no time to edge in a protest. Gerard decided that by the time Claudius commanded, for the benefit of the court as much as the prince, Hamlet to 'think of us As of a father', he must have demonstrated in the self-interested urgency of his reasoning that that was the very relationship it was impossible for anyone at court to envisage. He decided to make that line heavy with irony, the apex of the whole thrust of the first part of the speech. The second climactic moment would come with the proclamation that Hamlet was next in succession to the throne, an announcement which could effectively be made whilst Claudius himself was at the throne. Gerard thought immediately of the shabby plastic chair he had often encountered in examination rooms: one of these would have to represent the throne of Denmark, invested with regality through Gerard's dignity and bearing.

Gerard had next to create a setting for the scene within which he could move. He placed a chair upstage to represent the throne; he imagined that Gertrude was beside him, but forebore to indicate her presence with a chair! On either side members of the court stood and Hamlet, detached from the court, stood on his own at the front of the acting area as far right as was practical. It would be necessary, Gerard felt, to move to Hamlet at some stage in the speech, in order to identify clearly the character's location. The formality of the language suggested that Claudius should, after the first couplet spoken to Hamlet from the throne, address the queen and courtiers as he felt disposed. At the command 'throw to earth This unprevailing woe' Gerard moved from the throne to Hamlet, placing his hand on the prince's shoulder, but only momentarily, for as he spoke the line 'For let the world take note' he returned to stand before the throne, from which spot he made his political speech, this time directly to Hamlet, but with the consciousness that it was an appeal made in the presence of the entire court. Although the movement pattern was simple, Gerard felt that it expressed the king's intentions, and by crossing the stage to Hamlet he was able to separate the speech into two sections which in turn were but reflections of the shape of the argument in the mind of Claudius. There would be opportunity for imposing regal gesture in giving the homily on mutability, whereas in the second half of the speech Gerard decided that he would reserve any gestures for the final line, outstretching his hand to Hamlet, a stage picture with which he finished the piece.

Gerard had never seen a production of *Hamlet* so he looked at book illustrations of some of the productions of the Royal Shakespeare Company. From these he deduced that there was no historic period of costume to which designers turned; each seemed to create clothes from an indefinite past. It was important, though, that Gerard should envisage the costume he assumed he was wearing in the role, a full length richly embroidered gown, with wide trimmed sleeves courting bold gestures, the crown of state on his head. This Claudius is a warrior king who leads his forces to battle, and so wears riding boots in which he strides noisily across the stage.

5.2.3 *Douglas* by John Home

The third of these excerpts from period plays is taken from a tragedy by John Home, *Douglas*, performed in London for the first time in 1757. The play tells of a lad, Douglas, who is brought up by an old shepherd after he became separated as a baby from his mother. The mother believes that at the same time as she lost her son she became widowed and she has married, under pressure from her father, her second husband, Lord Randolph. The plot tells of the reunification of a mother with her long-lost son, a common story in eighteenth-century theatre. Sixteen years after the initial twin tragedies the mother and son meet and with an instinctive knowledge Lady Randolph recognizes her child. But lasting happiness does not ensue: the lad is killed and the grief-stricken Lady Randolph hurls herself from a cliff top to death.

The chosen selection comes from the first act of the play. In it Lady Randolph speaks to Anna, her serving woman, of the tragedy which struck sixteen years earlier. Anna has just remarked that perhaps Douglas still lives.

> No. It was dark December: wind and rain
> Had beat all night. Across the Carron lay
> The destin'd road; and in its swelling flood
> My faithful servant perish'd with my child.
> O hapless son! of a most hapless sire! –
> But they are both at rest; and I alone
> Dwell in this world of woe, condemn'd to walk,
> Like a guilt-troubl'd ghost, my painful rounds:
> Nor has despiteful fate permitted me
> The comfort of a solitary sorrow.

Tho' dead to love, I was compell'd to wed
RANDOLPH, who snatch'd me from a villain's arms;
And RANDOLPH now possesses the domains,
That by Sir MALCOLM's death on me devolv'd;
Domains, that should to DOUGLAS' son have giv'n
A Baron's title, and a Baron's power.
Such were my soothing thoughts, while I bewail'd
The slaughter'd father of a son unborn.
And when that son came, like a ray from heav'n,
Which shines and disappears; alas! my child!
How long did thy fond mother grasp the hope
Of having thee, she knew not how, restor'd.
Year after year hath worn her hope away;
But left still undiminish'd her desire.

(a) The original stage conditions

Mrs Moorcroft is taking the adult certificate of an examination in Dramatic Verse. It would be ungallant to state her age but she feels that this piece, with its dignified language underpinned by sorrow, is a suitable selection for someone with her own experience and maturity. Mrs Moorcroft was fortunate in that living in an attractive Yorkshire spa town she was near to Richmond where a delightful intimate Georgian playhouse is still used for theatrical performances. As did the Elizabethan stage, that at the Georgian Theatre juts out into the auditorium, Mrs Moorcroft discovered. However, there is an addition to it: a decorated frame, the proscenium arch, separates the rear part of the stage, in which the scenery is set up, from the front part where much of the action of the play took place in the eighteenth century. This acting area, the proscenium, is surprisingly shallow, measuring only fourteen feet in depth at Richmond. It is fifteen feet wide. Many examination rooms offer a performance space that size so it would be possible to reproduce the 'geography' of the proscenium of this theatre comfortably. Either side of the acting area is a door, the proscenium door, and through the two of these the performers made the majority of their exits and entrances. For examination purposes we are not concerned with the scenic area on the far side of the proscenium arch: performance is our business.

The rectangular auditorium is small. Immediately in front of the stage ten backless benches stand on steps in the pit. On three sides of the building is a row of boxes, the first of which on either side stands on the stage so that a spectator may with ease hold a whispered conversation with a performer. At the rear of the theatre, above the boxes, is the minute and uncomfortable gallery, a known haunt of immorality in Richmond's past. In *Douglas* Home carried on the Restoration convention of causing the actor to address the house partly in asides and partly by changes in the direction of the delivery, so that this key speech is not made to Anna alone but also to the various sections of the auditorium. In other words, the audience was a significant factor in the action.

(b) Study and interpretation

Mrs Moorcroft read the speech carefully and noted significant points about the way in which the story of Lady Randolph's early married life was told. Eighteenth-century people held a strong belief in the inevitability of what was 'destined', and so the phrase in line 3, the 'destin'd road' was an important one, for it was the road leading to the child's destruction. Two phrases follow which could only occur in poetic drama:

> O hapless Son! of a most hapless sire!

Mrs Moorcroft realized she must research Georgian acting styles in order to cope with such non-natural lines. A further sentence was significant in establishing the overall tone of the piece:

> . . . I alone
> Dwell in this world of woe, condemn'd to walk,
> Like a guilt-troubl'd ghost, my painful rounds.

A brooding air of melancholy and foreboding hung over the wooded landscape and its castle and this had to be transmitted in the acting. So too had the great determination of Lady Randolph in spite of the fact that she was in mourning.

One actress who had made the part of Lady Randolph her own, Mrs Moorcroft discovered, was Mrs Sarah Siddons. Biographies of Siddons were read and illustrations sought. Two pictures came to light. One was a watercolour by Mary Hamilton, painted when Siddons performed in Dublin in 1802, and useful as it showed not only Siddons's costume but also her stance or 'attitude'. Lady Randolph was clothed in a long black dress trailing over the floor and drawn in, beneath her bosom, by a gold braid. On the heroine's head was a diadem holding in place a long veil which reached to the ground and was used by Siddons to cover her arms. As she gestured the veil flew about emphasizing the movement. The second illustration was an engraving that appeared in 1819 in *The British Stage*, in many respects similar to Hamilton's. The costume consisted again of a black dress, this time with sleeves, and again with a veil. A coronet held a wimple as well as a veil in place. In each of the illustrations Siddons stands in an open stance, her legs well apart with her weight on the downstage leg and her arms gesturing widely. Movement appears to spring from her waist and shoulders.

As well as looking at pictures Mrs Moorcroft read about the style of acting Siddons employed. It seemed to be statuesque: a pose would be held for a number of lines and then, as the thought pattern changed, so a new attitude would be struck. This statuesqueness would break into moments of frenzy and dynamism so great that spectators were anxious lest Siddons should hurt herself.

Hysterics, shrieks and groans were the responses of the audience to these 'galvanizations'. Such descriptions were unnerving for the candidate to read but nevertheless Mrs Moorcroft realized that the play was written for this kind of acting, an alternation of attitudes and activity. To start with, it seemed to her, she must assume the attitude of a despairing story-teller and break this at the point at which Lady Randolph addressed her son and her husband. She would then strike another attitude to suggest her own spectral existence which in turn would change as she bewailed her son's loss of his inheritance. The final attitude she decided would be one of quiet resignation. Although in these attitudes Mrs Moorcroft's feet would be still, there would be plenty of scope for arm movement. Like many Georgian performers, Mrs Moorcroft looked in Henry Siddon's book *Practical Illustrations of Rhetorical Gesture and Action* for ideas on how she would convey through her arms such emotions as her sadness and indignation. As Mrs Moorcroft worked on the speech she realized the extent to which it was an address to the audience. Of course there were quiet moments when it would be appropriate to move to her servant and speak quietly, such as

> Nor has despiteful fate permitted me
> The comfort of a solitary sorrow

but such moments were rare.

Thomas Gray was most impressed with John Home's play and wrote that he had rediscovered the 'true language of the stage', missing since the death of Shakespeare. Mrs Moorcroft studied this language. As with Shakespeare's verse *Douglas* is written in iambic pentameters. The five stresses of each line help the actor to discover the meaning behind the text, the points that the writer wishes to emphasize; but they do more, for by wisely using these stresses the performer allows them to carry the verse along. Usually in each line one beat highlights the keyword of that particular line, although it falls only on a syllable:

> My faithful servant PERish'd with my child.

At other times the beat suggests words which need to stand in strong apposition to each other:

> The SLAUGHter'd father of a son unBORN.

The rhythm is so strong that there is little need to give technical attention to unstopped lines; in this case the metrical rhythm will preserve the linear pattern.

Home creates emphasis in other ways. Sometimes this is by the simple expedient of repeating a word:

> O HAPLESS son! of a most HAPLESS sire

in which the alliterative 's' is a further form of emphasis; and later:

> YEAR after YEAR hath worn her hope away

again accompanied by repeated sounds, this time 'h' and 'w'. In speaking the first example Mrs Moorcroft found that the noun was more important than the repeated adjective; not only did the initial letters of the nouns alliterate but Home also reduced each to a single syllable so that each could bear the full weight of a metrical stress. The second example differs in as much as Home has inverted his metre, beginning the first syllable of the line with a stressed beat rather than the second, and then righting the pattern so that each pronouncement of 'year' receives its metrical emphasis. At other times emphasis is created by the use of alliteration:

> Tho' DeaD to Love, I was compeL'D to weD.

This device is imaginatively used: in the first half of the line Home establishes the two sounds he will stress, 'd' and 'l', and reinvests in them in the second. More often alliteration occurs in a couple of sequential words, such as 'Solitary Sorrow' and 'Destin'D roaD'. Less frequently assonance is used but to excellent effect. See how the repeated 'ay' sound brings lightness, and thereby hope, to this line:

> And when that son cAme, like a rAY from heav'n.

Further help is given to the performer by the use of sibilants immediately before a caesural pause:

> . . . like a ray from heav'n
> Which shines and disappearS; alas my child.

The very slight, almost imperceptible, lengthening of the sibilant helps to give a fleeting image of the ray vanishing, reinforced by the joyful use of sibilants earlier in the line.

It was by attempting to place these details in the context of speaking the complete passage that Mrs Moorcroft learnt that Home was craftsman enough in writing dramatic verse to give her a vehicle which would help her along; she only needed to recognize wherein this help lay.

5.3 A SUMMARY OF ADVICE ON PREPARING EXCERPTS FROM PERIOD PLAYS

In looking at three senior candidates working on texts from period plays I hope you have gained some idea about preparing such pieces. We can summarize the main concerns of these candidates:

(a) Each acquainted him- or herself with the stage setting for which the selected play was written and was aware of the relationship of auditorium to stage. This was not solely an academic exercise but was undertaken because the physical interaction of the actor with his audience became evident from the study. In turn this helped the candidate to appreciate the style of acting employed within the theatrical conditions.

(b) The candidate then focused his attention on the text. He considered the role he was to assume and he looked at that role developing and interacting with other characters within the play.

(c) He studied the meaning of the pieces he was to perform and looked at the aids to performance the writer had offered in the rhythm, diction and stylistic devices.

(d) The candidate then went on to think about his solo performance. He clarified the stage setting he wished to create, the placing of accompanying characters, his own costume and his movement pattern and gestures. There were, too, such technical points as pace, climax, the direction of the playing, the introduction of the pieces, entrances and exits, and the final stage picture.

5.4 THE DRAMATIC SELECTION WITHIN THE CONTEXT OF THE RECITAL

Most candidates had to perform their dramatic pieces in tandem with at least one other. This leads to a fresh set of considerations. It will be sufficient to take one of the three candidates, Mrs Moorcroft, and look at her complete recital. She was required to present an excerpt from Shakespeare's dramatic verse as well as her own choice of playwright. As Mrs Moorcroft had chosen a tragedy, she wanted in her Shakespeare selection to avoid such tragic older-performer roles as Queen Margaret in *King Henry VI*. She therefore made her selection by editing several of the speeches of Paulina in *The Winter's Tale*, choosing the second act prison scene where the jealous Leontes has imprisoned Hermione his queen. Paulina, a bustling soul, offers to take Hermoine's daughter to Leontes hoping that the sight of the baby would bring him to his senses. Shakespeare's writing, as well as offering a role for the older performer, allowed, Mrs Moorcroft found, for character presentation together with touches of humour.

The candidate decided that she would give a very brief introduction to the recital and in this she mentioned that both pieces portrayed the attitude of women to children. Then she performed the Shakespeare piece. In the writing this seemed less emotionally charged than the Home and she felt that she should gradually scale the emotional peaks of the latter. Each piece was contextualized. She felt that there was time to do this as the examination extended for fifteen minutes. At the end of her second selection she held a final stage picture for a couple of seconds and then brought her recital to a close with a bow to the examiner–audience.

The problem of what to wear had taxed her ingenuity. Whilst she did not want to appear to be in costume she knew that wisely chosen clothes would give her confidence and help strengthen the two characterizations. A full black practice skirt and a dark blouse seemed appropriate. Simple props were allowed so she took with her a neat stage coronet and a long black veil resembling in shape and texture that in the illustrations of Siddons. Wisely she practised putting these on without the aid of a mirror so that on the day, quickly and purposefully, after the introduction to the Home extract, she retired to the side of the acting area, put on the headgear and walked on stage into the part. The addition of these simple tokens helped to create a visual distinction between the two roles. Additionally she ensured that her stage management of the Shakespeare piece allowed her to use different areas of the stage and to play directly to Emilia and the gaoler, the other two characters in the scene, rather than directing the action to the audience as she did in the character of Lady Randolph. These are all details but the time in which you can establish yourself as a performer is limited and details help to convince an onlooker that you have given your performance thought and polish.

5.5 THE EXPECTATIONS OF EXAMINERS

I asked a number of examiners about their expectations in viewing dramatic performances and their remarks are helpful not only in relation to this chapter but also to the next in which I shall consider the performance of contemporary drama. I have grouped the responses under the various academies. As might be expected there is a considerable overlap which I have let stand as this helps to identify the really important points.

(a) Associated Board

The Associated Board examiner looks for a projected performance. The candidate is expected to study the complete play – marks are lost if it is evident that this has not been done – and the performed extract must be set within the context of the play. He or she is expected to use movement and gesture suitable to the piece. He or she must be aware of the period in which the play is set and the acting style required. The candidate should be competent at creating his or her own stage, peopling it, as required, with other characters. He or she is expected to use the examiner as a token member of the audience and not, as is sometimes done, as another character to be played against.

(b) Associated Examining Board

In the A-level in Theatre Studies the examiner evaluates the candidate's understanding of the text by means of performance, discussion in the *viva-voce*, and the performer's notebook. The candidate must correctly use his or her body and voice in order to communicate theatrically. A candidate may use props and costumes and is given credit for these, although it has to be remembered that the rubric states the performance is given in 'rehearsal conditions'. Background study helps the candidate to be knowledgeable about the original performance conditions but it is important that the performer, in presenting the piece, is communicating with a present day audience.

(c) *Guildhall School*

The Guildhall School looks for the candidate's sensitive and imaginative response to the content and mood of the play, to the character portrayed, and for an awareness of the shape and structure of the scene that has been excerpted; the examiner expects the candidate to communicate through 'character and interpretation'. A vocal and physical technique is deemed necessary and the use of voice and speech must be appropriate.

(d) *LAMDA*

LAMDA examiners look for spontaneity of performance. The character which the candidate presents must be credible; 'each moment', states the syllabus, 'is important and should be lived', an art which requires sensitivity, relaxation and concentration. The dramatist's intentions must be realized and communicated by the candidate and it must be evident that the character performed is clearly understood. An important criterion is that by the end of the performance the examiner feels entertained. A knowledge of the social and literary conditions in which writing of all genres was originally undertaken helps to give the candidate's performance a feeling of authenticity. Senior candidates are expected to be conversant with the historic presentation of Shakespeare.

(e) *London College of Music*

The London College of Music examiner looks for spontaneity and liveliness in the candidate's performance. He or she expects the candidate to give an authentic picture of a character that bears comparison with any other appearance in the course of the play. Certainly a feeling for the speech style and the movement of a period is expected. From grade 6 the candidate is expected to give evidence in performance and spoken description of the style of production which the chosen play will require and this, of course, relates back to the original performance conditions even though the candidate may choose to transpose the play to another setting.

(f) *Mountview*

At Mountview dramatic excerpts are usually presented by candidates working in pairs; however solo performance is not precluded and in this the examiner looks for a dynamic presentation of a living character. The candidate's use of space is noted and credited.

(g) New Era

The New Era examiner looks for signs that the candidate is giving a portrayal of life. This arises from an understanding of the role, the candidate's vision and technical ability. The candidate is to *be* the character and the portrayal must be a truthful one consonant with the part in the play as a whole. An interpretation of the character must be given and if this is lacking marks are lost. This character is interpreted through the candidate's total use of him- or herself, through voice, body, gesture and movement.

(h) Royal Academy of Music

A candidate entering for one of the Academy's licentiate examinations must demonstrate in performance an understanding of the style of the play from which the selection has been made, and that he or she has totally acquired the character which must be understood in the context of the complete play, including, most importantly the moment's prior to entry. It is imperative that the candidate makes a dramatic impact.

(i) Poetry Society

The Poetry Society offers an examination in dramatic verse speaking and, as the following note from the syllabus indicates, the focus is on voice:

> Whilst examiners are fully aware that bodily movement and gesture are essential for the complete realization of dramatic verse in performance, candidates are advised to choose extracts which give them the opportunity to interpret and convey meaning, character and mood *mainly* by the use of voice.

Thus the examiner is looking for a competent but unobtrusive technique in verse speaking with a flexibility that can easily convey 'meaning, character and mood'.

(j) Trinity College

The Trinity College examiner looks for a true interpretation of the character in relation to the context of the complete play. The candidate has to demonstrate an ability to deal with the costume of the period, imagined, of course, but made 'real' by the candidate and the movement and gesture appropriate to this. The manners of the period need to be conveyed and the style of speaking must be suitable to the period in which the play was written; the candidate must be aware of the author's intention in writing the work and ensure that the performance reflects this. The Trinity College representative did not feel that it was necessary for the candidate to have a knowledge of a play's original theatrical conditions; a portrayal of the manners of the period were of greater importance and should certainly be expressed in performance.

5.6 THE PERFORMANCE SPACE IN THE EXAMINATION

Various boards have differing policies about the provision of a performance space and, in part, these are influenced by the philosophy governing the objectives of the examination. Both the Poetry Society and the New Era representatives spoke of the need for as large a space as possible for performance and a Poetry Society examiner, following this up, mentioned the exhilaration of projecting one's performance through space. The Associated Board and Trinity College representatives believed that a large room was preferable to a hall and that they would not wish candidates to perform on a stage for any of the examinations. Satisfactory large rooms and studios are used for higher grades and diplomas at the headquarters of LAMDA and the London College of Music. Candidates for the Mountview examinations perform in the school's studios and stage lighting may be used. The opera stage of the Royal Academy of Music is available for the LRAM examinations, so giving the candidate the chance to make decent entrances and exits. At their various provincial examining centres most of the boards rely on local representatives to arrange premises but the satisfactoriness of these is variable. Associated Examining Board candidates enjoy the security of working in their home base. Candidates for diplomas and higher grades would be wise to ask the examinations administrator or the local representative of a board either to allow them to look at the room to be used or to send them a specification of it. The scale of the performance can then be prepared rather than suffering the inconvenience of rapid adaptations on the spur of the moment.

I ought to remark that the performance should be presented to the examiner. In several instances I have examined in a hall used by the teacher of the candidates and found that a candidate was performing with his back to me as I was sitting in the part of the room which was normally the acting area.

If the room is oddly shaped or cramped, the examiner will bear this in mind in evaluating your work. This is merely another challenge which both candidates and touring professionals face in presenting their work!

5.7 RESOURCES

5.7.1 Bibliographical details of books mentioned in the text

Aeschylus (ed. R. Fagles) (1977) *The Oresteia*, Penguin Books, Harmondsworth.

Booth, M. (ed.) (1965) *Eighteenth Century Tragedy*, Oxford University Press, London (this contains John Home's play *Douglas*).

Gray, T. (ed. P. Toynbee, L. Whibley and W. H. Starr) (1971) *Correspondence of Thomas Gray*, Oxford University Press, Oxford.

Grimal, P. (1986) *Dictionary of Classical Mythology*, Blackwell, Oxford.

Harvey, P. (1937) *Oxford Companion to Classical Literature*, Oxford University Press, London.

Kelly, L. (1980) *The Kemble Era*, Bodley Head, London.

Laver, J. (1983) *Costume and Fashion: A Concise History*, Thames and Hudson, London.

Machiavelli, N. (trans. G. Bull) (1961) *The Prince*, Penguin Books, Harmondsworth.

Manvell, R. (1976) *Sarah Siddons: Portrait of an Actress*, Heinemann, London.

Shakespeare, W. (ed. H. Jenkins) (1982) *Hamlet*, Methuen, London.

Shakespeare, W. (ed. J. H. P. Pafford) (1969) *The Winter's Tale*, Methuen, London.

Siddons, H. (1822) *Practical Illustrations of Rhetorical Gesture and Action*, Sherwood, Neely and Jones, London.

Yarwood, D. (1967) *Outline of English Costume*, Batsford, London.

The British Stage was a periodical publication which had a limited life in the early nineteenth century. Copies may be found in larger libraries such as the British Library, London and the Bodleian Library, Oxford. Illustrations from it are sometimes reproduced in biographies.

5.7.2 Books on acting

Barkworth, P. (1980) *About Acting*, Secker and Warburg, London.

Bates, B. (1986) *The Way of the Actor*, Century, London.

Callow, S. (1985) *Being an Actor*, Penguin Books, Harmondsworth.

Gielgud, J. (1963) *Stage Directions*, Heinemann Educational, London.

Mackenzie, F. (1936) *The Amateur Actor*, Thomas Nelson and Sons, London.

Newton, R. G. (1967) *A Creative Approach to Amateur Theatre*, J. Garnett Miller, London.

Redgrave, M. (1953) *The Actor's Ways and Means*, Heinemann Educational, London.

Scher, A. (1988) *Desparate to Act*, Lion's, London.

Sher, A. (1985) *Year of the King*, Methuen, London.

Stanislavsky, C. (1980) *An Actor Prepares*, Eyre Methuen, London.

5.7.3 The period play in its historical context

Hartnoll, P. (1968) *A Concise History of the Theatre*, Thames and Hudson, London.

Nagler, A. M. (1952) *A Source Book in Theatrical History*, Dover Publications, New York.

(a) Greek drama

Bieber, M. (1961) *The History of the Greek and Roman Theatre*, Oxford University Press, London.
Dover, K. (1982) *The Greeks*, Oxford University Press, Oxford.
Swaddling, J. (1977) *The Greek Theatre*, British Museum Publications, London.
Webster, T. B. L. (1956) *Greek Theatre Production*, Methuen, London.
A wide range of Greek plays in English translation is published by Penguin Books in the Penguin Classics series.

(b) Elizabethan and Jacobean drama

Brown, J. R. (1969) *Shakespeare's Plays in Performance*, Penguin Books, Harmondsworth.
Edwards, C. (ed.) (1979) *The London Theatre Guide, 1576–1642*, Bear Gardens Museum, London.
Goodwin, J. (ed.) (1964) *Royal Shakespeare Theatre Company, 1960–1963*, Max Reinhardt, London.
Harrison, G. B. (1954) *Introducing Shakespeare*, Penguin Books, Harmondsworth.
Hodges, C. W. (1973) *Shakespeare's Second Globe*, Oxford University Press, London.
Joseph, B. L. (1951) *Elizabethan Acting*, Oxford University Press, London.
Leech, C. and Craik, T. W. (1975) *The RevelsHistory of Drama in English, Vol. iii, 1576–1613*, Methuen, London.
Nagler, A. M. (1981) *Shakespeare's Stage*, Yale University Press, New Haven.
Spencer, T. B. (ed.) (1964) *Shakespeare: A Celebration*, Penguin Books, Harmondsworth.
Wells, S. (1977) *Four Major Productions at Stratford-upon-Avon*, Manchester University Press, Manchester.
Yarwood, D. (1984) *English Interiors*, Lutterworth Press, Cambridge.

(c) Georgian drama

Burke, J. (1976) *English Art, 1714–1800*, Clarendon Press, Oxford.
Dodd, J. S. (1779) *Critical Remarks on Mrs Jackson's Performance of Lady Randolph in the Tragedy of 'Douglas' at the Theatre Royal in Covent Garden, London.*
Hazlitt, W. (ed. W. Archer and R. Lowe) (1895) *Dramatic Essays*, Walter Scott, London.

Joseph, B. (1959) *The Tragic Actor*, Routledge and Kegan Paul, London.

Lawrence, W. J. (1935) *Old Theatre Days and Ways*, G. G. Harrap, London.

Leech, C. and Craik, T. W. (1975) *The Revels History of Drama in English*, Vol. iv, 1750–1880, Methuen, London.

Mackintosh, I. and Ashton, G. (1975) *The Georgian Playhouse*, Arts Council of Great Britain, London.

Mackintosh, I. and Sell, M. (eds) (1982) *Curtains*, John Offord, Gosport (contains a gazetteer of Georgian and Victorian playhouses).

Nicoll, A. (1980) *The Garrick Stage*, Manchester University Press, Manchester.

Southern, R. and Brown, I. (1973) *The Georgian Theatre, Richmond, Yorkshire*, Georgian Theatre (Richmond) Trust, Richmond.

5.7.4 Books on costume, make-up and period deportment

Barton, L. (1961) *Historic Costume for the Stage*, A. and C. Black, London.

Chisman, I. and Raven Hart, H. E. (1934) *Manners and Movement in Costume Plays*, Kenyon Deane, London.

Corson, R. (1965) *Fashions in Hair*, P. Owen, London.

Corson, R. (1986) *Stage Make-Up*, Prentice Hall, Hemel Hempstead.

Hope, T. (1963) *Costumes of the Greeks and Romans*, Dover Publications, New York.

Oxenford, L. (1951) *Design for Movement*, J. Garnett Miller, London.

Selbie, R. (1977) *The Anatomy of Costume*, Bell and Hyman, London.

5.7.5 Some places to visit

Bear Gardens Museum, Bear Gardens, Bankside, London. Exhibits relate to the theatres of Shakespeare's day.

Bradfield College, Bradfield, near Pangbourne, Berkshire. A miniature version of a classical Greek theatre. Productions of Greek plays in the original language are given in alternate summers. The theatre is not freely open to the public and for permission to view application must be made to the Bursar.

Geffrye Museum, Kingsland Road, Shoreditch, London. A series of room interiors from 1600 onwards; invaluable when considering interior scenes in period plays.

Museum of Costume, Assembly Rooms, Bath, Avon.

St George's Theatre, 49 Tufnell Park Road, Tufnell Park, London. Balconied stage modelled on Elizabethan lines, where seasons of Shakespeare's plays are given.

Theatre Museum, Covent Garden, London. The national collection of theatrical ephemera. Some material relates to the Georgian theatre.

The Theatre, Richmond, Yorkshire. A restored Georgian theatre complete with bookshop and museum gallery. Frequent tours during the day and performances in the evenings.

Theatre Royal, Westgate Street, Bury St Edmunds. Built in 1819, this theatre reflects the shape of the late Georgian playhouse. Tours by day and performances at night.

Victoria and Albert Museum, Cromwell Road, South Kensington, London. The Costume Court is useful in considering the effect of costume on stance and movement. Various period rooms are also helpful in considering the setting of interior scenes.

French's Theatre Bookshop, 52 Fitzroy Street, London W1P 6JR. The United Kingdom's principal stockist of plays, both period and modern as well as other books on theatre and drama. An annual catalogue is produced and books may be obtained by post.

6

In rehearsal :
Contemporary drama

6.1 CONTEMPORARY DRAMA: TIME AND SPACE

Many boards give candidates an opportunity to present an excerpt from a contemporary play. Sometimes lists of set pieces are given in the syllabus; at other times the onus for the choice is placed on the candidate, which throws up the question, 'What is meant by a *contemporary* play?' Many would understand that this means a play by an author who is at present living and writing but some boards would extend the span; thus the New Era stipulates that a scene from a 'modern play' may be given. The Guildhall School issues a caveat that the setting of the contemporary play must be in the present day; however, the normal understanding is that whilst the author must be one of our contemporaries the setting may be of any period past or present.

In the previous chapter we considered the original performance conditions of plays and these must still be kept in mind for they determine the style in which the play is written, influencing the actor's approach to the text; a community pageant play written to be performed on a large scale by a cast of several hundred local people will be in a different vein from a play commissioned by the members of a theatre club to be performed in their intimate playhouse. Sometimes a play is written in the expectation that it will be given a particular type of staging. Thus a play envisaged as a promenade production by its author, with the audience standing and moving informally around the action, will differ from a play written to be performed 'in the round', with a static audience surrounding the performance area.

6.2 CHARACTERIZATION IN CONTEMPORARY DRAMA

As with period plays you will need to consider carefully the relationship of the character you are portraying to the play as a whole and to think about its development within the framework of the plot. Your chosen character's relationships with other people are important as you have to present a microcosm of these in the excerpted performance. The language he or she uses is a clue and if you search below the level of the words you can discover what it is that motivates the person. Thus a character may be sardonic in speech. Why? Perhaps because beneath the surface the character is lonely and distrustful of the people who surround him or her. This must be hinted at in your performance, even if there is no direct reference to such a quality within the confines of the excerpt.

In considering period plays we saw that costume can be a major help in conveying the essence of a character. It sets the character within its historical period and also tells us something about the person's psyche. Today, chains of clothing stores offer much the same kind of wear throughout the United Kingdom, but clothes may still be used to suggest specific characteristics: the untidily dressed Bohemian with his wide vision of life contrasts with the fastidiously tidy person whose view is cramped and self-sufficient. As with period plays a token piece of clothing can suggest an extension of the character you are playing; many female candidates, for example, use a handbag to reinforce their characterization, or they bring along a selected pair of shoes to influence their walk. Men may introduce an occupational feature in their clothing such as the waxed jacket of the man who spends long days in the open air or the boots of the labourer.

6.3 KEY TEXTS

In this chapter I am taking excerpts from five plays and making some suggestions about the ways in which candidates could prepare these pieces with the help of their teachers. Ideally we ought to have a conversation about each, for your own ideas are as valid as mine; however you can still think of what I suggest as part of a two-way process in which you offer agreement or disagreement and modify my remarks accordingly. The selected pieces are: a speech of Mr Fox from *Fantastic Mr Fox*, a dramatization of Roald Dahl's novel, which would be suitable for performance by a boy of eight or older; Mrs Hoff's opening speech from *Hoff the Cat Dealer* by Andrew Davies, suitable for a girl of ten or older; a speech of the Hostess in *The Business of Good Government* by John Arden and Margaretta D'Arcy, a part suitable for a female of fifteen and upwards; a speech of Mrs Holly from *Suddenly Last Summer* by Tennessee Williams, suitable for a mature female candidate; and finally a speech of the Reverend Elmer Penn from *Savages* by Christopher Hampton, suitable for a mature male candidate. As before, my intention is not to instruct you *how* to perform the text but to introduce you to a number of guiding factors and leave you, the performer, to make your own decisions.

6.3.1 *Fantastic Mr Fox* by Roald Dahl

Fantastic Mr Fox is a charming children's play. The adaptor, Sally Reid, gives clear stage plans and elevations together with directions. However, the adaptor wisely points out that settings and movements may be left to the performer's imagination and you would do well to regard them as starting points for your own interpretation. Although I envisage that the candidate selecting this piece is between eight- and ten-years-old there is some leeway in the age range.

Your first task is to read the play, a job you will enjoy as it is full of lively humour. Mr Fox has three enemies – Boggis, Bunce and Bean, all of whom are objectionable farmers. In this scene Fox has just made his way into the Mighty Storehouse of Bunce. He has brought his three small sons, and Mr Badger accompanied by his offspring, with him. They look around the shelves at the delicious packs of chickens and geese in the poultry store:

> Look, I know my way around these farms, blindfold. For me it's just as easy below ground as it is above it.
>
> (*Puts his head through imaginary floorboard. Curtains open to reveal inside of BUNCE's Mighty Storehouse, packed full of ducks and geese.*)
>
> Yes, I've done it again!
>
> (*Jumping on to stage, others follow, gape in wonder.*)
>
> I've hit it smack on the nose. Right in the bull's eye. Come and look!
>
> (*MR BADGER and three SMALL FOXES scramble up steps.*)
>
> This, my dear old Badger, is Bunce's Mighty Storehouse! All his finest stuff is stored here before he sends it off to market. Just feast your eyes on *that*. What do you think of it, eh? Pretty good grub.
>
> (*MR BADGER and SMALL ONES run forward to grab at food.*)
>
> Stop! This is *my* party, so *I* shall do the choosing. We mustn't overdo it. Mustn't give the game away! Mustn't let them know what we've been up to. We must be neat and tidy and take just a few of the choicest morsels. So, to start with we shall have four plump young ducks!
>
> (*Reaches up for four from shelf.*)
>
> Oh, how lovely and fat they are. No wonder Bunce gets a special price for them in the market. All right, badger, lend me a hand to get them down. Your children can help as well . . . There we go . . . Goodness me, look how your mouths are watering . . . And now . . . I think we had better have a few geese . . .
>
> (*MR BADGER and SMALL FOXES help MR FOX as he talks.*)
>
> There will be quite enough . . . we'll take the biggest . . . Oh my, oh my, you'll never see finer geese than these in a king's kitchen . . . Gently does it . . . that's the way . . . And what a couple of nice smoked hams . . . I adore smoked ham, don't you, Badger?

Actions speak louder than words, so start by going through the play again, making a list of the things that Mr Fox does: in that way you can learn a lot about his character. My own list states that he takes much poultry from the three farmers; that he outwits them often; that he can smell the farmers a long way off; that he is quick at digging a tunnel; that he bravely guards his family; that he is a great schemer; that he is generous to the other digging animals; and that he gets on well with the diggers with the exception of Rat. From these points we see that Mr Fox is a most energetic, sociable animal, good at organizing his digger friends; he also has a contempt for the farmers, and in invading their property takes risks which show us how cheeky he is. Now many of these characteristics must be evident in your portrayal of Fox. 'How?' you ask. In several ways. When Fox speaks to Badger and his young ones he has to do so with authority so that the other animals look up to Fox and do as he suggests. In performing this role you must learn to speak with authority and it will help you to do this if you watch an 'authority figure' such as your headteacher at school. As you speak you must expect to be obeyed. You also want to show the energy and liveliness of Fox. This is done partly by your speaking and also by the way you stand and move. At once we have another problem to solve: how exactly are you going to move? Some candidates would want to perform the excerpt on all fours – but would you be able to do that throughout the play? I suspect you'd get very tired indeed and you would find this posture limiting. So you will probably stand upright in a stance that suggests alertness: but you must still be a fox! I saw an actor indicate this by the watchful way he held his head, carefully listening from time to time, his nose high in the air as if he were checking with his sense of smell any sounds he heard. However, you may find other ways to suggest Fox. A further question you might ask yourself is 'Shall I wear a mask to suggest that I am a fox?' One can be made from some brown felt or you might wish to make a paper-sculpture face. If you do decide on a mask there are several points to bear in mind: the mask must be firmly secured, for you don't want to feel during your performance that your head is unsafe; the mask must not muffle your voice and it must allow you to be dynamic. If you find an animal mask gets in the way of your performance, then don't use it; and that rule goes for any other costume accessory. It is possible for these to impede your performance as well as enhance it.

Now let us look at the words Fox is given to say. Read through the excerpt again. Do you notice that Fox speaks in many short sentences? Why does he do this? They show that he is an excitable, impatient animal wanting to get on with doing things rather than talking overmuch. Another characteristic of Fox's speech is that many words are emphasized, sometimes through repetition; for example, when Fox is talking to the Badger family he repeats the word 'mustn't' three times, and occasionally a word which Fox emphasizes is printed in italics, such as '*that*', '*I*' and '*my*'.

By this time you are ready to start thinking about the staging of the excerpt. How can you suggest that you are breaking through into the storehouse? Some candidates may want to mime this action using their hands and arms to suggest Fox scrabbling through the floorboards and then squeezing into the store room, while other candidates will want to use and adapt any furniture that is in the room, such as tables and chairs, and crawl beneath these to indicate the tunnel.

Look at the text and see what you have to make 'real' in this scene. First of all there are the other animals – Badger and his family and the cubs of Mr Fox. Then there are the shelves on which the wrapped poultry are lying ready to be sold. At the end of the excerpt Fox talks about hams and these are hanging from the ceiling. How are you going to arrange these imaginary items? Let us consider the shelves first. Your immediate response might be to imagine the shelves running across the back of the acting area but you would soon find the difficulty of turning away from the examiner in order to reach the poultry, and in a solo recital it is extremely difficult to perform with your back to the audience. How about creating the shelves along one side of the stage? – in that way you can speak most of your lines outwardly. The same with the hams hanging from the ceiling. If they are towards the front of the stage you can point to them without turning away. A bigger problem is: where are the other characters going to stand? We have already seen that Fox is the leader in this expedition, so why not have the other animals sheltering behind him for most of the time until, towards the end of the piece, they help Fox take goods down from the shelves? There are always problems in getting the examiner to 'see' characters you are creating. After Fox's injunction, 'Come and look!' he might help Badger into the store. When he shouts 'Stop!' at the animals he must hold up his arms and repel them, and when the animals are helping to unload, Fox could take a goose at a time and hand it to the smaller creatures. What is more, when Fox is speaking to Badger and the others he must look directly at them, into their eyes: this, too, helps to make them a reality.

You are now ready, with the help of your teacher, to begin to perform the piece in rehearsal. At first you will do this with the text in your hand, but after a couple of lessons you will find that you can remember the words and your hands are then free to use. These must become quite as expressive as your head in conveying the character and I hope that you have asked yourself by this time whether you, as Fox, ought to wear some scruffy leather gloves for your digging activity. As you rehearse let the performance grow until you feel that in Fox you have a rounded character.

6.3.2 *Hoff the Cat Dealer* by Andrew Davies

The next selection is taken from *Hoff the Cat Dealer*, a short play by Andrew Davies, and the excerpt, which would suit a girl of between ten and twelve, is the opening speech of Mrs Hoff. The play is about Hoff who has lost his job as a car worker, and Prowler the amazing talking cat who helps to make the Hoffs wealthy. There is a strong moral in this humorous piece:

If you set your heart on something
You will find your wish come true.

(MRS HOFF *alone. She speaks to the audience.*)
No good staring in through my kitchen window. Hoff's
not back from work yet. Anyway you wouldn't want to
know us. We're just ordinary.

We're as ordinary as you.
If you want to know what we do,
Hoff works at the car works.
A bit of a car comes along to Hoff
And Hoff screws in four screws:
Not the sort of work you'd choose
But it pays for the children's shoes.
And I clean people's houses,
Do the jobs they don't like to do.
Too often I've seen my reflected face
Staring up from the bottom of a rich man's loo.
I want my turn. I want a good time.
I want to be rich. Is that a crime?

When you have read the play through, jot down your first impressions of Mrs
Hoff. Then go through the text a second time making a note of everything you
learn about her. My list makes the following points: at the start of the play Mrs
Hoff stresses that her family is an ordinary one; they are not well off so Mrs Hoff
has to go out to work as a part-time cleaner; she is a practical hard-headed
woman and as soon as she sees Prowler the cat she tells her husband to get rid of
him; she has a nose for making money – for example, it is her idea that Prowler
should appear on television; she is the one in the family who chooses to become
rich; she doesn't like cats although they bring the Hoffs a lot of money; she has
no qualms about selling Prowler to an unsatisfactory buyer; she initiates the
cat-selling mail-order business; she plans the large new house to which her own
relatives are invited. Now, if you had to choose a few words to sum up Mrs
Hoff's characteristics, I wonder what they would be? My own list is that she is
unfeeling, greedy and pushing.

How can you make a reality of this person? Start by compiling a dossier on
Mrs Hoff. This will help you to create a background for her. You could make a
form containing a list of questions that Mrs Hoff has to answer. These few
questions can start off your list:

What is your age?
What is your Christian name?
How old were you when you were married?

What other part-time work have you done?
How many children have you?
Do you have any hobbies?
Do you make your own clothes?

When you have completed your list of questions pretend you are Mrs Hoff and fill in the answers. Try to see this woman as clearly as you can. Try to understand why she is mean and greedy. Have events in her life made her so?

Once you have created a background for Mrs Hoff make a drawing of her as she appears at the start of the play. In this let us see some of the characteristics you were considering earlier. You can make this as elaborate as you like, the more detail the better. Find a quiet corner, sit down and look at your picture until you have memorized the details. Then close your eyes and try to picture yourself as Mrs Hoff – feel the clothes she is wearing, adjust your posture so that you sit in the way she would, feel inside yourself the same kind of longing for easy money and think of some of the ways you could get this. Try writing, as Mrs Hoff, a letter in which you express your innermost feelings; mention in this what you want most urgently.

At home do some everyday actions in the way you feel Mrs Hoff would do them, such as the cleaning, tidying a room or doing your hair. These simple activities will help you to become this character. When you are shopping, look at women whom you feel can teach you something about Mrs Hoff. One may be moving in the way you feel she does, another will be shouting across the road in a harsh voice at a child, another will be pushing in the queue to get on the bus. When you get home try out in the character of Mrs Hoff the activities you have seen. In this way you will be using both your own feelings and your observations as a help in finding the character.

Go back to the drawing and show this to your mother. She may be able to find you some of the clothes you have sketched Mrs Hoff wearing. Dressed in these try moving and gossiping as you feel your character would. It may be a good idea to select one or two items that you can quickly put on in the examination room as a token costume. Suitable garments would be an apron, a headscarf and a trodden-down pair of shoes. Remember to check in your syllabus that a costume is not prohibited.

How does Mrs Hoff speak? She has had a very hard life and this may have left her with a whining tone which makes her sound as though she is continually complaining. We have seen, too, that she is determined to get her own way and this will make her voice stridently assertive. However you finally decide to convey her speech remember that she must be heard and understood by the audience.

Now that we have created a three-dimensional character the next job is to work on the excerpt considering the direction. Mrs Hoff is alone in her kitchen speaking to the audience. She accuses people of staring in through the window, so the playwright has adopted the convention of allowing the audience to look through an imaginary 'fourth wall', which he removes once the play begins. Mrs Hoff's main task is to set the scene and this she does by talking about her family. It would be an over-easy approach to have Mrs Hoff standing still delivering the whole speech to the audience. She needs to be motivated and to react to the situation she finds herself in. You need to know some facts about Mrs Hoff's immediate circumstances. What is she doing in the kitchen before she addresses the audience? There are a number of answers, such as scrubbing the kitchen floor, doing the washing up, ironing. . . . If props are allowed in your examination take along a bucket and scrubbing brush and in performance intersperse your activity with remarks to the audience. Where do the pauses in the speaking occur? These must be made so that the audience can take in the information which Mrs Hoff is giving, and they occur where Mrs Hoff finishes with one subject and prepares to go on with another. For example, 'We're as ordinary as you' marks the end of the introductory information, and her remark 'But it pays for the children's shoes' closes the information about the rest of the family before she goes on to talk about herself at some length. How she uses the pauses is a problem you must solve. Does she continue with her cleaning? Or unstack the kitchen chairs? Or empty her pail? You have to decide too which is the most important statement Mrs Hoff makes., I would plump for one of two alternatives: either 'I want my turn' or 'I want to be rich'. These remarks highlight Mrs Hoff's selfish determination. When you want to emphasize a statement such as this, it may be spoken very directly and deliberately to the audience as this convention has been established from the start of the excerpt.

The verse section is marked by a strong rhythm which is indication enough to the listener that we have swung from prose to verse. I think that very little by way of conscious poetry speaking is needed: the metre and the rhyming scheme will see you through. All of your speaking will be concerned with establishing this particular character and on making contact with the audience. For a few moments Mrs Hoff is a chorus introducing the household which will figure in the play.

6.3.3 *The Business of Good Government* by John Arden and Margaretta D'Arcy

The next piece I've selected is suitable for a fifteen-year-old girl or indeed someone older: it is a speech of the Hostess in *The Business of Good Government* by John Arden and Margaretta D'Arcy. This is a Christmas play which was written for the people of Brent Knoll to perform in their village church. The staging is simple and the writing unpretentious, two points to remember in your presentation. The off-stage characters have sat around the acting area listening to the performers whilst they waited to tell their own part of this old and well-known story. The excerpt marks the first time the Hostess has appeared in the action. She sweeps busily with a broom as she speaks:

> It's not as if they were all paying for their rooms neither – half of 'em come here with a piece of yellow paper – 'A Government chit, madam, it'll be charged to your credit from the beginning of the next Revenue Period – take it to the Town Hall'. The way my house is at the moment, you'd think *I* was running the Town Hall. Civil Servants . . . then there's the Military – *they* don't pay neither. 'Haw haw, landlady, I want accommodation for a corporal and thirteen men of Number Eight Detail, three nights altogether, breakfasts and suppers, find their own dinners: but you'll have to provide cooking facilities . . . Oh yes, and covered storage for the transport. See the place is clean'. Oh, I could lie down and die! To say nothing of the rest of 'em. 'Have you got a room, please?' 'Could you let us have a bed missus?' 'Just a corner, just a mattress, just a bit of straw – every house in the place is full, we've been all round the town.' I know very well they're full. *I'm* full! No vacancies! Not any more. I mean it. Why should I have my premises made a scapegoat for administrative incompetence and I don't care who hears me!

Let us think first of all about the character of the Hostess. She runs the inn at Bethlehem at which Mary and Joseph arrive later. We can see that she is a bustling character by the tone of her remarks and by the way she gets on with the cleaning whilst speaking. She appears to be a character who needs plenty of other people around her so that she can rehearse life's difficulties to them. Obviously she loves the challenge of her work. She has an engaging habit of enlivening her conversation with imitations of other people. Shortly after the excerpted speech, when Mary and Joseph arrive in Bethlehem, we see a new side to her personality. She is more than a brusque person; she has a great capacity to sympathize with others and determines that in spite of the inconvenience she will take in the couple. Her practical nature is shown by her realization that she must fetch the midwife for Mary. However, once the baby is delivered the responsibility of looking after the mother and child weighs heavily upon her, and when the midwife urges Mary and Joseph to lodge in her own house the Hostess quickly points out the virtues of this arrangement.

With these characteristics in mind you must begin to picture how you will make the Hostess a reality for your audience. You may agree with me that her broom is a vital extension of her character and that without it the portrayal would be incomplete. Therefore find a well-used and business like broom through which you can express your capacity for hard work. At Brent Knoll the costumes were neither historical nor modern, but a kind of compromise which suggested the essence of the character. Thus Joseph was shown wearing a heavy blanket over a coarse jersey, with his trousers tucked into wellingtons – obviously a working man without much money. The Hostess, who concerns us here, looked like a peasant woman from one of Brueghel's paintings with her long skirt, apron and head-scarf. As you are presenting several pieces you need some adaptable clothes. For this piece you could quickly put on a wrap-round skirt and an apron. A pair of clogs would make ideal footwear with their workmanlike clatter on the floor. If these are not to be found, see what other kinds of footwear would suggest a bustler and support the overall appearance of the character.

Let me give you a few pointers towards the presentation of the piece. Your sweeping of the room must be a practical job: sweep the acting area as you would clean out the attic at home and, like the Hostess, make sure that you do this properly! When you speak directly to the audience you will need to let up but then go back to the place at which you stopped and carry on from there. This attention to detail does give truth to your performance which a desultory 'mime', half indicating that you are sweeping, would lack. Your next decision must be when to stop work and talk to your listeners. Some of the speaking accompanies the activity but at other times the speaking has precedence, depending on the importance of what is being said. The most important point the Hostess makes is that her inn is full. Obviously this statement demands that it is made without any extraneous distraction. I suspect that the Hostess is rather pleased with her ability to mimic the various characters who come into her life. She does this vocally, of course, finding a suitable voice for each, but she also gives a hint of the person's physical qualities. Momentarily we have a character within a character and in order to convey this the sweeping must cease. One of the preparations you can make for your performance is to see how many ways you can find to hold the broom: lean on it; hold it vertically with both hands, changing this to a horizontal hold; stand the broom on end, and so on. I'm not suggesting that you employ all of these in your performance but my point is that often candidates bring a prop to the examination and don't fully utilize it.

We will go on to think about words. In their introduction to the play the writers point out that they have avoided pretentious, theatrical language and that they saw no reason why the workaday characters should speak in rural voices. Rely then on the idiom of the writing. What you will need to think about is the way in which the various characters whom the Hostess imitates speak: the civil servant, the soldier and the travellers. You may be fortunate enough to 'hear' these voices in your head but some will have to work consciously. Consider the changes in speaking you can make. Within the space of a few tones the pitch of your voice may be raised or lowered; you can also, within limits, alter the rate of your speaking as well as the dynamics of your voice. Then you may add to this a prevailing characteristic of the imitated speaker according to your conception: the civil servant, perhaps, speaking in a cultured and slightly bored voice, the soldier in enthusiastic, rough and ready tones . . . but *you* must decide on this. Remember, however, that there must be a unity of character: the imitations are all made by the Hostess and in the mimicry she must not escape from her own character. There will be a need for rapid changes of voice as the Hostess slips back effortlessly into her own speech patterns.

In a monologue of this nature a few strong pauses are needed, too, to help the audience assimilate the meaning and to break up the gossip naturally. Two places for pause have been indicated by the writers; you may feel that your own interpretation requires others to be made. In these pauses you may return to your sweeping.

Is the Hostess speaking to herself or to the audience? The writing suggests that she speaks occasional phrases to herself such as her muttered, disjointed 'Civil Servants . . .' but on the whole the writers hint that this is a delivery directed to the audience. She might even deliver some of the speech to the business end of her brush.

As the speech begins it would be appropriate, because of the way in which the play is set, for the Hostess to enter from the side, sweeping as she does so, allowing her character to be savoured until she addresses people with her first line. There is no exit direction at the end of the extract and it would be an appropriate interpretation for her to challenge the audience with her final sentence, glaring defiantly.

6.3.4 *Suddenly Last Summer* by Tennessee Williams

The next piece is in strong contrast with the pastoral telling of the Christmas story, although in its own way it is simply the telling of a story based on a Greek legend. It is taken from the third scene of Tennessee William's sultry melodrama *Suddenly Last Summer* and the speaker is Mrs Holly.

> Yais, she has, she's had an elevator installed where the back stairs were, and, Sister, it's the cutest little thing you ever did see! It's panelled in Chinese lacquer, black an' gold Chinese lacquer, with lovely bird-pictures on it. But there's only room for two people at a time in it. George and I came down on foot. – I think she's havin' her frozen daiquiri now, she still has a frozen daiquiri promptly at five o'clock ev'ry afternoon in the world . . . in warm weather . . . Sister, the horrible death of Sebastian just about *killed* her! – She's now slightly better . . . but it's a question of time. – Dear, you know, I'm sure that you understand, why we haven't been out to see you at St Mary's. They said you were too disturbed, and a family visit might disturb you more. But I want you to know that nobody, absolutely nobody in the city, knows a thing about what you've been through. Have they, George? Not a thing. Not a soul even knows that you've come back from Europe. When people inquire, when they question us about you, we just say that you've stayed abroad to study something or other. (*She catches her breath.*) Now. Sister? – I want you to

please be *very* careful what you say to your Aunt Violet about what happened to Sebastian in Cabeza de Lobo. . . . Just don't repeat that same fantastic story! For my sake and George's sake, the sake of your brother and mother, don't repeat that horrible story again! Not to Violet! Will you?

An explanation of the context is needed. The author has based his play on several Greek legends in which perverse people are eaten: to be consumed is seen as a just punishment for moral depravity. Catharine Holly had been engaged to Sebastian Venable. He had used her as a bait to procure young men for his own pleasure and in consequence he was pursued, cut down and devoured during the couple's holiday at Cabeza de Lobo. Catharine's story of the event was not believed and she has been confined to St. Mary's Hospital in the hope that when she is less shocked the account will change. Mrs Venable has sent for Catharine to hear for herself the description of Sebastian's death: she has also sent for Mrs Holly, Catharine's mother, and her brother George. The play takes place in the exotic Victorian Gothic mansion in which Mrs Venable lives in the Garden District of New Orleans. Mrs Holly and George have just arrived and Mrs Holly is overwhelmed by the setting as well as highly perplexed by Catherine's assertions. Thus you see that the piece is suitable for a mature candidate. An American voice is required: the woman is so much a product of the States it would be impossible to present her as of any other nationality.

The period setting is important in giving an atmosphere with its fantastic garden, which resembles a tropical, prehistoric forest, in an adjoining conservatory. Mrs Holly gives an inkling of the exoticism of the interior in her description of the lift. Throughout the speech Mrs Venable is off-stage and Mrs Holly's references to her must impress the audience with the respect that her removedness demands. The over effusive Mrs Holly is in a house which normally quells any ebullience and in the near presence of a woman who intimidates all her acquaintances. Her enthusiasm is battling against these forces.

One of the challenges for the performer is planning the stage and creating the illusion that other people are present in the drawing room. It is spacious and in it are Catherine, seated, who is referred to as 'Sister', George, an elegant young man, very restless in the strange atmosphere, and Mrs Holly who has not yet had time to settle herself. This means that a mobile Mrs Holly will direct her conversation sometimes to a stationary Catherine and sometimes to George whose position may change. Fortunately she uses his name several times which helps to establish that she is still speaking to him, and it may be wise to ensure that this is lightly stressed so that the audience picks up the point. It is possible to suggest that George is on the move by following his figure with your eyes correctly focused. Mrs Holly's movements and eye contact will, of course, depend on which of her two children she is speaking to; for example, the urgency of her plea not to repeat the 'fantastic story' to Mrs Venable suggests that Mrs Holly should be very near to Catharine, perhaps holding her hand or laying her own hand on the girl's shoulder. As well as creating two unseen characters on stage you have also to bear in mind that you must make the ubiquitous Mrs Venable a reality. Know in which direction she has gone to have her aperitif and acknowledge this as you speak about her.

Let us turn from the stage management to the text so that we can determine the speaking, moves and gestures required. Firstly there is the American southern dialect. If you get an opportunity to hear this reproduced on tape or radio that is helpful. Don't worry too much about individual words as you listen but trace the melody of the speaker's voice. Try humming this. Listen, too, to the pace of the words, and the way in which a word is held and then a 'catch-up' in time made in the phrases following. Once you've got this pattern fixed you can start to add the words of the text. Try listening to yourself on tape speaking the part. Note whether acquiring an accent has robbed your voice of range and immediacy. If it has, try speaking to your friends and family in the southern voice, read from the newspaper using it, in fact, try to find as diverse a range of opportunities to speak the dialect as possible. In this way spontaneity and the modulatory variations which accompany this will return.

Mrs Holly's speech gradually leads up to the point she wants to hammer home – that Catharine must change her account of Sebastian's death – so the opening remarks about the lift are inconsequential. The first sign of urgency comes with her sentence '. . . the horrible death of Sebastian just about *killed* her'. How are you going to convey this urgency? Is this a hidden stage direction to make your way over to Catharine and to contact her in some way? Or can you create the urgency more naturally by moving away from her and firing the words over a distance? A moment later Mrs Holly becomes the remorse-stricken mother, sorry that she has neglected to visit her daughter in hospital. Two problems arise here: how do you suggest this mother and daughter relationship? And how do you show that the mother's affection is determined by her desire for financial gain, for only Catharine is able to unlock Sebastian's will from the judicial procedure Mrs Venable has instituted? These considerations must overlay Mrs Holly's assurances of secrecy. It is then that she reaches the climax of her pleading with Catharine. Having taken you thus far through the speech I must leave you to work out your own interpretation for it is yourself whom you bring to the part. In this task you are not asked to imitate anyone else but to make the characterization entirely your own. Observation of people like Mrs Holly, your own understanding of her character, externals such as clothes, shoes and accessories which help to give a formal identification to the person, are all a help in your work; do remember, though, that there is an instinctive response within you to this character which primarily brings her to life.

6.3.5 *Savages* by Christopher Hampton

The concern of Christopher Hampton's play *Savages* is the indiscriminate slaughter of the Brazilian Indians in contemporary South America. Alan West (his name has the ring of symbolism about it) an anthropologist with an intense sympathy for the native Brazilians, is captured by guerillas. A series of cameos surrounds this central theme, presenting the audience with the responses of various people living in Brazil to the 'Indian problem'. In flashbacks we see West's relations with his fellow whites and one of these, Episode 11, is with an American missionary, the Reverend Elmer Penn. Penn explains his own policy in running the mission.

> You see, we felt when we arrived, and you must understand that when Maybelle and I arrived here five years ago it was so primitive it was like something out of the pages of the *National Geographic Magazine* – we felt that what was very important was to make a clear distinction, clear enough to be unmistakable to the Indians, between what they had in the past and what we were offering them for the future. Well, now, after the first steps, when the only thing you really need is a little courage and frankly nerve, and believe me, if there's one thing even a Stone Age savage can understand, it's raw courage – you consolidate. Now when I say consolidate, that probably sounds quite easy to you, but what it really involves is more than three years of very very hard work, in which you have to learn their language, teach them the Gospel in terms they can understand, show them that your medicine is better and more effective than the shaman's, win them away from their own primitive beliefs and, well, I suppose one has to be honest about this, make them dependent on you. Well, when you have achieved all that, there comes a moment, and I suppose judging that moment correctly is the most difficult job we have in the civilization process, there comes a moment when you have to move from the defensive to the offensive. And when that moment comes, you have to say to the Indian, look, either you must go forward with us, or you must leave the flock. You see, for a long time the new concepts you've introduced them to co-exist with a lot of the bad old ways and there just has to be a confrontation, when you say to them, if you don't want to renounce the stimulants and intoxicants that are preventing you from becoming a useful member of the community, if you don't want to accept what we do for you, why you're just going to have to go your own way. It's a very delicate task and it's really impossible to avoid stepping on a few cultural toes, but if as I say you choose the moment carefully, you'll only lose a very small number of them. And of the rest you can truly say:
>
> > The race that long in darkness pined
> > Have seen a glorious light.

Penn represents a very different point of view from that of West. West is passionate to preserve the Indian culture, including its social customs, its language, its mythology, its integrity. This is something for which Penn has scant regard: he has arrived in Brazil to proclaim a foreign faith, a gospel presented in American terms, to moralize and to impose: he speaks of changing 'the lives of these savages', for that is how he sees the Indians. The meeting between West and Penn is a clash of fundamentally differing viewpoints.

In performance it would be simple to create a parody of all that Penn stands for. Balance this: he is a person of dynamic faith and he believes that he is working for the good of the Indians by building up an enclosure of harmony. As an insurance against parody, slightly earlier in the play Carlos Esquerdo, Alan West's captor, shares with him his concept of the 'New Beatitudes'; it is by these that men rising against those of Penn's ilk live; they are the counter-weight to Penn's beliefs. Major Brigg, a man who brings a British 'solution' to the Indian crisis, who has scant respect for their values and who, in his own way, wreaks as much havoc as Penn in passing on a 'flu epidemic to one of the tribes under his protection, holds beliefs running parallel to those of Penn. Although Penn doesn't appear with Brigg or Esquerdo, their own characters, as cyphers in the plot, affect your portrayal of Penn and the message they give is plain: he must be a credible person.

The scene is set in the main room of Penn's bungalow; all is hygenic, tidy and functional and this must be expressed in the character of the clergyman for he is surrounded by symbols of Western efficiency – a filing cabinet and a deep freeze unit. Your only way to present these objects is through the character. Similarly something of the out modedness of his own religious belief is suggested in a Victorian harmonium standing in the room and his love of dated missionary hymns. Here again this has to be suggested in your portrayal of Penn. Stage directions state that during the conversation West is seated in a comfortable armchair and Penn sits on the higher desk chair, a good position from which superiorly to preach his gospel. No indication is given by the playwright of Penn's clothes; you have to bear in mind in dressing for the recital that this is a tidy person, a trait which could be presented visually.

You have to make two decisions about the presentation of this speech: is it to be static? And does silence have any part to play in it? Let us deal with movement first. If you take the point that Penn is preaching at West, then he will want to reinforce his message with gesture and maybe movement. The thrust of the argument is that there comes a time when one has to be on the offensive. You may feel that you can strengthen this assertion by the use of gesture; if I were playing this part I would rise at this stage of the argument in order to tower over West. Penn seems to become aware that his words are dogmatic, and in the sentence beginning, 'You see, for a long time the new concepts . . .' he takes a less belligerent line, which could be an indication that he gets down to West's eye-level by sitting. I suggest that you go through the text marking the places you feel are the most forceful and imagine how Penn is going to present this strength. A long speech such as this begs that a number of pauses are made in order to show how Penn's thought processes are passing from one set of ideas to another, and this is where the actor must realize the value of silence. Work through the speech again and group the ideas into blocks. Where there is a change of gear this suggests that Penn needs some kind of breathing space to order his thoughts. Of course, not all of the pauses will be the same, and to determine their length you must go through the same process as Penn, tracing in your mind this shaping of the next stage of the argument. In pausing, concentrate on the thought process so that the audience may concentrate on you.

In this example I am not going to offer further hints on speaking the text nor about the stage management of the section, for the earlier examples in this chapter have mapped out procedures. You must, however, consider the position of Alan West in the acting area; whether he is a static captive audience; Penn's relationship with West; the way in which he creates the illusion of West's existence; the acquisition of an American voice; and the use of modulation in order to express your ideas with interest and clarity.

6.4 RESOURCES

6.4.1 Bibliographical details of works mentioned in the text

Alcock, J. (ed.) (1987) *Playstage. Six Primary School Plays*, Methuen Children's Books, London (contains *Hoff the Cat Dealer* by Andrew Davies).

Arden, J. and D'Arcy, M. (1963) *The Business of Good Government*, Methuen, London.

Dahl, Roald (adapted by S. Reid) (1987) *Fantastic Mr Fox*, Puffin Books, Harmondsworth.

Hampton, C. (1974) *Savages*, Faber and Faber, London.

Williams, T. (1961) *Suddenly Last Summer, Orpheus Descending, Something Unspoken*, Penguin Books, Harmondsworth.

6.4.2 Background reading

Phillips, G. D. (1981) *The Films of Tennessee Williams*, Art Alliance Press, Cranbury, New Jersey.

Spoto, D. (1985) *The Kindness of Strangers: a Life of Tennessee Williams*, Bodley Head, London.

Books on acting listed in Section 5.7.2 also relate to this chapter.

7

Presentations by duos and small groups

7.1 DUO PRESENTATIONS

Much of this book is about solo performances in examinations. In this chapter I extend the subject to include selections for two people and for small groups to perform. This is an exciting new development in the field of drama examinations and there is no reason why, even if you are primarily interested in solo performance, you should not take an occasional examination jointly with one or a small group of friends. It will prove to be an enriching experience.

In the first part of this chapter I am going to discuss selections for two people to perform. Before we arrive at key texts, however, it would be useful to look at the boards which offer examinations in duo acting. The Associated Examining Board, in its A-level Theatre Studies gives the candidate who takes acting as the skill option the opportunity to present two pieces, one of which is as a duo; the choice of pieces is left to the candidate with the stipulation that set books for other parts of the examination are not to be used. The Guildhall School offers grade examinations in duo acting; except for the lowest grades two contrasting pieces are presented by pairs of candidates; there is also an opportunity to perform either a mime or an improvisation as a duo or singly; again the choice of pieces is left to the candidate although certain stipulations are made at the higher grades. The examinations of the Mountview are designed to be sat by two candidates who together perform a set selection; from grade 6 candidates choose their own selections as part of a programme of poetry and drama.

You must bear in mind certain principles if you are permitted to select your own pieces. Obviously the chosen excerpt must suit your age and that of your partner, as far as its content and quality are concerned. If both you and your partner are going to be evaluated in the same examination then your respective roles must be of equal importance. Usually simple furniture, chairs and tables, is provided and any other props must be brought by the candidates. Either a costume which can be rapidly changed or a practice dress may be used for most examinations. As is customary with nearly all speech and drama examinations you must provide the examiner with a copy of the text of your excerpt. Always, of course, consult your examination syllabus to check if there are any variations from these common practices.

Much of the advice I have given in earlier chapters is relevant to duo acting and I suggest that you look through these bearing in mind such topics as the selection of suitable pieces, the social and theatrical context of the play, costume, movement, gesture and performance style; you must also consider programme building where this is appropriate to your examination. You will find, too, that Chapters 8 and 9 contain much relevant information.

7.2 KEY TEXTS

In order to appreciate the considerations which have to be made for duo performance let us look at three pairs of candidates as they prepare their two-handers for presentation to the examiner.

7.2.1 *Our Town* by Thornton Wilder

Bill and Rosie, two eleven-year-olds, have decided that they are going to take grade 1 of the Mountview Drama Performance Grades. The set piece which appeals to them is a conversation between George and Emily in *Our Town* by Thornton Wilder, for they find that they can easily identify with the characters in it although they are five years older than themselves. In writing *Our Town* Wilder wanted to present his audience with the innumerable details of life as lived by the families of Grover's Corners in New Hampshire but, in contrast, he wanted the staging to be very simple. Realistic scenery is replaced by a few chairs, a couple of tables, a bench, and two step ladders. The tops of the latter objects indicate the upstairs of the Gibbs's and Webbs's houses where George and Emily are doing their homework. At the same time as these two characters are working at the tops of the ladders Dr Gibbs is sitting at the table, which represents the kitchen, reading. A concealed choir, belonging to the Congregational Church, can be heard practising.

GEORGE	Hsst! Emily!
EMILY	Hello.
GEORGE	Hello!
EMILY	I can't work at all. The moonlight's so *terrible*.
GEORGE	Emily, did you get the third problem?
EMILY	Which?
GEORGE	The *third*?
EMILY	Why yes, George, that's the easiest of them all.
GEORGE	I don't see it. Emily, can you give me a hint?
EMILY	I'll tell you one thing: the answer's in yards.

GEORGE	!!!In yards? How do you mean?
EMILY	In *square* yards.
GEORGE	Oh . . . in square yards.
EMILY	Yes, George, don't you see?
GEORGE	Yeah.
EMILY	In square yards of *wallpaper*.
GEORGE	Wallpaper – oh, I see. Thanks a lot, Emily.
EMILY	You're welcome. My, isn't the moonlight *terrible*? And choir practice going on – I think if you hold your breath you can hear the train all the way to Contoocook. Hear it?
GEORGE	M-m-m- What do you know!
EMILY	Well, I guess I better go back and try to work.
GEORGE	Good night, Emily. And thanks.
EMILY	Good night, George.

Our Town is set in 1901. Some research on life at that time was needed and in their school library Bill and Rosie looked for photographs of houses, interiors, people, clothes and everyday activities in American small towns at the beginning of the century. The material gleaned from this search was a basis for discussion as the pair traced the progress of the two characters through the play noting their interaction and their relationships with other people. They were trying to give 'body' to their characterization for the couple, as presented in the excerpt, hold little human interest.

Wilder envisaged that both performers would sit at the tops of step ladders. To Bill and Rosie this seemed an impractical way of staging a piece in an examination and the chance that two step ladders were on tap seemed beyond the bounds of possibility. They therefore decided they would each sit at a small table allowing these to represent the two rooms of separate houses and at first it seemed best to imagine that the dwellings were on opposite sides of the street until it dawned on the pair that it was unsatisfactory to perform the whole excerpt in profile. Moving the tables on their axes solved nothing as this ensured that whilst one played the scene towards the examiner, the other person was playing away from him. Besides this, if the two characters caught sight of each other too easily, then the scene would become totally static. This last consideration prompted them to place the tables eight feet away from each other, both facing the audience; each represented a desk placed immediately before an upper window of two neighbouring houses on the same side of the street. In order to be able to speak to the other each performer had either to lean over the top of the table, and so through the imagined window frame, or climb on to the desk top (eventually Rosie's move) and peer through the frame. With this solution their performance gained visual interest.

The two candidates had to come to terms with the New Hampshire dialect. They learnt that Americans enjoy savouring words more than do English people and thus it was that Wilder had placed the repeated word 'terrible' in italics; in speaking it Emily had to summon up the magic of the warm evening. In a recital performance there was no other way of conveying the moonlight than by her wondering voice. Rehearsals taught them, too, that the conversation about the arithmetic problem required pauses as Emily struggled to help George. Obviously the complete conversation can't be *sotto voce* and they had to discover a sentence on which they could pass from the whisper implied in George's first 'Hsst!' into quiet projected speech. They discovered too that the tone of this brief conversation passes from mundane problems about area to a lyrical enjoyment of the evening. All were pointers to the range of speaking that the text demanded.

George and Emily demonstrate in their rehearsals useful pointers: duo acting highlights the need to be conscious of the physical relationship of each character; it reveals that the dialogue must be passed from one character to another; pauses must jointly be utilized; candidates must jointly understand the tone and style of the excerpt for there must be a harmonization within the performances.

7.2.2 *The School for Scandal* by Richard Sheridan

The next example focuses on the relationship between two characters in emotional and physical terms, as well as introducing the challenge of historical style when two people are working together.

Jeremy and Kate are taking a grade 6 duo acting examination in which an excerpt from an eighteenth-century comedy is stipulated. These young people are sixteen, and a text they are both studying for the GCSE English examination is Richard Sheridan's sparkling comedy *The School for Scandal*. From this they have excerpted Act 2 scene 2, a caustic and witty conversation between the elderly Sir Peter and his young country-bred wife, Lady Teazle. The candidates are allowed up to six minutes for the piece and, once they can run the scene with pace, they will find they have time enough. I have not given the text of this selection as it is lengthy. However, it is easily obtainable from a library.

As with solo period pieces the performers must have a clear idea of the theatrical conditions in which the play was first performed. Richard Sheridan wrote his comedy in 1777 for the Theatre Royal, Drury Lane, London, of which he was manager. This was one of the two patent theatres of the city and the building held 1800 people, although we must remember that this large audience was crammed into a smaller area than would be permitted today. In fact fourteen years after his play was first presented there, Sheridan decided to enlarge the auditorium.

The theme which Jeremy and Kate chose to work on shows the audience the relationship between Sir Peter and Lady Teazle. In the previous scene Sir Peter has already told the audience his difficulty: six months previous, to that time an 'old bachelor', he had married a young country woman. Immediately after the marriage Lady Teazle proved to be a wild spendthrift, rapidly making inroads into Sir Peter's fortune. She has also joined a company of scandal-mongers presided over by Lady Sneerwell. In spite of these defects, Sir Peter dearly loves his young wife.

At the beginning of the excerpted scene Sir Peter is taking Lady Teazle to task for her extravagance in buying flowers for their London house during the winter. Lady Teazle uses her own kind of logic to combat her husband's protestations: '. . . am I to blame because flowers are dear in cold weather?' Sir Peter's counterblast is to remind Lady Teazle of the restricted rural life she led before she married him but she undercuts him by describing in detail its duties such as inspecting the dairy, looking after the poultry, combing the dog, playing cards with the clergy and reading sermons to her aunt. Sir Peter points out that he has made his wife a 'woman of fashion, of fortune, of rank' and Lady Teazle insinuates that her position would be on the ascendant if she were Sir Peter's widow. She goes on to say that as Sir Peter has made her fashionable she must spend to remain so. Tiring of the argument, 'our daily jangle', she announces her intention of going to see Lady Sneerwell, a name which causes Sir Peter to fulminate against the pack of gossips. 'What,' asks Lady Teazle with sweet reasonableness, 'would you restrain the freedom of speech?' She tries to entice her husband to accompany her but he remarks that he will drop in later 'just to look after my character'. The scene finishes with Sir Peter paradoxically admiring the 'charming air' with which his wife contradicts each of his expostulations and claiming that when they are quarrelling Lady Teazle appears at her best.

Jeremy and Kate compiled from the play text a dossier on Sir Peter and another on his wife. It could be over-easy to present Peter Teazle as a buffoon and his wife as a yokel upstart and the dossiers were useful in providing material which could be used in the selected scene. More than any other characteristic, the basic honourableness of each character has to permeate the acting. Later research gave the pair some facts about the first performers of these two roles. That of Sir Peter was played by Thomas King, then a forty-seven-year-old man, the comedian of the Drury Lane company. William Hazlitt, a noted theatre critic of the Georgian stage, described his playing of the part as 'amorous, wheedling . . . hasty, choleric, peremptory'. Mrs Frances Abington took the part of Lady Teazle. Although she was middle-aged when the comedy was first staged, she played the part with a girlishness and an articulation so precise that an eye-witness remarked that every syllable was conveyed 'distinctly and even harmoniously'. Not only did Jeremy and Kate gain some hints which helped them in the portrayal of the characters, they also realized that they were part of the great tradition of English acting.

There were still further discoveries to be made if a scholarly as well as artistic presentation of the scene was to be given. Kate found it difficult to envisage what the Teazle's town house would look like so she examined photographs of Georgian interiors in architectural works. She discovered one point which proved to be of importance in staging the play: furniture such as upright chairs and sofas were not positioned about the room as now but around its edge. It was for this reason that the backs of many of the chairs were upright. Therefore the couple, if they did sit down, would not do so in an easy relationship with each other but formally, either in line or opposite each other. They looked too at pictures of clothes of the period for these would make a difference to their stance, movement and gesture. Kate was especially interested in one of the Georgian dresses, noting its bulk around the skirt area and the extent to which it was pinched in at the waist. She also studied the underwear worn by the fashionable, for these garments caused constriction around the waist and rib cage and also helped to bulk and frame out the skirt. She tried to imagine the effect on one's carriage of wearing such clothes, realizing that they would make her stance rigid and that in any movement she must be conscious of the skirt sailing behind her. Jeremy noticed that the men's clothes were more comfortable, although they were heavy. He saw in full-length portraits that men tended to stand with their feet turned out so that the white stockings, which were visible as far as men's knees, did not give their wearers' legs the impression of being bandy.

Having digested all this material it was time to start rehearsing the scene. Not all of the notes their teacher gave them can be recorded here; instead I've made a summary of some of the more important decisions. It was agreed that four chairs would be used, formally arranged, two on either side of the acting area, facing straight across the stage. This would help define an imagined proscenium. Entrances and exits would be made downstage, slightly below the rectangle formed by the chairs. It was through the stage left proscenium door that Kate, as Lady Teazle, made her entrance followed by Jeremy in his role. In common with many of the actors in theatrical portraits they came to the front of the proscenium, leaving a wide space between themselves through which they might hurl abuse at each other. Both actors found it difficult to bear in mind that a Georgian play was addressed as much to the audience as to the other characters. In speaking her opening lines Kate realized that Lady Teazle often mimicked her husband, and so she made her 'Sir Peter, Sir Peter' an imitation of his 'Lady Teazle, Lady Teazle'. She realized that as the scene progressed Lady Teazle often picked up a key word in her husband's previous speech or hinted at his old-fashioned 'Aye' by using an archaic 'Nay' in reply, a further mark of imitation. The first subject in the selection is extravagance, and then the tenor of the piece alters as Sir Peter reminds his wife of her former life. It seemed at that point a movement was necessary in order to emphasize the change of topic. Jeremy and Kate's teacher had found a snippet by Sir Jonah Barrington on style in Georgian comedy and they decided this could be useful:

> . . . whenever [the performers] made a speech [they] walked across the stage and changed sides with the performer who was to speak next, thus veering backwards and forwards like a shuttlecock.

The restricted space of the examination room, so much smaller than the proscenium of Drury Lane, would not allow a move to be made on every speech but at least the convention could be employed occasionally.

Later they discussed whether Sir Peter's recollection of his wife sitting, before her marriage, at her tambour was in fact an implied stage direction and decided that perhaps Kate should sit on one of the chairs leaving Jeremy free to stand in the rectangle as he described her rustic life.

Much of the time the two characters seemed to stand apart from each other although they occasionally altered their axes, and Kate wondered whether they should come near to each other at the first sign of their underlying good humour breaking through. She plumped for Lady Teazle's remark, 'But, Sir Peter, you know you promised to come to Lady Sneerwell's too'. Here was an opportunity to show a closer relationship between the pair, a chance for Lady Teazle to move over to her husband and perhaps take his hand or lay her hand on his sleeve. Georgian prompt books suggest that Lady Teazle usually left by the opposite proscenium door from the one she entered by, signifying that she leaves the house to go to Lady Sneerwell's. Later Sir Peter, of course, goes off the way he entered, back into the inner recesses of the house. After his wife has left the stage Sir Peter is alone and this gives him a chance to speak directly to the audience: Jeremy knew that he must do this with a welcoming warmth of tone, not only feeling affection for his wife but also wanting to interest the audience with his family affairs; it was as if he had stepped out of the play briefly in order to make this reassuring contact with the audience.

Yet again, in describing this selection I've concentrated on the preparatory material. Much of the acting stems directly from your perception of what is required. No one can really tell you *how* to play a part – only you can do that. But I can give you clues to the way in which you may study a role and so feed your imagination.

7.2.3 *Waiting for Godot* by Samuel Beckett

For the last of these three studies in duo acting let us look at Alaric and Rod. They are taking Theatre Studies as part of an A-level course. They are required to demonstrate an individual theatre skill to the examiner and both have chosen acting from a list of options. They must present two pieces, both excerpted from published works, which demonstrate a contrast in acting approach and techniques. It is stipulated that one piece must be performed as a solo and the other must be presented with the help of another student. The boys have decided that the piece they will work on together is a conversation between Estragon and Vladimir taken from *Waiting for Godot* by Samuel Beckett. Both students are being examined together in the *Godot* excerpt and the rubric states that in this case each part should offer 'adequate opportunity for aassessment'. There is no difficulty with the roles of Vladimir and Estragon in ensuring this, for each character is an imprint of the other. A further requirement is that each candidate must keep a working notebook which becomes a record of the process involved in the demonstration of the skill. After reading the play several times the two students focused on passages which could serve as their excerpt. In most of these they felt that the similarities of Vladimir and Estragon were in evidence and they wanted to explore the differences between the characters; they therefore chose a conversation from the second half of the play.

ESTRAGON	Well?
VLADIMIR	What was I saying, we could go on from there.
ESTRAGON	What were you saying when?
VLADIMIR	At the very beginning.
ESTRAGON	The beginning of WHAT?
VLADIMIR	This evening . . . I was saying . . . I was saying . . .
ESTRAGON	I'm not a historian.
VLADIMIR	Wait . . . we embraced . . . we were happy . . . happy . . . what do we do now that we're happy . . . go on waiting . . . waiting . . . let me think . . . it's coming . . . go on waiting . . . now that we're happy . . . let me see . . . ah! The tree!
ESTRAGON	The tree?
VLADIMIR	Do you not remember?
ESTRAGON	I'm tired.
VLADIMIR	Look at it.
	They look at the tree
ESTRAGON	I see nothing.
VLADIMIR	But yesterday evening it was all black and bare. And now it's covered with leaves.
ESTRAGON	Leaves?
VLADIMIR	In a single night.
ESTRAGON	It must be the Spring.
VLADIMIR	But in a single night!
ESTRAGON	I tell you we weren't here yesterday. Another of your nightmares.
VLADIMIR	And where were we yesterday evening according to you?
ESTRAGON	How do I know? In another compartment. There's no lack of void.
VLADIMIR	(*sure of himself*). Good. We weren't here yesterday evening. Now what did we do yesterday evening?
ESTRAGON	Do?
VLADIMIR	Try and remember.
ESTRAGON	Do . . . I suppose we blathered.

VLADIMIR	(*controlling himself*). About what?
ESTRAGON	Oh . . . this and that, I suppose, nothing in particular. (*With assurance.*) Yes, now I remember, yesterday evening we spent blathering about nothing in particular. That's been going on now for half a century.
VLADIMIR	You don't remember any fact, any circumstance?
ESTRAGON	(*weary*). Don't torment me, Didi.
VLADIMIR	The sun. The moon. Do you not remember?
ESTRAGON	They must have been there, as usual.
VLADIMIR	You didn't notice anything out of the ordinary?
ESTRAGON	Alas!
VLADIMIR	And Pozzo? And Lucky?
ESTRAGON	Pozzo?
VLADIMIR	The bones.
ESTRAGON	They were like fishbones.
VLADIMIR	It was Pozzo gave them to you.
ESTRAGON	I don't know.
VLADIMIR	And the kick.
ESTRAGON	That's right, someone gave me a kick.
VLADIMIR	It was Lucky gave it to you.
ESTRAGON	And all that was yesterday?
VLADIMIR	Show your leg.
ESTRAGON	Which?
VLADIMIR	Both. Pull up your trousers. (*Estragon gives a leg to Vladimir, staggers. Vladimir takes the leg. They stagger.*) Pull up your trousers.
ESTRAGON	I can't.
	Vladimir pulls up the trousers, looks at the leg, lets it go. Estragon almost falls.
VLADIMIR	The other. (*Estragon gives the same leg.*) The other, pig! (*Estragon gives the other leg. Triumphantly.*) There's the wound! Beginning to fester!
ESTRAGON	And what about it?
VLADIMIR	(*letting go the leg*). Where are your boots?
ESTRAGON	I must have thrown them away.
VLADIMIR	When?
ESTRAGON	I don't know.
VLADIMIR	Why?
ESTRAGON	(*exasperated*). I don't know why I don't know!
VLADIMIR	No, I mean why did you throw them away?
ESTRAGON	(*exasperated*). Because they were hurting me!
VLADIMIR	(*triumphantly, pointing to the boots*). There they are! (*Estragon looks at the boots.*) At the very spot where you

left them yesterday!
Estragon goes towards the boots, inspects them closely.

ESTRAGON   They're not mine.

VLADIMIR   (*stupefied*). Not yours!

ESTRAGON   Mine were black. These are brown.

VLADIMIR   You're sure yours were black?

ESTRAGON   Well, they were a kind of grey.

VLADIMIR   And these are brown? Show.

ESTRAGON   (*picking up a boot*). Well, they're a kind of green.

VLADIMIR   Show. (*Estragon hands him the boot. Vladimir inspects it, throws it down angrily.*) Well of all the –

ESTRAGON   You see, all that's a lot of bloody –

VLADIMIR   Ah! I see what it is. Yes, I see what's happened.

ESTRAGON   All that's a lot of bloody –

VLADIMIR   It's elementary. Someone came and took yours and left you his.

ESTRAGON   Why?

VLADIMIR   His were too tight for him, so he took yours.

ESTRAGON   But mine were too tight.

VLADIMIR   For you. Not for him.

ESTRAGON   (*having tried in vain to work it out*). I'm tired! (*Pause.*) Let's go.

VLADIMIR   We can't.

ESTRAGON   Why not?

VLADIMIR   We're waiting for Godot.

ESTRAGON   Ah! (*Pause. Despairing.*) What'll we do, what'll we do!

VLADIMIR   There's nothing we can do.

ESTRAGON   But I can't go on like this!

VLADIMIR   Would you like a radish?

ESTRAGON   Is that all there is?

VLADIMIR   There are radishes and turnips.

ESTRAGON   Are there no carrots?

VLADIMIR   No. Anyway you overdo it with your carrots.

ESTRAGON   Then give me a radish. (*Vladimir fumbles in his pockets, finds nothing but turnips, finally brings out a radish and hands it to Estragon, who examines it, sniffs it.*) It's black!

VLADIMIR   It's a radish.

ESTRAGON   I only like the pink ones, you know that!

VLADIMIR   Then you don't want it?

ESTRAGON   I only like the pink ones!

VLADIMIR   Then give it back to me.
Estragon gives it back.

ESTRAGON	I'll go and get a carrot.
	He does not move.
VLADIMIR	This is becoming really insignificant.
ESTRAGON	Not enough.
	Silence.
VLADIMIR	What about trying them?
ESTRAGON	I've tried everything.
VLADIMIR	No, I mean the boots.
ESTRAGON	Would that be a good thing?
VLADIMIR	It'd pass the time. (*Estragon hesitates.*) I assure you, it'd be an occupation.
ESTRAGON	A relaxation.
VLADIMIR	A recreation.
ESTRAGON	A relaxation.
VLADIMIR	Try.
ESTRAGON	You'll help me?
VLADIMIR	I will of course.
ESTRAGON	We don't manage too badly, eh Didi, between the two of us?
VLADIMIR	Yes yes. Come on, we'll try the left first.
ESTRAGON	We always find something, eh Didi, to give us the impression we exist?
VLADIMIR	(*impatiently*). Yes yes, we're magicians. But let us persevere in what we have resolved, before we forget. (*He picks up a boot.*) Come on, give me your foot. (*Estragon raises his foot.*) The other, hog! (*Estragon raises the other foot.*) Higher! (*Wreathed together they stagger about the stage. Vladimir succeeds finally in getting on the boot.*) Try and walk. (*Estragon walks.*) Well?
ESTRAGON	It fits.
VLADIMIR	(*taking string from his pocket*). We'll try and lace it.
ESTRAGON	(*vehemently*). No no, no laces, no laces!
VLADIMIR	You'll be sorry. Let's try the other. (*As before.*) Well?
ESTRAGON	(*grudgingly*). It fits too.
VLADIMIR	They don't hurt you?
ESTRAGON	Not yet.
VLADIMIR	Then you can keep them.
ESTRAGON	They're too big.
VLADIMIR	Perhaps you'll have socks some day.
ESTRAGON	True.
VLADIMIR	Then you'll keep them?
ESTRAGON	That's enough about these boots.
VLADIMIR	Yes, but –

ESTRAGON   (*violently*). Enough! (*Silence.*) I suppose I might as well
                       sit down.
                       *He looks for a place to sit down, then goes and sits down
                       on the mound.*
VLADIMIR   That's where you were sitting yesterday evening.
ESTRAGON   If I could only sleep.
VLADIMIR   Yesterday you slept.
ESTRAGON   I'll try.
                       He resumes his foetal posture, his head between his knees.

In this passage Vladimir is clearly in charge: it is he who questions Estragon
about the previous day; he who examines Estragon's leg; he who finds the boots
and eventually gets them on Estragon's feet; he who feeds Estragon with a black
radish; and finally he who watches whilst Estragon sleeps.

The casting was a difficult business. Both students had ideas about the
portrayal of the two characters. They decided to alternate the roles in early
rehearsals until each actor seemed to fit the right mould. Their teacher pointed
them to the next step: they would need to gather information about each
character from the text and alongside this task to think about ways in which the
play could be presented, for the traditional iconography of the two tramps
established by Roger Blin in the first production had, in the play's many revivals,
worn thin. Estragon's boot figures in the play and so, in other episodes, does
Vladimir's hat, and they decided that these traits were pointers to the inner nature
of each character: Vladimir was the cerebral, a ready-made philosopher whose
head can never quite adjust to the hat and Estragon was the earthier of the two.
Vladimir is also a bit of a theologian caught in a web of problems about
redemption, personal salvation and rejection. Furthermore he is a quaint
naturalist passing on to Estragon the folklore about the shrieking mandrake root.
His theological and horticultural interests combine in his recognition of the
willow tree, the tree on which traditionally Judas, the betrayer of Jesus, hanged
himself. Estragon is a very different person: he tells bawdy jokes, he is a poet, he
has a longing to break away from Vladimir although he can't muster the
will-power to do this, he longs for sleep which is a symbol of death and his
thoughts run on hanging himself from a tree branch. As the two students
pondered on the nature of the characters, they realized that their names revealed
something about them: Estragon took his name from the bitter herb, tarragon,
whilst Vladimir's name suggested a mysterious Russian emigré.

The setting was a problem. At the start of the selection Vladimir refers to a tree
which forms an important part of the play's iconography. The tree is seen in a
number of guises: at one stage it is the tree of damnation from which Judas
committed suicide and the cluster of ideas around it hark back to the tree in the
garden of Eden, the tree of the knowledge of good and evil; but the tree, too,
represents life in its covering crop of leaves and hence it represents salvation and

is akin to the tree on Calvary, the cross on which Jesus was crucified. With these complex ideas centred on the tree it seemed necessary to show that it was special in some way: was it to be a man-made tree with its branches espaliated into a cruciform shape? Or was it an ordinary tree with its branches painted, perhaps in red as a symbol of martyrdom and salvation? These and similar ideas the pair discussed at length. What would your solution to this challenge be?

Rehearsal was a time in which the relationship between Estragon and Vladimir was examined. Of necessity and as part of the problem-solving element of the examination the candidates' work is self-directed; however, Alaric and Rod were introduced to a number of theatre games by their tutor which helped them understand how changes in their relationship could be made evident. One consisted of taking a small section of the text and creating a parallel improvisation around the situation, after which the actors discussed not only what they felt and did but their instinctive physical responses to the emotional and cognitive side of the performance. For this they used the first few lines of the excerpt. Rod decided that he and Alaric were two alcoholics who had spent a blissful night and the next morning were attempting to pierce the haze to relive those few happy hours. After the improvisation had developed they discovered how they had related spatially at the beginning of the situation: how Alaric had come up to Rod and taken him, right at the start, to look at the riverside where the evening had begun and Rod had to be introduced to the scene as if he were visiting it for the first time; they noticed how Alaric took the hem of Rod's jacket as he led him to the site; they thought too how Rod had continually wanted to move away from the scene of so much happiness. All of these responses, movement, gesture, the use of space, the use of the other person, eye focus and tone of voice fuelled the rehearsal of the brief opening sequence of the *Godot* excerpt.

Dressing and undressing each other was another game they played, safeguarded by a pre-arranged limit to the amount of clothing to be shed. They tried this activity at different speeds in a variety of roles using as many different kinds of costume as the costume hamper in the wardrobe allowed. Soon they realized that there was an art to putting on clothes in front of an audience, and the achievement of this gave the actors the flexibility, alongside the portrayal of intense concentration which arouses interest in the audience, to tackle Beckett's seemingly simple stage direction: '*Vladimir succeeds finally in getting on the boot*'.

The lads themselves invented the 'What have I got in my pocket?' game in which each arrived at rehearsal with several selected objects in his pocket with which to amaze or entertain the other. The relationship they built up through this very simple and sometimes seemingly stupid game brought to life another section of Beckett's text, the business of discovering turnips and a radish in Vladimir's pocket, as well as proving that many viable theatrical ideas arise from a simple basis. I'd like to stress that the rehearsals did not consist of blocking in a series of moves and of repeating memorized lines in a variety of ways. Flexibility allowed the characters to grow and this in turn influenced the actors' relationship with each other, and if *Godot* is not about relationships, then what is at the heart of the play? In a helpful set of guidelines for teachers issued by the Associated Examining Board the advice given is: 'The aim of this skill [i.e. acting] is that the actor should examine the character and the extract afresh'. The two candidates I have described worked in that spirit.

Earlier in this section I mentioned that each candidate was required to produce a working notebook which was submitted in advance of the examination to the examiner. In this the candidates are asked to detail the stages of the process which culminate in the demonstration of the acting skill and to look at the character and the excerpt within the context of the complete play. I have seen working notebooks which were no more than a bland diary of events. The Board sees the business of staging an excerpt as a learning process in which one is meeting problems and considering a variety of solutions to them. It would be helpful therefore if, in the light of watching Rod and Alaric at work, I mentioned a number of points which ought to figure in their notebook. This is not a definitive list and your own notebook would no doubt contain equally valid material.

The choice of play was a good starting point; the reasons for this were given in personal and contextual terms. A statement of Beckett's intentions in writing the play helped to give balance to the candidates' own reasons for the choice, and a consideration of the critical reception the play originally and subsequently received helped to determine its worth as a selection piece. Thus they were balancing personal opinion with historical and literary evidence. The candidates' perception of Vladimir and Estragon was also important. Alaric and Rod searched the text for references to the earlier off-stage life of the characters and noted their findings. A description was given of the development of the performance. Notes on the design and stage management of the piece were also given. The theatre games which Rod and Alaric played were an important factor in shaping the production and a statement on the nature of these, the insights that they gave and their practical application in performance, were important areas to cover. They made a retrospective examination of what they had learnt from the whole exercise and considered how process and product could have been improved and developed. Thus the record was as much about their thinking as about the practical contingencies of the preparation period.

In marking the A-level work the examiner considers the candidate's presentation on two fronts: the understanding of the skill of acting and the demonstration of the skill. In addition to giving a practical presentation each candidate, as we have seen, supports his or her work with a notebook and has an interview with a visiting examiner. Thus the examiner has a three-fold conspectus of the candidate's understanding. The examiner has to consider to what extent the material presented was appropriate and whether a satisfactory contrast between the two chosen pieces was achieved and allowed the candidate to present a range of acting skills. Moreover it has to be decided if the candidate was sensitive to the piece in determining the most appropriate performance style.

When evaluating the candidate's demonstration of acting skill the examiner looks at the way in which the candidate uses his or her total powers of expression – voice, body, space, listening and response; the faithfulness and sincerity of the characterization is important too. The candidate's skill in using performing aids is also evaluated; such items as props, token costume and lighting, if used, must be effective in their employment. There is too the candidate's ability to engage and hold the audience which is creditworthy. To some extent the criteria adopted by the Associated Examining Board differs from the more traditional approach of some other boards and that is why, for the sake of clarity, I have adjoined the candidate's performance to the examiner's expectations.

7.3 EXAMINATIONS IN GROUP PERFORMANCE

Examinations in small group performance are also offered by a number of boards and as their nature varies a summary of these is needed.

(a) Associated Board

The Associated Board offers two grades in acting for groups of four to six candidates: improvisation forms the basis of the content of the junior grade and developed improvisation and text-based performance of the senior.

(b) Associated Examining Board

In the Associated Examining Board's A-level in Theatre Studies all candidates must take part in a group project realizing an original drama presentation created by the group. From five to nine candidates are allowed in each group.

(c) The General Certificate of Secondary Education (Southern Examining Group)

The GCSE offers a unit in group acting with three to six candidates in each group: the performance is text-based.

(d) Guildhall School

The Guildhall School holds a series of grade examinations, many of which contain a balance of improvisation and text-based performance. The leeway for group size is three to twenty candidates.

(e) LAMDA

LAMDA holds several examinations in the subject. Freedom of choice is allowed and the work may consist of either improvisation or text-based performance. Two sizes of group are allowed: up to five and up to ten candidates.

(f) Mountview

Mountview group performance grades consist of text-based and improvised work with groups numbering from four to twelve candidates; a bonus is that the work is presented in a small theatre.

(g) The Poetry Society

The Poetry Society offers a group programme examination for three or more candidates in which the group presents a programme of poetry on a chosen theme.

(h) Trinity College

Trinity College offers grade examinations in group drama which consist of either the presentation of a scripted play in part or in whole, or of a prepared improvisation. At a senior grade a programme of dramatic excerpts is stipulated. The examinations are for groups of five or more candidates.

7.4 THREE GROUP EXAMINATIONS

Instead of presenting key works or case studies illustrating the preparation for this type of examination I would like to comment on three of them: the group project of the AEB A-level in Theatre Studies, the group performance in the GCSE Theatre Arts (SEG), and the Group Programme of the Poetry Society.

7.4.1 The Associated Examining Board: Group Project

I have been fortunate in having the opportunity to examine a number of group projects in the AEB A-level Theatre Studies examination and I have been delighted by the range of the work and the dedication of the groups in their preparation. The stipulation is that each group has to devise an original theatrical presentation for which it has total responsibility. The tutor advises but does not choose the theme nor direct the piece. The presentation lasts between fifteen and thirty minutes, depending on the size of the group, which numbers from five to nine candidates. After the presentation the group discusses its work with the visiting examiner. There is no reason why candidates should not draw on other sections of the examination for inspiration and some of the most successful group presentations I have seen have used the study of plays or the theories of theatre practitioners as a spring board. Let me give you an example.

A group at a sixth form college had developed an interest in the theories of the French writer Antonin Artaud. Here was a man who had little time for conventional theatre and the safe divide between acting area and audience area. He saw theatre as an elaborate ritual which impinged directly on the spectator causing his own emotions to become as shattered as those of the character personated. For this ritual Artaud envisaged a hangar-like building surrounded by a gallery in which audience and actors could freely mix. Presentations were to be by means of movement and drama, incoherent yells and screams, processions, banners, larger-than-life puppets – in fact any theatre artefact which would make a direct assault on the senses of the audience. The latter part of Artaud's life was dominated by fits of depression and for some years he was committed to an asylum. This was the starting point for the students' preparation. The great turmoil in the mind of Artaud was the nexus of the production. The set was a blazing white box on to which lights were trained. Everyone except Artaud wore a doctor's white coat. In contrast Artaud was dressed in the costume he liked to wear for effect, the court dress of an eighteenth-century aristocrat, a strange conceit for a man who passionately believed that all men, with or without rank, learning or wit, should be open to the experience of theatre. Beyond the fact of Artaud's madness there was little by way of a narrative line in the presentation: one was simply bombarded by Artaud's ideas about the nature of theatre. This particular group project left one unnerved; in itself it had demonstrated the force of Artaud's concept of a theatre of cruelty.

One of the virtues of the group project is that the academic interests, the popular enthusiasms and the technical expertise of each member may be woven into the presentation. On another occasion I saw a project which reflected the social concerns of the group, many of whom lived in an inner city area. The tutor running the course was keen that each student should master, over the two years of their study, a number of theatre skills, including such peripheral ones as photography, photomontage and film making. These were all employed in a documentary project on the problems caused by sub-standard housing. The breadth of presentational techniques could have engendered a fragmented presentation but the social commitment of the students proved to be the cohesive force holding the show together.

Such freedom of approach makes demands on the evaluative skill of the visiting examiner, for as the presentation progresses he or she is assessing the various parts of the show to which individuals have contributed, including as wide a range of talents as song-writing, choreography, lighting, orchestration, editing and design. The examiner has three headings under which to evaluate the work. The first is the content of the programme. Here, in looking at the subject matter, he or she weighs up its quality, its suitability for the group and the effectiveness with which it is presented. The second area the examiner considers is the mastery of theatrical technique and in this both the group as a whole and the individual performers are assessed. Lastly the examiner looks to the group for the critical appraisal of its members of their work which is pursued in the discussion following the show. It should be stressed that this is a performance: the group may use set, costume, lighting and props and an audience of students may be invited. Through this exercise the students can gain a personal and experiential knowledge of the way in which theatre works.

7.4.2 The General Certificate of Secondary Education (Southern Examining Group): Theatre Arts

The Theatre Arts examination of the Southern Examining Group for the General Certificate in Secondary Education is the culmination of a new and exciting course introducing students to theatre as an audience and as practitioners. It is worth remembering that for many students in rural areas professional theatre is a rare commodity and that some young people have far more experience of performing than of watching theatre. The acting component in the Theatre Arts course allows small groups of three to six candidates to present either a one act play, or scenes from a longer play, or a thematic work, or a compilation; unlike the A-level Theatre Studies course in which each group directs its own work, in the Theatre Arts course the teacher directs the pieces presented. This is demanding as any one class could contain as many as ten groups and obviously some areas of the preparation must be left to the candidates. The laudable intention that the GCSE is for all pupils, whatever the standard of their attainment and ability, means that the teacher has to accept the best each candidate is able to offer and use this positively in the work which will be examined. There is no hiding in the backstage for the inept. The range of examinable components, too, is daunting for the teacher although challenging and exciting for the pupils: acting is merely one of a number of elements which, taken as an option, constitutes a highly flexible course.

7.4.3 The Poetry Society: Group Programme

The last of these examinations I would like to look at is the Poetry Society's Group Programme of poetry. In this a group of more than three candidates builds a programme around a chosen theme. Although the main emphasis is on poetry speaking the presentation may also include prose, movement, music and improvisation as well as the candidates' own writing.

Many of the anthologies I have seen are highly imaginative but there can be some pitfalls, due to the candidates' misunderstanding of the spirit of the examination. The choice of theme poses the group a challenge as there are a number which have worn threadbare. How often have I listened to programmes on such themes as 'Nature', 'Animals', 'The Weather' or 'Spring' knowing, before their introduction, the poems which inevitably will be used? The difficulty with these themes is that the kind of poems collected speak little of the everyday experience of the candidates. Instead an insipid romanticism makes the recital not only unreal but also mawkish. There are more serious and personal issues which concern young people: you have opinions to express on the place of women in society, on hostages, on the rape of the environment, on the misuse of animals and so on. One difficulty is that traditional anthologies don't cover these subjects and you have to become acquainted with new poets and new writing, using poetry magazines, privately printed books of verse and the poetry column of periodicals such as the *Listener* and the *Spectator*. You must show that poetry is relevant to you now and engages your intellect as well as your emotions.

There are over-easy solutions to the problems of presentation. This is exemplified by the group of five candidates in which each person presented a poem and was then silent and disengaged for the remainder of the programme. Admittedly this is an extreme example but it does point to the need for the group to present work *as a group*. I'm not necessarily advocating choral speaking, which is a sophisticated and complex art form requiring considerable powers of aesthetic judgment, but I am asking you to look very carefully at the poems you have chosen and to see to what extent they are suitable for solo voices or, in suitable poems, how many voices could appropriately be used. Sometimes an extra voice in a poem highlights the questioning that goes on in the poet's inner self; sometimes, too, a work divided amongst a number of speakers highlights its many facets. The division of the time available between poetry speaking and commentary demands careful consideration and here again the right deployment of the speakers can emphasize that the programme is the offering of a group. Similarly the use of a reiterated chorus throughout the recital may stress the theme and its corporate nature.

Another neglected aspect of the group recital is the visual: many candidates adopt an 'all or nothing' approach. I have seen a group costumed, constantly on the move, dancing, playing instruments – and throughout felt that the poetry speaking was almost an after-thought; in contrast there was the group which stood in a line to speak the poems in turn, remaining so throughout the recital. Obviously any grouping must serve the literature, and the visual impact must be an enhancement of the spoken word. There may well be a case for movement by some of the group whilst others speak the text. The poems in Edith Sitwell's 'Façade' are an example of verses with strong rhythms in which sound is of paramount importance and to which movement could be made. Discernment will help you to decide which poems to use. On the whole, though, poetry demands a stillness and non-dramatic approach by the group. There are no rules; so develop your artistic sensibility.

I would like to give an example of a Group Programme that is balanced and imaginative; this was prepared by four pupils at St Helen's School, Northwood – Julia, Lisa, Marie-Claire and Natalie – with the help of their teacher, Mrs Carol Lamont. The pupils had decided on the theme 'Whispering Fear'. Their final selection consisted of the poems given below which were spoken in the order printed.

'The Witches' Spell' by William Shakespeare

> Double, double, toil and trouble;
> Fire burn, and cauldron bubble.
> Fillet of a fenny snake
> In the cauldron boil and bake;
> Eye of newt, and toe of frog,
> Wool of bat, and tongue of dog,
> Adder's fork, and blind-worm's sting,
> Lizard's leg and owlet's wing,
> For a charm of powerful trouble,
> Like a hell-broth, boil and bubble.
> Double, double, toil and trouble;
> Fire burn, and cauldron bubble.

'Dream of a Witch' by Jennifer Noble

> Under a big black hat she sat
> Over a cauldron that bubbled and spat;
> By her side on a rush green mat
> Crouched the witch's thin black cat.
> Her face was covered an ugly green,
> In her eyes a wicked gleam;
> Sharp, crooked teeth far from clean
> Provided a wonderful sight to be seen.
> Into the pot, white burning hot,
> Went frogs and eels, snails, the lot;
> One wary lick at the large wooden spoon
> And then she peered into the gloom.
> I shuddered; felt it was my doom
> To die in this great witch's room.
> I shrank against the bulging wall,
> Felt a broomstick straight and tall –
> I clutched it, and then with one jump
> Sailed over the witch's hump
> Out of the door and up to the moon.
> The witch shrieked loudly, waved her spoon.
> I woke up sharply to the starling's tune.

'Mushrooms' by Sylvia Plath

> Overnight, very
> Whitely, discreetly,
> Very quietly
>
> Our toes, our noses
> Take hold on the loam,
> Acquire the air.
>
> Nobody sees us,
> Stops us, betrays us;
> The small grains make room.
>
> Soft fists insist on
> Heaving the needles,
> The leafy bedding,
>
> Even the paving.
> Our Hammers, our rams,
> Earless and eyeless,
>
> Perfectly voiceless,
> Widen the crannies,
> Shoulder through holes. We
>
> Diet on water,
> On crumbs of shadow,
> Bland-mannered, asking
>
> Little or nothing.
> So many of us!
> So many of us!
>
> We are shelves, we are
> Tables, we are meek,
> We are edible,
>
> Nudgers and shovers
> In spite of ourselves.
> Our kind multiples:
>
> We shall by morning
> Inherit the earth.
> Our foot's in the door.

'Moonlight' by Kathleen Carvell

> The moonlight spreads an eerie glow

Across the darkening skies,
And silently across the lawn
A ghostly bird flies;
The trees rustle and the pond ripples,
The wind whispers and sighs
And silently across the lawn
A ghostly bird flies.
The quietness of the peaceful eve
Is broken by low cries
As silently across the lawn
A ghostly bird flies

'Midnight Wood' by Raymond Wilson

Dark in the wood the shadows stir:
    What do you see? –
Mist and moonlight, star and cloud,
Hunchback shapes that creep and crowd
    From tree to tree.

Dark in the wood a thin wind calls:
    What do you hear? –
Frond and fern and clutching grass
Snigger at you as you pass,
    Whispering fear.

Dark in the wood a river flows:
    What does it hide? –
Otter, water-rat, old tin can,
Bones of fish and bones of man
    Drift in its tide.

Dark in the wood the owlets shriek:
    What do they cry? –
Choose between the wood and river;
Who comes here is lost forever,
    And must die!

The group decided to present a 'frame' to the recital. The four girls listlessly sat together; a distant noise was heard which the girls, breaking away from each other, investigated. As the sound changed to a rhythm and then to music – the theme from *The Phantom of the Opera* – the girls put on masks and began, as witches, to dance. They were ready for the first of the poems.

'The Witches' Spell' was a mixture of solo lines and group speaking; the masks were discarded at the end of the piece. 'Dream of a Witch' was spoken by Lisa to accompany a mime by Julia and Natalie, involving the witch described and the child who saw her. 'Mushrooms' was again a mixture of solo and unison speaking; a feature was a gradual increase in dynamics throughout the piece. 'Moonlight' gave an opportunity for the group to create a rhythmic movement which suggested the flight of the ghostly bird introduced in the poem. The final piece, 'Midnight Wood', allowed rather more mobility with its four stanzas divided for speaking amongst the group whilst the non-speakers moved rapidly on each italicized question and then froze for the remaining lines of the verse.

To mirror the opening sequence the girls reassembled as for the opening group, no longer bored and enervated but eager and ready to tell of their adventures suggested by each of the poems spoken.

The candidates were delighted that their programme, on presentation to the Poetry Society, was warmly commended by the examiner.

What then are the objectives of the candidates in the Group Programme? Through their group approach to the text a number of people are discovering the depths of meaning in a selection of verse and presenting their discoveries to the listener with as much care, sound judgment and technical accomplishment as they can muster. The individual members of the group are also listening with care to the poems whether they themselves are speaking or silent, for it is only through such absorption that an audience, in turn, will listen with complete attention.

7.5 RESOURCES

7.5.1 Bibliographical details of works mentioned in the text

Beckett, S. (1956) *Waiting for Godot*, Faber and Faber, London.
Sheridan, R. (ed. F. W. Bateson) (1979) *The School for Scandal*, Ernest Benn, London.
Wilder, T. (1970) *Our Town and Other Plays*, Penguin Books, Harmondsworth.

7.5.2 Key works: Further reading

(a) Sheridan

Barrington, J. (1869) *Personal Sketches of His Own Times*, Henry Colburn, London.
Bingham, M. (1972) *The Track of a Comet*, George, Allen and Unwin, London.
Darlington, W. A. (1951) *Sheridan*, Longman, Green, London.
Loftis, J. (1976) *Sheridan and the Drama of Georgian England*, Blackwell, Oxford.

Porter, R. (1982) *English Society in the Eighteenth Century*, Penguin Books, Harmondsworth.
Ranger, P. (1986) *A Master Guide to 'The School for Scandal'*, Macmillan, London.

(b) Wilder

Harrison, G. A. (1984) *The Enthusiast*, Houghton Mifflin, Boston (a biography of Thornton Wilder).
Wilder, T. (ed. D. Gallup) (1985) *The Journals of Thornton Wilder*, Yale University Press, New Haven.

(c) Beckett

Coe, R. N. (1964) *Beckett*, Oliver and Boyd, Edinburgh and London.
Cooke, V. (ed.) (1985) *Writers on File: Samuel Beckett*, Methuen, London.
Esslin, M. (1968) *The Theatre of the Absurd*, Penguin Books, Harmondsworth (ch. 1).
Fletcher, J. *et al.* (1978) *A Student's Guide to the Plays of Samuel Beckett*, Faber and Faber, London.
Pountney, R. and Zurbrugg, A. (1981) *York Notes: Waiting for Godot*, Longman, London.
Scott, N. A. (1965) *Samuel Beckett*, Bowes and Bowes, London.

7.5.3 Further reading on group examinations and the examples given

Barker, C. (1977) *Theatre Games – a New Approach to Drama Training*, Eyre Methuen, London.
Hart, J. (1986) *Teachers' Guide. Drama and Theatre Arts. GCSE*, Southern Examining Group, Guildford.
Nixon, J. (1987) *GCSE Coursework – Drama*, Macmillan, London.
Southern Examining Group (1987) *Drama and Theatre Arts. Coursework Memorandum*, Southern Examining Group for the GCSE, Guildford.
Spolen, V. (1963) *Improvisation for the Theatre*, North Western University Press, Illinois.
Stout, A. K. (1965) *Aspects of Drama and the Theatre*, Sydney University Press, Sydney (a chapter by L. R. Chambers gives an informative account of the theories of Antonin Artaud).

8

Readings, talks and discussions

8.1 A SURVEY OF THE CHAPTER

In addition to your performance of verse, prose and drama, many boards examine further aspects of performance and I've grouped some of these together in this chapter so that we may consider suitable methods of preparation. The subjects I am going to deal with are sight reading, prepared reading, prepared talk and extempore talk. I would also like to think about the discussion which sometimes follows both types of talk, as well as the more formal viva voce which often follows a programme of performed pieces.

8.2 SIGHT READING

Mark shedules show that the framers of various syllabuses regard sight reading as an important accomplishment for a performer. Unfortunately some candidates feel that they are disadvantaged because they have no natural skill in this subject, but brief, regular practice will ensure that you become adept. Just a couple of minutes every weekday will bring a surprising and obvious improvement after a month or so. Sight reading may include prose or verse or both and sometimes a dramatic piece. Each of these I would like to consider in turn.

8.2.1 Sight reading: Prose

Let us start with prose reading. The examiner will hand you either a book or a typed sheet containing the prose. Take this to the spot in which you are going to read it and make sure that as much light as possible is on the paper. This may mean standing a little nearer to a window than you would wish or stationing yourself under a light. The older you are the more important it is to find the lightest spot in the room for after the age of twenty eyes deteriorate.

The examiner will not expect you to start reading straight away: you have a little while for preparation. Exactly how much time usually depends on the examiner. Use this time economically. Rapidly look at the title and the name of the author if these are given and then skim through the text itself: don't try to read every word! You are establishing certain things. First of all the content of the piece – sometimes the title prepares you for this – and what the author's most important points are. Secondly, you want to know the atmosphere of the piece. Two authors might write about a tree: to one it is a joyous symbol of growth and to another it is an object of terror with its gnarled branches and hoots of owls from within. You must be prepared to interpret the intention of the writer. Thirdly, senior candidates should get a clear impression of the voice of the writer. A text by D. H. Lawrence on miners washing at the pit-head after a day's work rejoices in the sensuous elements of steam and lather on human skin, but the writer of a socialist tract, outraged that men are degraded by spending the day in the filth of coal dust, would adopt a very different voice. Voice influences style and this is something you must come to terms with. Lastly, in your preliminary scan be aware of the vocabulary. Those responsible for selecting sight reading pieces avoid unusual words, nevertheless look out for any words which are likely to give you trouble. This sounds a formidable list of things to do but don't worry; with practice you can establish all of this quickly and much of it simultaneously.

A candidate may wonder whether to sit or stand for the reading. The subject of the piece should guide you. If the prose is formal or oratorical, or respect for the text deems that you ought to stand, then do so; but many pieces of prose consist of recollections or a passage from a diary, in which case the informality of the writing would suggest you could sit to read. Much the same criteria apply to poetry. Narrative poetry, full of activity and with a dynamic rhythm, may best be spoken standing; quiet, reflective poetry could be tackled whilst sitting. Whether standing or seated hold your script high enough not to have to look down at it. An ideal position is one in which you can raise your eyes and not your head when you want to look at the audience.

Now it is time to read. Announce both the title and the author if they are given. This opening announcement prevents you rushing headlong into the piece. Avoid using as a title something which is only classificatory, such as 'Sight Reading: Grade Four'! Now take the opening sentence and set the pace with that. Attempt to read it fast enough to maintain your listener's interest but slow enough to give you confidence and prevent you tripping over words. Much of the reading I hear is taken too fast. As you speak let your eyes read ahead for half a dozen words. This is important, for then you meet the vocabulary which you will speak in a moment and the gist of the writer's thought. You are also prepared for that awkward word which you spotted earlier. Simply pronounce this in what seems a sensible way to you and have no further worries about it. You *may* have mispronounced it but that won't worry the examiner unduly. Don't stumble, don't repeat your attempt: one stab, right or wrong, is sufficient. Reading ahead has another important purpose: it allows you to look occasionally at the listener. This eye contact is important, for you are not just transmitting words; you are communicating a meaning and this momentary contact between you and the examiner can be used most effectively when you want to emphasize words or phrases. As you come to the end of your reading slow down to ensure that an impression of finality is given.

Let us try a test piece of sight reading. Begin by skimming through the following piece establishing the meaning, vocabulary, atmosphere and voice.

'Stonehenge' by W. H. Hudson

> As a child I had stood in imagination before it, gazing up awestruck on those stupendous stones or climbing and crawling like a small beetle on them. And what at last did I see with my physical eyes? Walking over the downs, miscalled a plain, anticipating something tremendous, I finally got away from the woods at Amesbury and spied the thing I sought before me far away on the slope of a green down, and stood still and then sat down in pure astonishment. Was *this* Stonehenge – this cluster of poor little grey stones, looking in the distance like a small flock of sheep or goats grazing on that immense down! How incredibly insignificant it appeared to me, dwarfed by its surroundings – woods and groves and farm-houses, and by the vast extent of rolling down country visible at that point.

The paragraph tells of a disapppointment: the contrast between the writer's imagined view of Stonehenge and the apparent smallness of the reality. This is the type of piece which might be set for grade 5 or 6 so there are presumably no great difficulties in the vocabulary. The atmosphere is one of double amazement; there is the image that the child has of Stonehenge and then that of the adult visitor. What of the voice? The author is not querulous about the dwarfing; he accepts his disappointment and attempts to describe graphically what it is that the stone circle is dwarfed by. The climax of the paragraph for me comes in Hudson's exclamation: 'Was *this* Stonehenge . . .!'

Now try reading the passage aloud. Remember not to hurry and do read ahead. Know where your imagined listener is sitting and occasionally look at him, especially when you want to make an emphasis. Right – off you go!

What did you discover in your reading? One point, I hope, that became obvious was that the piece allowed for several pauses to be made. The first of these, a rhetorical pause, is after the question, 'And what at last did I see with my physical eyes?' This pause is a chance for you to contact the listener before embarking on the next section. Similarly, after the word 'astonishment' you can pause, willing your listener to wonder what it was that caused this reaction. You might also have noticed that in describing past impressions the writer is recollecting and possibly needs time to do this, and so a slower pace would be appropriate than when Hudson had the view of the downs and the stones in front of him – then you can give a slightly quicker factual commentary until the last phrase of the final sentence, where a slowing down not only suggests that your reading is complete, but also allows the listener to visualize the immense plain stretching to the horizon.

I suggested earlier regular practice. Almost any material that comes to hand can be used as long as it covers a wide range of prose. Look around the house for bits and pieces: the newspaper, advertising mail, books lying about – any of these will give a couple of minutes' sight reading. Anthologies of essays are also useful and several are suggested in the Resources section of this chapter.

8.2.2 Sight reading: Verse

It is generally considered more difficult to read verse at sight than prose, so poetry appears as sight reading only after the candidate has had some experience of reading prose. The ploy I would suggest to you is much the same to start with, though. Begin by looking at the title and gain an impression of the content. Ask yourself, 'What is the writer saying?' Try to feel, too, where the poet's sympathy lies: what does he feel about the subject? Feeling will in part suggest the pace at which the verse is to be read. Here I would say that much of the verse I listen to in examinations is read much too quickly. A poem is more than content: form comes into focus. Notice the shape of the first stanza and then quickly check that the others are the same shape: you don't want to be left with an uncomfortable suspicion half-way through the poem that you have mislaid a line. You may meet a solidity of text – and at once you should question whether a sonnet is in front of you. If so, try rapidly to see the 'shape' through which the poet's argument progresses. Or the solidity may be due to the fact that an Augustan poet such as Pope has been selected and you discover that the material is presented in rhyming couplets.

Discover the poet's voice in the verse. Admittedly this is difficult, and if you can't rapidly reach a decision you may have to make a neutral response to the text and imperceptibly begin to suggest the voice as the reading progresses. For example, once you have placed a poem as an Augustan piece then you would be looking for the voice of satire, for sharply barbed wit and, if the poet is Pope, a love of names and technical terms.

Here is an opportunity to arrive at quick decisions in response to a text:

'Christ Crucified' by Richard Crashaw

> Thy restless feet now cannot go
>   For us and our eternal good,
> As they were ever wont. What though
>   They swim, alas! in their own flood?

> Thy hands to give Thou canst not lift,
>   Yet will Thy hand still giving be;
> It gives, but O, itself's the gift!
>   It gives tho' bound, tho' bound 'tis free!

How did you get on? The title pinpoints the subject. The content is concerned with devotional ideas in relation to the subject, rather than working in a descriptive territory. In each verse there is an antithesis which your speaking must recognize: the first verse tells of Christ's feet fastened and yet swimming – in his own blood, we are left to presume – and the second tells of the nailed hands which can make gifts. The subject matter, the apparent simplicity of the verses and the meditative tone would suggest to you that here is a poem which must be taken at a slow contemplative pace. Now try speaking the poem aloud.

We make discoveries in speaking. What are yours? I realized by the end of the first line that, because of the complexity of ideas, the listener would be following the thread of these with all of his attention and that I would have to give an indication of line endings, especially as altered pronunciations do not now allow me to rhyme 'good' with 'flood'. Therefore I had to draw out very slightly the vowel sound of 'go' and lead in to the second line. Again, the complexity of the material suggested to me that, although I always want to preserve the rhythm of a line, I had to emphasize and pause on 'swim' in line four in order to get this new idea across, the freedom of Christ's feet, and then the even more unusual idea of the element in which they swam introduced by the word 'alas'. Certainly 'own flood' must be brought to the listener's attention and that may be achieved by a slowing down on the two words. In the second stanza I discovered that the recurring forms of 'give' and 'gift' need to be sorted out and I can only do this by my responsive modulation; it is imperative that, with due awe, using a slower pace and gaining a subtle contrast in the two words, I give the listener the paradox in the juxtaposition of 'bound' and 'free'. In the examination, when you have finished the reading, you may feel that you have not done justice to the poem; the examiner understands this, for perfection will not be reached in a single encounter with a poem.

Often candidates too quickly 'let go' of the atmosphere they have created in the reading by walking over to the examiner's desk to return the script barely before the final word is spoken. Maintain for a couple of moments the concentration you have brought to the piece; stand still and think about the author's message with which you have been entrusted and then simply relax your concentration. Remember to return the examiner's script!

8.2.3 Sight reading: Dramatic text

Sight reading from a play is usually set by a board offering examinations in acting. The procedure varies. Sometimes the candidate is given information about the character, at others there are only the words of the character from which to make deductions about the kind of person to be portrayed. Sometimes notes on moves or gestures are included in the piece: these should serve as an indication rather than as directions to be slavishly followed.

Much of the advice about prose reading at sight applies here as well. Make a preliminary survey of the piece. Get a clear grasp of who the character is and how that character is presented through the words spoken in the excerpt. In skimming the text search out any unusual words and phrases. Work out the frame of mind – happy, emotionally upset or very angry – the character is in. Visualize the pattern of movement implicit in the piece. You will be doing very well if you manage all of that.

When the examiner asks you to begin, remember that this is more than a reading. You are communicating through your body how another person acts, feels, thinks and speaks. Therefore the words must be heartfelt. You must be the character you are portraying. So again you realize the need to read ahead in the text if only to allow yourself time to relive the character's emotions. Remember, too, that silence is an important part of your performance. Pauses, silences on some moves, times of thinking, will all help to add truth to the reading.

Certain simplifications in movement and gesture have to be made as you are holding the script. Get into the habit, if you are right-handed, of holding the text in your left hand; this will then leave your right hand free. If you are successfully reading ahead you will be able to use your eye focus from time to time to help to establish other characters on stage to whom you are speaking. Unless the piece is an example of audience address, there will be no need to look directly at the examiner.

As an example let us take a speech from a play suitable for a female candidate. Have a look through the following:

> MOTHER: They're laughing at me; that's what's the matter with them. They're laughing at an old woman who has had a misfortune. I told you what kind of place the world was, Cuthman, and I shall put a stop to it. I tell you, I've a sense of humour, but I won't be laughed at. (*She . . . rounds on the MOWERS.*) I don't know who you are, but I'm glad I wasn't born in your part of the country. Where I was born we knew how to behave; we knew better than to laugh at an old woman who had come to grief. We were very respected in the village where we come from, I may tell you; but as it happens we decided to travel. (*The MOWERS give an even louder roar of laughter.*) All right, all right! One of these days you'll laugh for too long, you'll laugh yourselves into trouble, take my word for it.

Your initial reactions are probably something like this: 'I have to portray an old woman who is being laughed at by a group of mowers. Obviously she is very angry at their ridicule. I wonder what has happened to her to make them laugh? It may be that the mother has been humiliated in some way. As well as speaking to the mowers she is also talking to someone called Cuthman and, as she is labelled 'Mother', he is probably her son. Where am I going to place these people? Keep things simple! Cuthman can be downstage left and the mowers in a gaggle downstage right. I will begin above left centre and then I can move down to Cuthman and across to the mowers.' Spread out in print your reasoning appears to take a long time but many of these ideas and decisions are made simultaneously and, with practice, your mind's eye can visualize the scene. You are now ready to perform the speech. Try it!

What have you discovered through this trial run? Probably that it is very difficult to be angry at the start of a piece. Your indignation has to grow like spreading fire. You could begin at left centre and by the time you mention Cuthman's name and storm downstage left to him your anger has grown inside you considerably. A stage direction in the text sends Mother over to the mowers, and that move can be indicative as she storms across the front of the acting area by now very angry indeed. She might suddenly contain all of her rage as she thinks back to her youth, icily saying, 'Where I was born . . .'. As you mention that you had decided to travel, a remark which causes the mowers to break into hilarity, you might start to move upstage grandly and then stop in your tracks at the mowers' hoot of laughter. The last sentence seems to be spoken directly to the group. I'm sure that you will remember to stay within your character at the end of the piece, creating a silent tableau, before you retract from the role.

You may have recognized that this particular speech is taken from Christopher Fry's play *The Boy with a Cart*. It is the story of Saint Cuthman journeying with his old Mother through Sussex until he arrives at Steyning where he builds a great Saxon church. The mowers became hilarious when they saw that Mother's mode of transport was in a wheelbarrow pushed by Cuthman out of which she had fallen.

Regular practice is needed with dramatic pieces such as this. A book to use is one composed of suggested audition pieces, then you can practice a different piece every couple of days and for the sake of gaining experience it doesn't matter whether the excerpts are for men or women. Getting into the habit of rapidly summing up the theatrical potential of a speech and then putting it into practice is your principal task.

8.3 PREPARED READING

Some boards require a candidate to read a prose passage selected by the examiner from a book which the candidate has prepared. Others give a set book and stipulate a limited number of chapters, three or four, from which the examiner will choose a passage.

When you are allowed a choice you will obviously select a book which appeals to you and presumably one that you would want to read in its entirety, even if the selection is to be made from a limited number of chapters. In that way you will gain an idea of the characters in the novel, how they relate to each other and how each individual behaves. You will then need to consider the chapters from which the examiner will select paragraphs. Look through these carefully, noting any words of which you are uncertain of the pronunciation. Use a dictionary to determine the correct pronunciation and check this with your teacher. You must also know the meaning of all the words in the key chapters and again your dictionary may be helpful. If there are only two or three key chapters it would make an interesting exercise to tape record these. You can then play the tapes at your leisure, sometimes following the words in your book and at other times simply listening to the tapes. In that way you will easily gain an idea of the content and structure of each chapter which will stay with you when you undertake your reading.

Preparation may be undertaken on thematic lines; here I will consider the presentation of characters, descriptive writing and action. In order to pin my remarks on to an example I have chosen *Silas Marner* by George Eliot, the pen name of Mary Ann Evans, and I am supposing that the key chapters from which the examiner will make his selection are five, six and seven. The book tells of Silas Marner, a linen weaver, who has settled in the village of Raveloe. He is an isolate, finding consolation in a growing pile of gold. This is stolen from his cottage by Dunstan Cass, the squire's son, who later disappears, Some time after this incident Silas finds an orphaned girl with a head of golden curls standing outside his cottage. He takes her in and brings her up as his daughter. She becomes the replacement for the stolen coins. Many years later, with the draining of a pond, the body of Cass, together with the stolen gold, is discovered.

When you begin to think about the characters you may find it helpful to list them and make some notes on each. Thus the beginning of your list would look like this:

Silas Marner:
elderly; a weaver; a stranger in the locality; has difficulty in communicating with other people; capable of responding; very upset at the loss of his gold; gives others the impression at times that he has gone mad.

Bob, the butcher:
jolly; smiling fellow; a bit secretive; a slow speaker; a mild man.

The farrier:
very persistent in trying to find out things; not put off by guarded answers.

Mr Snell:
landlord of the Rainbow Inn; quiet; placatory.

Mr Macey:
a musical man; very long-winded; enjoys telling stories; elderly;
moralizes.

This exercise will help you sort out who the characters are and, more
importantly, you can use the information you have collected to deduce how each
character would speak, so that if the excerpt chosen by the examiner contained a
conversation you could indicate changes of voice to make your reading alive.

Let us see how this works in practice. After the first paragraph in Chapter 6 the
butcher, the landlord and the farrier converse. The landlord starts. We know
from the information the novelist has given us that he rarely plays a part in the
chatter going on in his inn and that in this case he begins in 'doubtful tones', so
you might decide that the landlord's speaking would be rather slow and very
deliberate. However, the butcher is also a slow-spoken man so he must be
differentiated from the landlord; we know that the butcher speaks in a 'husky
voice' and this could be the distinctive factor. Soon the farrier enters the
conversation. He has a very different temperament, persistent in his questioning
and rapidly leaping to conclusions, prompting you possibly to make him a rapid
speaker who easily becomes excited. By tackling the direct speech of the text in
this way you will show the examiner that you possess the vocal range to make the
print live.

One of George Eliot's strengths is her ability to describe places and people.
Many candidates consider description difficult to read; they feel that there is little
to 'get their teeth into', so in order to think about the possibilities for speaking let
us take one of the descriptive passages in which Eliot paints for us the feelings of
Marner as he trudges home in happy anticipation of his supper:

> When Dunstan Cass turned his back on the cottage, Silas Marner was not
> more than a hundred yards away from it, plodding along from the village
> with a sack thrown round his shoulders as an overcoat, and with a horn
> lantern in his hand. His legs were weary, but his mind was at ease, free
> from the presentiment of change.
>
> Silas was thinking with double complacency of his supper – first,
> because it would be hot and savoury; and secondly, because it would cost
> him nothing. For the little bit of pork was a present from that excellent
> housewife Miss Priscilla Lammeter, to whom he had this day carried
> home a handsome piece of linen; and it was only on occasion of a present
> like this that Silas indulged himself with roast meat. Supper was his
> favourite meal, because it came at his time of revelry, when his heart
> warmed over his gold; whenever he had roast-meat, he always chose to
> have it for supper.

You can latch on to two of Marner's feelings: his physical weariness, shown in
the slowness with which he makes his progress from the village, and the old

man's pleasant anticipation of his treat of roast pork. These are your two highlights. Your sympathetic tone of voice must convey the plodding weariness that runs through the first paragraph: but be subtle about this for after all you are the narrator, a person who is an onlooker, and not Marner himself speaking. The second paragraph gives you an opportunity to suggest the succulence of the supper, simply by dwelling, almost imperceptibly, on such flavoured words as 'hot', 'savoury' and 'roast-meat'. Just as Marner's heart is warmed at the thought of the meal so something of that same warmth must colour your vocal tone, and the best way to do that is to be completely responsive to the idea of a pleasant hot meal eaten in one's own small cottage.

Obviously some thoughts about pace are needed, for the reading would seem pedestrian if you took it all at the same pace. Our considerations about the first paragraph suggested that this should be spoken slowly. The pleasing thoughts about supper will no doubt speed the pace a little but you must be subtle. Don't make a sudden change in pace simply because you have arrived at the new paragraph. An interjection occurs when we learn a little about Miss Lammeter. No longer is the focus on Marner and so the narrator may give the new information in a purely factual voice which will allow him to speed up his pace slightly. However, I would repeat that these variations I have mentioned must be made gradually and not be obtrusive.

Candidates often feel happier when they are given an excerpt in which there is some kind of action. *Silas Marner* is not a violent novel and descriptions of activity happening in it are muted, but nevertheless the skilful writing gives the reader opportunity to create a quiet suspense. Try reading the following paragraph and as you do so ask yourself where the most dramatic moments occur, for it is around these that you must plan the shape of your reading:

He rose and placed his candle unsuspectingly on the floor near his loom, swept away the sand without noticing any change, and removed the bricks. The sight of the empty hole made his heart leap violently, but the belief that his gold was gone could not come at once – only terror and the eager effort to put an end to the terror. He passed his trembling hand all about the hole, trying to think it possible that his eyes had deceived him; then he held the candle in the hole and examined it curiously, trembling more and more. At last he shook so violently that he let fall the candle, and lifted his hands to his head, trying to steady himself, that he might think. Had he put his gold somewhere else by a sudden resolution last night, and then forgotten it? A man falling into dark waters seeks a momentary footing even on sliding stones; and Silas, by acting as if he believed in false hopes, warded off the moment of despair. He searched in every corner; he turned his bed over and shook it and kneaded it; he looked in his brick oven where he laid his sticks. When there was no other place to be searched, he kneeled down again and felt once more all round the hole. There was no untried refuge left for a moment's shelter from the terrible truth.

My own choice for the dramatic climax is the sentence beginning 'At last he shook so violently . . .'. Eliot's writing suggests that this should be so for she has Marner trembling more and more violently until that point is reached. Of course, another highly dramatic moment comes when Marner first notices that his hoard of gold is missing. From the earlier dramatic moment until the later one is an opportunity for you to convey this frenzy of activity by increasing the pace of your reading. You will need compensatory pauses or a slower pace later on, and immediately before the question 'Had he put his gold somewhere else . . .?' would be an appropriate place for a dramatic pause. An increase in dynamics often accompanies increasing pace which will help to suggest mounting tension. But within this, too, contrasts will be needed and the question may be asked with searching quietness. After this question Eliot lists a further bout of activity, separating Marner's actions by a series of semicolons. Here again, increasing pace would be suitable until, in the final sentence, the deep despair of the old weaver is slowly spelt out. Thus pace and dynamics help to convey tension and excitement. Occasional dramatic pauses may also be used.

Many of the points we covered in the earlier paragraphs of this chapter on sight reading apply to prepared readings: the way in which you hold your book, reading ahead, getting the true tone of the passage, occasional eye contact with the listener – these are all important considerations. So, too, are some of the points made in Chapter 4 about the performance of prose excerpts. If you are entering for an examination in prepared reading, you may care to consider the possibility of using *Silas Marner* as a key text; young people aged from fourteen to sixteen will find it an interesting account of a changing society set in the previous century.

8.4 PREPARED AND EXTEMPORE TALKS

A prepared talk is set in some of the examinations of the Associated Board, the English Speaking Board, the General Certificate of Secondary Education (English, Oral Communication), the Guildhall School, LAMDA, the London College of Music, the New Era and Trinity College. Some of the above boards also set an extempore talk. The points I would like to cover in this and the next section will be helpful to candidates entering for the above examinations.

8.4.1 The prepared talk

Begin your work on the prepared talk by checking your syllabus for information relating to the following questions:

(a) Do I get a choice of topic for my talk or is it set?
(b) How long is the talk to be?
(c) Am I asked to imagine a specific audience?
(d) Am I invited to bring exhibits or to give a demonstration as part of my talk?
(e) Are there any other stipulations?

Boards expect most talks to be fairly brief, varying in length from two to ten minutes. Time keeping is important and heavy examination schedules mean that an examiner will usually ask you to bring your talk to a conclusion if you go over the allotted time.

Occasionally candidates are asked to let the examiner know the type of audience for which the talk is intended: if you are at school it would be in order to say that you have members of your class in mind as the recipients. I have listened to talks delivered as if to a political meeting, members of a local history society, the Women's Institute, people who have attended a cookery demonstration, a literary circle, a football club, an inventors' collective and so on. You then have to tailor your talk to meet the interests of that particular group and marks are awarded for your success in doing this. A couple of boards allow for an audience to listen to the talks so that you are in a 'real life' situation.

Syllabuses sometimes state that candidates are allowed to bring exhibits. Soon I will be giving you some advice about using illustrations but your exhibits need not be limited to this: if your talk is on angling then you could take your rod, flies and other interesting paraphernalia. One of the most spectacular talks I attended was given by a candidate who was a cookery student; she brought with her a small spirit stove and demonstrated how to prepare an exotic dessert. There may be further regulations. For example, some boards expect the candidate to conduct a discussion with members of the audience or to answer questions on the talk posed by the examiner.

At the outset it is easiest, if the topic has not been set by the board, to choose this and then to decide on your audience. Choose a subject which really interests you and on which you can speak with authority. Begin to think of ways in which you can make this subject absorbing to your audience. Let us watch Oliver as he prepares for his examination. He is very interested in wild flowers and has been allowed to have the end of his parents' town garden as a wild area in which to foster them. Oliver is going to speak about creating this garden. His first task is to gather some ideas for the talk and he begins by jotting down possible subjects as they occur to him in any order. His list soon looks like this:

(a) Different kinds of wild flowers
(b) How I made my wild garden
(c) Butterflies
(d) Grasses
(e) Problems I have encountered
(f) Creating the country in the town

(g) Our need for conservation groups
(h) Visitors to the wild garden.

There is obviously no shortage of material here! In fact, as Oliver is only allowed three minutes to speak on this topic, he realizes that he has more than he can cope with, especially as he does not want to appear to be pouring a quart into a pint pot. He decides he will focus on how he initially planned and set up the garden, so from his list he chooses points (b), (e) and (f). It seems appropriate to speak very briefly about the countryside in the town and then go on to speak about the design and establishment of the wild garden, mention one or two problems and end on a note about his successes; this is not a lack of modesty for the listener wants to hear of these. Oliver now has a flexible plan in mind which he can easily change if he so wishes.

It is now time to decide on his audience and he settles for a group of his peers. He must decide if visual material will help him communicate with his friends. Some photographs could do this, although he feels that they will be far too small. This is an important decision. The imagined group, plus the examiner, need to see large, practical visual material. Instead he decides to have a changing diagram. He begins by drawing the shape of the garden on a large sheet of card with a felt tip pen. He includes the small pond in the back corner and the stump of a felled tree which is a feature of his garden. In order to gain a feeling of progression Oliver will, as he gives his talk, mark with a broad pen the various areas which have grown up in the wilderness. His other visual aid consists of one of his successes: in one corner of the garden a spread of yellow-rattles is visible amongst the grasses and Oliver pots up one and brings this to the examination, together with a couple of dried samples of the plant which he can shake so that the examiner may hear the seeds rattling in the pods, the origin of the plant's popular name. That, he decides, is enough material to take with him: a little well used will gain him more marks than a muddled plethora.

Now Oliver can begin to shape his talk. He knows the rough outline; he must consider at what point he is to introduce the diagram of the garden – perhaps after the opening short section on the country in the town – and at what point it is best to produce the yellow-rattles. These, he decides, he will keep in a box out of sight so that their appearance will create a surge of interest. He would like to make a few notes but these he is going to keep to a minimum. A couple of postcards serve very well. They are easier to manage than sheets of paper and Oliver can hold them unobtrusively in his left hand. He simply chooses a title for each of the sections of the talk and makes a note of subsections and visual material underneath each. This is a copy:

A Wild Garden.
(a) Introduction: the country in the town;
       disappearing wild life;
       the duty of conservation.

(b) From derelict patch to wild garden.*
(c) Challenges and successes;
      plants smothered by grass and nettles;
      wild visitors to the garden;
      the yellow-rattles.*

The two asterisks in Oliver's notes are a reminder to him to produce his visual material at those points. Had there been much material he would have done well to number the exhibits.

Instead of making notes Oliver might have memorized a number of key words which would help him preserve the shape of his talk. The list might consist of:

Conservation
Garden plans
Planting
Challenges
Successes.

Oliver's talk is almost complete. One tip: he could learn the first and last sentences of his talk. By doing this he will open in an arresting way and his assurance will help him sound authoritative. Oliver planned his first sentence: 'Just imagine a city with no grass, no trees, no plants in it!' Wisely Oliver knows too how his talk will end. This sentence must be a pithy summation of what he has said. Knowing the content of Oliver's talk, are you able to compile this sentence for him? Although these two sentences may be committed to memory it is unwise to learn any more of the talk. Pauses for thought and the odd interjection are part of the personality of a speaker and help to make the talk alive and spontaneous.

Oliver needs to practice his talk a couple of times. He can easily try it out on his family or his teacher so that he gains in confidence. As he practices he must time the talk and ruthlessly cut out any material which is going to hold him up. So that he knows how much time he has at his disposal, he plans to take a watch with large clear hands into the examination room; keeping an eye on it he can judiciously edit his talk if he finds time creeping up on him.

Having seen Oliver prepare his talk I will itemize the process he went through. This may be of help in your preparation:

(a) Choose your topic;
(b) Identify your audience;
(c) Decide on the area you are going to cover and the ordering of your talk;
(d) Decide whether to include exhibits or illustrative material;
(e) Shape the talk and make brief notes;
(f) Prepare the introductory and closing sentences;
(g) Practice the talk within the allotted time span.

Rather than working intensively on one talk, prepare and give several: in that way you will learn about adaptability and keep your interest and communication fresh and alive. Listen to talks, too. There may be a chance to hear a young people's debating society at work. Don't forget that talks form an important part of the programme of Radios Three and Four and that it is possible to read some of the talks in the weekly edition of the *Listener* which is in many libraries.

When you are giving your talk remember that the usual principles about performance apply. Choose a suitable place to stand, or sit if that is appropriate, so that there is a divide between yourself and your audience. If a lectern is available, use that to keep your notes on, if not, hold them in your hand. If exhibits are allowed a small table is normally in readiness in the room. Prior to your talk set out your material and pin or prop up any diagrams; don't forget to take drawing pins or tape with you if you think these will be useful. Decide in advance whether you are going to stand behind your display table or to the side of it. My own preference, as I don't wish to be hidden, is to stand at the side when I am giving a lecture. Don't rush your talk; allow both yourself and your audience time to think. Remember, too, that a well-held pause between each section of your talk is vital if the listener is to appreciate the overall structure of it. Imagine that the audience is sitting around the examiner; he won't want you to rivet him with a fixed stare so deliver parts of the talk to various imaginary people. On the other hand don't neglect the examiner; important points should be made to him and remember the value of eye contact when you want to make an emphasis. At the start, quickly come to the point of your talk. Oliver, rather than beginning, 'I have come here today to talk to you about the wild flower garden I made last year . . .' simply began with the title 'A Wild Garden', paused a moment and then started with his pre-planned first sentence. Above all, determine to interest your listeners, reach out to them emotionally and sympathetically for they want to hear an interesting talk: when you feel you have gained a rapport, there is every chance that you are holding the audience's attention.

You may wonder what are the examiner's evaluative criteria when listening to your talk. Firstly one is interested in its content. Sometimes I am very impressed by the amount of research which has gone into the preparation, although I don't want to be bombarded by impersonal facts. Secondly, one notices the structure of the talk: this would include the arrangement of the content and the clarity with which you deal with the topic. Thirdly one is interested in the delivery, which will include the use of your voice, your ability to use visual material and, above all, in your enthusiasm for your topic.

Choosing a suitable topic for your talk can be a difficult task. In order to give you an idea of the range of topics that is encouraged by boards, to complete this section I list the titles of a small proportion of the talks the boys of Oxford School gave as part of their GCSE Oral Communication examination:

The ozone problem and our response.
Dolphins: are they intelligent?
The politics of acid rain.
Nicaragua and its problems.
The five pillars of Islam.
The importance of imagination in today's world.
Artificial football pitches.
The censorship of books.
Violence in computer games.
The Zeebrugge disaster.
AIDS and its effect on the public.
Deforestation.
Nutrition in school.
The privatization of the electricity industry.
The re-introduction of capital punishment.
The access ban on my house.
Cruelty to animals in sport.
Age-rated films.
'Death Row'.
Should prostitution be made legal?
Plumbing, heating and ventilation.
The development of martial arts.
My prize: a trip to America.
Do teenagers respect their parents?

8.4.2 Extempore talks

Many of the points we have covered about prepared talks apply also to extempore talks; the difference, of course, is that with the latter the examiner chooses the subject and gives it to you either shortly before the examination or during it. The various syllabuses make clear when you are given the topic, or choice of topics, and how long you have to prepare your talk. Take to the examination a pen, notebook and several postcards for your notes. When the examiner gives you the topic, don't panic. Nearly everyone immediately imagines that they know nothing about a subject which is suddenly introduced. Decide quickly what kind of response the topic needs. For example, it may be a controversial question and you have to line up the pros and cons and make a decision. The topic 'Should traffic be banned from town centres?' suggests that kind of approach. You may be presented with a somewhat open title and left to deal with the subject in your own way. In this category I have set 'The English Weather' and 'Antiques'. You don't have any reference books to hand so the examiner does not expect your talk to be a highly factual one. He wants instead your own enthusiastic, personal responses; for him that is where the interest will lie. He does expect you to give your responses in an organized way and that is how much of the planning time is to be used. Jot down on your notepad any ideas which come to mind about the topic. If we use 'The English Weather' as an example such ideas might be:

Idyllic sunny days at the sea-side;
Cold weather: a bane to the elderly;
Snowballing;
The dullness of a predictable climate;
Cloud formations;
Hazardous fogs: where have the 'pea-soupers' gone?;
What to wear in the rain.

Look at this job lot of ideas and decide which can be used and how these can be structured into a talk which progresses naturally from one point to another. Now you can make a few notes on your postcards. As before, a list of key words may be sufficient. With an extempore speech you have to be more flexible than with a prepared one for you don't know from experience how the various points are going to fit into the time allowed. You can use personal anecdotes if you so wish but when you have related one do offer some kind of comment on it: you may want to point out what you have learnt through the incident or how a chance encounter changed your ways of thinking about a problem. It is even more necessary than with a prepared talk to take a watch into the examination room so that, according to the time, you can adapt the structure of your talk as you give it.

8.5 DISCUSSION

Sometimes the examiner holds with you a discussion on your prepared or extempore talk. He or she wants to know where your interests lie and their opening remarks are made to set you speaking. Often these are conveniently in the form of a question, such as 'Why did you choose this subject?' 'Because I like it,' is a blocked response which doesn't advance the discussion; but if, in the case of the talk on the wild garden, Oliver explains that his grandmother had several old-fashioned herbal books and identification manuals and that he first became interested in this topic by identifying the plants which grew on the sides of the disused railway cutting, then Oliver puts his enthusiasm into some sort of context and allows the examiner to pick up on the points he has offered.

Try then to open up to the examiner in as positive a way as possible. After a prepared talk be ready to give leads and to take the conversation into areas which you think are fruitful for discussion; after all, it is you and not the examiner who is the expert on the chosen subject. Give some prior thought to the ways in which you could direct the conversation, remembering that this is a discussion time, not the examiner's question time, so don't be afraid to ask him his opinion on your chosen topic, and when he gives it, please listen, for this is an important part of conversation. Try to see the examiner's point of view and judge how much of this you agree with and where any possible differences are to be found. Without being arrogant or antagonizing the examiner you can put alternatives. Remember that these are often complementary and not opposing viewpoints.

The subject chosen for Miriam's extempore talk was 'Fashion', a topic in which, somewhat untypically, she had very little interest. Nevertheless, her talk was not without merit but she wondered how she would acquit herself in the discussion. She decided to take the bull by the horns and began, 'I'm not really interested in fashion because . . .' and then went on to explain how she had a scale of values which put other things, such as support for mothers in Bangladesh, as a far higher priority. Feeling that she ought to make at least oblique reference to the subject she went on to say that she bought most of her clothes at the Oxfam shop. Now in the opening of the discussion she has given the examiner a couple of useful leads to work on, aid for the Third World and the Oxfam shops. So even if you have a negative attitude to a subject try, like Miriam, to make a positive statement. Miriam was sensible enough, as the discussion progressed, to use a degree of tact as well for she noticed that the examiner wore a well-cut suit. How easy it would have been to have denigrated all interest in fashion. But she didn't. The same need for tact was brought home to me some years ago when I was examining a diploma candidate. My fellow examiner was an elderly gentleman who listened courteously as the candidate held forth on the hypocritical values of the Victorians. 'Do you realize, young man,' the examiner asked at length, 'that I am a Victorian?' So keep your wits about you: try to clarify in your own mind who it is you are having a discussion with. Remember that the examiner is not an Aunt Sally for you to knock.

8.6 *VIVA VOCE* OR QUESTIONS

More formal than either the conversation or the discussion is the time devoted to a viva voce, sometimes referred to as 'Questions' in the syllabus. In this the examiner asks specific questions and looks for factual content in the answers. The areas on which the questions will be based are itemized in the syllabus. Questions tend to be asked on the following areas according to the board's policy and the seniority of the grade taken:

(a) The performer's use of his or her body;
(b) The sounds of English;
(c) The techniques of speech used in performing specified material;
(d) Poetic form;

(e) Specified writers;
(f) Various literary periods;
(g) The pieces performed in the examination.

Let us look at each of these items in turn.

Every performer uses the body in a presentation whether this is in poetry speaking, giving a talk or acting. The questions on the performer's use of the body often refer to the method of breathing, projection and articulation. Some of this is covered by practical exercises in the next chapter and books are listed in the Resources section which will amplify your knowledge. In answer to my question I am sometimes given a speech learnt by rote and, suspecting that the candidate hasn't fully appreciated the sense of the definition, a subsequent question will show that the rote answer holds little meaning for them. For example, in answering questions on breathing candidates sometimes refer to 'the diaphragmatic and inter-costal method', yet they remain unaware of the significance of these two, admittedly formidable, terms. Therefore try to describe processes in your own words and be prepared to explain any technical terms you use. Make sure, too, that this area of theory does not become divorced from your performance. One should inform the other.

A couple of boards expect candidates for the junior grades to know about the sounds of English and their classification into various groups. Thus there are various classifications of vowels and consonants. Ensure that you understand why each sound has a place in its group. Practise making the sounds yourself and listen to them in the speaking of your pieces.

The examiner may ask you about speech in relation to certain kinds of texts, perhaps those which you have performed. He or she may want to know purely technical points, such as the use of the suspensive pause to determine the shape of spoken poetry. He or she may be interested in the style of speaking, asking questions, for example, about pointing or tackling blank verse. You will become conversant with these techniques through working on your pieces and noting technical pointers as they are given by your teacher. When I was a student I used to write each technical pointer I was given on an index card which I filed alphabetically. This system was handy for rapid reference. Chapters 3 to 6 contain information on speaking specific types of text.

For some question sessions you will need to know about the various forms of poetry. In Chapter 3 we have thought, for example, about ballad and sonnet forms. You may be asked about other verse structures such as the Spenserian stanza. Poetic genre such as narrative verse and lyric verse are a fruitful ground for the questioner. Try to base your questions on what you have learnt through your own performances of these, backing your knowledge by appropriate reading.

In the senior grades of some examinations candidates are asked about specific writers, sometimes poets and other times playwrights. Try to read at least one major work of each person on your list and as you study this jot down some of the things that impress you about it. Not all candidates are certain what to look for. If your stipulated author is a playwright, be aware of the kind of plots they construct; of the characters in them and how they inter-relate, asking yourself whether we can learn about the writer's view of humanity from these roles; look at the places and period in which the play is set and enquire whether there is a reason for this; look at the form of the writing, whether, for example, it is verse or prose; think about the vocabulary the playwright uses as well as the imagery which often reveals a writer's thinking.

Let us suppose that John Webster is one of the specified writers and that you are reading *The Duchess of Malfi*. The plot is one of increasing terror until in Act 4 the audience sees murderers and madmen engaged in horrific rituals. In Webster's portrayal of the Duchess we see a noble person, but one self-willed and flouting social convention by upsetting hierarchy and marrying beneath her. The characters who surround her – Ferdinand, the Cardinal and Bosola – form a trio mechanically plotting to destroy the marriage, mental powers and life itself of the Duchess. Renaissance Italy is the setting for this tragedy, a land seen by Englishmen as the European centre of intrigue and elaborate murder. Much of Webster's text is written in blank verse; it isn't of a regular iambic pattern, such as Shakespeare's, but in the dozen years since the latter's final play was written the verse has become much freer, with extra syllables and as many enjambed as stopped lines which give a fluidity to the actor's speech. Images of corruption, disease and death are to be found which make for a darkly brooding tragedy. Obviously you would try to see a production of *The Duchess of Malfi* and make a note of your response to the interpretation of character and location within that. This kind of preparation is of greater value and has more meaning than the rote list consisting of the writer's dates and three facts about his work unrelated to personal discoveries with which I am frequently presented.

You may be required to know about the literature of a period. Your experience of this is of greater value than merely knowing a few 'facts' about, for example, the Romantics. Try reading a couple of the shorter poems of each of Keats, Shelley, Wordsworth and Coleridge. Look at the subjects they chose and the language employed. Consider the aims of these writers, especially the two latter who were striving to express themselves in the plain language of the everyday. Broaden your scope, looking in art books at illustrations of Romantic painting: Constable and Turner capture on canvas the ideas and atmosphere of the Romantic poets. Enjoy these explorations and in your answers convey this pleasure to the examiner.

The pieces you perform are sure to be used as the basis for some questions. Obviously you will have thought about your selection but have you tried to formulate your thoughts into words? Try to be conversant with a couple of other works by each author and see where these have points in common or contrast with your selection. Know a little about the circumstances within which each writer worked: what influenced and shaped his work? Why do you feel his writing is relevant today?

If you are well prepared for your *viva voce* you will enjoy it. Hopefully the examiner will respond to you and share some of his own enthusiasm. Question time should be a friendly exchange of informed minds.

8.7 RESOURCES

8.7.1 Bibliographical details of works mentioned in the text

Eliot, G. (1971) *Silas Marner*, Penguin Books, Harmondsworth.
Fry, C. (1945) *The Boy with a Cart*, Frederick Muller, London.
Hudson, W. H. (1982) *Afoot in England*, Oxford University Press, Oxford.
Martin, L. C. (ed.) *Poems of Richard Crashaw*, Clarendon Press, Oxford.

8.7.2 Aspects of oral communication

Barrett, H. (1981) *Speaking Practically: An Introduction to Public Speaking*, Holt, Rinehart and Winston, Eastbourne.
Bergin, F. J. (1981) *Practical Communication*, Pitman, London.
Jay, A. (1974) *Communication of Ideas by Words and Visual Aids*, British Institute of Management, London.
Wise, A. (1966) *Looking Ahead: Your Speech*, Longman, London.

8.7.3 Further reading in preparation for the viva voce or questions

This section of the examination is wide ranging and therefore the list given below appears to be a collection of disparate books. It does however indicate the categories of books which will be found useful in your preparation.

Armstrong, J. M. (1987) *Consonant Characters*, White Rose Studio, 21 Otley Road, Leeds LS6 3AA.
Bentley, E. (1966) *The Life of the Drama*, Methuen, London.
Blamires, H. (1984) *A Short History of English Literature*, Methuen, London.
Clark, K. (1969) *Civilisation*, British Broadcasting Corporation and John Murray, London.
Denes, P. B. and Pinson, E. N. (1973) *The Speech Chain*, Anchor Press, New York.
Gombrich, E. H. (1952) *The Story of Art*, Phaidon Press, London.
Herbert, D. (1960) *The Penguin Book of Narrative Verse*, Penguin Books, Harmondsworth.

Holdsworth, R. V. (1975) *Casebook: 'The White Devil' and 'The Duchess of Malfi'*, Macmillan, London.

Honour, H. (1981) *Romanticism*, Penguin Books, Harmondsworth.

King, N. (1982) *York Notes: The Duchess of Malfi*, Longman, London.

Lucie Smith, E. (ed.) (1965) *The Penguin Book of Elizabethan Verse*, Penguin Books, Harmondsworth.

McAllister, A. H. (1963) *A Year's Course in Speech Training*, University of London Press, London.

Nicoll, A. (1962) *British Drama*, George G Harrap, London.

Rumsey, H. St John (1939) *Speech Training for Children*, Frederick Muller, London.

Webster, J. (ed. J. Russell Brown) (1974) *The Duchess of Malfi*, The Revels Plays, Manchester.

Williams, T. G. (1961) *English Literature. A Critical Survey*, Pitman, London.

Wilton, A. (1981) *Turner and the Sublime*, British Museum Publications, London.

8.7.4 Practice pieces for sight reading

The following two collections of pieces are helpful for senior students who wish to master changing styles in prose as part of their preparation for the sight reading test.

Norwich, J. J. (1982) *Christmas Crackers*, Penguin Books, Harmondsworth.

Williams, W. E. (ed.) (1951) *A Book of English Essays*, Penguin Books, Harmondsworth.

The following books of audition pieces are a useful source of sight reading material from plays:

Bolton, B. and Richmond, J. (eds) (1964) *New Drama – Men*, Samuel French, London.

Bolton, B. and Richmond, J. (eds) (1964) *New Drama – Women*, Samuel French, London.

Harvey, A. (1973) *Solo*, Samuel French, London.

Pertwee, E. G. (1951) *For the Actress*, Samuel French, London.

Stoker, J. (ed.) (1978) *Make Your Own Choice: Speeches for the Younger Actor*, Samuel French, London.

Stoker, J. (ed.) (1975) *Make Your Own Choice: Speeches for the Younger Actress*, Samuel French, London.

8.7.5 The English Speaking Board

Teachers and all candidates undertaking work in oral communication will find much of use and interest in the publications of the English Speaking Board. A book list is available from the Board's headquarters: The English Speaking Board, 32 Norwood Avenue, Southport, Merseyside PR9 7EG.

9

The performer in training

9.1 THE PERFORMER'S BODY

Nowadays surgeons think of human bodies as machines which they must help to function properly and so they have at their disposal various 'spare parts' such as artificial hip-joints or heart valves with which they can replace parts that have become damaged. A performer, too, may think of the body as a mechanism which, for the purpose of giving a satisfactory performance, must be kept in good working order.

9.2 EXERCISES FOR THE PERFORMER

In the first part of this chapter I am going to suggest specific exercises which keep those parts of the body used in the speech process working at an optimum. As in the preceding chapters, I am assuming that you are working with a teacher and that these exercises will be carried out in conjunction with his or her advice.

9.2.1 Relaxation

Stress and tension are two hazards of modern living. In order to work effectively a performer's mind and body must be relaxed. Most of the exercises which follow assume that you are in a state of relaxation so you see why this is placed first and the importance of it. Use these exercises to help you to become relaxed and also use them to imprint this feeling of relaxation so that when you are about to perform you can mentally recall relaxation without having to perform the exercises.

(a) Lie down on the floor on your back with your arms to your sides and your legs resting along the floor. Stretch your right arm into the air above you, attempting to get it as near the ceiling as you can; then let it collapse beside you. Feel the relaxation in this arm. Go through this process in turn with your left arm, your right leg and your left leg. After each stretch be aware of the contrasting relaxation.

(b) Press each part of your body that touches the floor into the ground and then, in contrast, allow your body to relax on the surface of the floor. Repeat this process a couple of times. Let the impression of relaxation sink into your muscles so that eventually, without going through the exercise, you can recall the relaxation.

(c) Lie on your back. Gently inhale. Then very gently blow air to a spot on the ceiling. As you blow let tensions drift away from your mind and body;

(d) Lie on your back. Inhale slowly through your mouth: as air fills your lungs let it also fill you with dynamism. Slowly exhale: as air leaves your lungs so too tension leaves your body. Repeat this as a pattern of slow breathing.

(e) Play quiet, relaxing music. Lie on your back. Feel relaxation gradually overtaking you. Remain on the floor in this state.

(f) Lie on the floor. Listen to the sounds you can hear outside the room; after a minute bring your attention inside the room and listen; then bring your attention inside yourself, listening to your heartbeats and pulse. Hold your concentration within you. Let this help you to relax.

(g) Sit on an upright chair. Slump forward, your arms hanging between your legs. Stay as relaxed as this position allows. Slowly straighten your spine, neck and head to the original sitting position. Repeat twice.

(h) Lie on the floor. Stretch and then relax in turn your fingers, wrists, forearms, complete arms, shoulders, spine, legs and toes. Then continue to lie on the floor in a relaxed state.

Begin your physical preparation for a speech session with one or more of these exercises. Collect additional relaxation exercises which you find helpful. It is a good plan to write each on a separate index card and file under various categories such as 'Relaxation', 'Breathing', 'Projection', etc. May I repeat the important point I made earlier: retain within yourself the feeling of relaxation you experienced and recall this later in the day, allowing it to penetrate and calm your body.

9.2.2 Limbering

Limbering exercises, together with relaxation, help to free the performer's mind and body so that one is geared to the requirements of the text. We may group limbering exercises into those that are general, and those specific to the speech organs:

(a) *General exercises*

(i) Breathe in and as you do so slowly raise your arms bringing them above your head; allow your finger tips to touch; as you stand on your toes, stretch the whole body upwards. Feel dynamism coursing the length of the machine. Lower your arms and relax your body as you exhale.

(ii) Stand. Flop forward from your waist, knees straight, fingers either pointing at the floor or touching it. Slowly, inch by inch, straighten your spine; allow the straightening to work through your neck; lastly bring your head up. Stand easy, but erect, for a moment. Repeat twice.

(iii) Lie down on your right side. Curl up into as small a bundle as possible. Gradually uncurl and explore with all parts of your body as much of the personal space around you as you can reach from a stationary position. Gradually retract your body into a small space. Repeat, but this time lie on your left side at the start. This exercise is fun when accompanied by music. As well as using obvious exploratory mechanisms such as fingers and arms, try using the small of your back, your hips, your chest, etc. The aim is to reach the furthest arcs of your personal space with as many parts of your body as possible.

(iv) Stand easy. Begin by raising yourself on to your toes. Repeat this rhythmically and quickly. Minimally increase the speed and apply more effort so that the elevation turns into small jumps on your toes. Feel relaxation throughout all the parts of your body that are not employed in making the bounces.

(v) Any energetic dance to lively music is an appropriate form of limbering.

(b) Specific exercises

Those areas used in the speech process which we can exercise are the throat, shoulders and waist. It is important that these are relaxed and limbered as tension here can inhibit breathing and the effective functioning of the resonators. Let us begin with the neck area. The larynx is situated here as well as part of the series of chambers, the resonators, in which sound is built up.

(i) Stand easy. Let your head flop backwards. Feel the stretch in your neck. Flop your head forward, allowing the neck area to relax. Appreciate this relaxation.

(ii) Stand easy. Keeping your shoulders still and as relaxed as possible, draw your head towards your right shoulder; continue the circle by drawing it back as you look upwards; continue round to your left shoulder and so to the front. Allow your head to balance easily on the support of the neck. Repeat this exercise, working the circle in the opposite direction.

Your shoulders need to be relaxed and limbered as well:

(iii) A simple exercise is to stand easy. Draw your shoulders upwards as far as they will go, aiming to touch your ears with them. Now allow your shoulders to fall back into position. Pause whilst you appreciate the relaxed feeling. Repeat the process several times then stand easy.

(iv) Stand easy. Working with your right shoulder, raise it upwards, then pull it backwards and then allow it to adjust to its normal position. Relax for a moment before repeating the process twice.

(v) Repeat the previous exercise with the left shoulder.
(vi) Repeat exercises (iv) and (v) with both shoulders working simultaneously.

Your diaphragm is used in the process of breathing and speaking so your waist area may be relaxed and limbered:

(vii) Stand with your feet slightly apart. Flop forward from your waist. Slowly upright yourself, allowing your arms to extend straight in front of you. By the time you are upright your arms are at right angles to your body. Continue the process by raising your arms above your head. Feel the stretch from your waist. Slowly lower your arms and stand ready for speaking.

(viii) Stand with your feet slightly apart. Flop forward from your waist. Let your arms hang loosely from your shoulders. Keeping both feet firmly on the floor, slowly raise your arms to your right side, until they are stretching outwards level with your shoulders; continue to make a circle with your arms so that they rise above your head, stretching the whole of your body upwards; your arms pull round to the left, your trunk following and then they fall loosely in front of you. Repeat this exercise in the opposite direction. At the end of the process feel the relaxation around your waist area.

(ix) A modified 'Plough' is another way of stretching and strengthening your waist muscles. Lie on your back. Raise your knees until they are level with your head then raise your feet upwards so that your weight is supported on your shoulders; by this time your legs should be rising towards the ceiling. Let your legs pass over your head with your weight still supported on your shoulders. Now reverse the process. Bring your legs above your head, pointing them to the ceiling; bring your knees towards your face and then easily rock into a sitting position.

(x) Stand with your feet apart. Raise your right arm. Make a large arc with it, bending forward as you do so so that your right hand can touch your left foot. It doesn't matter if you can't make contact to start with, just aim to get your hand in the right direction! Reverse the exercise and stand upright. Repeat twice. Then take the same exercise but raising your left arm. Your left arm will articulate with your right foot.

(xi) Raise your arms to shoulder height in front of you; at the same level swing them to the right; now swing them to the left. Repeat twice. Lower your arms and rest for a moment. Repeat the complete exercise.

Don't force any of these exercises. Take that at your own pace and as your agility allows. Regular practice will increase flexibility and you will find that you are able to stretch more efficiently. Look out for further exercises for the neck, shoulder and waist areas, write them on to cards and add them to your file. Colour code them if you wish.

9.2.3 Stance

While we are thinking about the physical aspects of speech I would like to consider stance, as this can be improved with practice:

(a) Try walking across the room on the diagonal. Your head is balanced on your neck with your eye focus immediately to the front; your shoulders hang easily. Walk around the room several times conscious of this stance. Now increase your alertness by stretching, only fractionally, your spine from the small of your back.

If you can practise this exercise in a hall or studio which allows extra room, inhale before your travel and exhale as you walk across the diagonal of the room, remembering to add that extra growth from the small of your back. If no hall is available, you can easily adapt the exercise when you are walking in the street, consciously breaking it into a cycle of a quick inhalation and a slow exhalation and allowing a moment's relaxation, even though you are still walking, before the next inhalation.

(b) Now we transfer the exercise. Instead of moving, you are going to practise the stance whilst stationary. Place both feet firmly on the ground, slightly apart. Feel your head balanced on your neck column. Feel your arms hanging from the cross-beam of your shoulders. Your hands can rest lightly against your thighs. Now, without introducing unwanted tension, stretch your spine very gently upwards, making the stretch come from the small of your back.

When a neutral position is needed for speaking, the above posture serves effectively. Notice that some parts of your body are relaxed and some are alert, ready for the breathing and speech process to take place. Alertness and freedom from inhibition are the qualities needed for performance, rather than an attempt at total relaxation.

9.2.4 Breathing

Breath is the fuel which powers speech and without effective breathing speech is unsatisfactory. When we inhale air it is stored in our lungs. We need to practise a gradual exhalation so that air is used economically in the speech process. When we speak the air passes through the trachea, or windpipe, to the larynx; here sound is created by the vocal folds vibrating. This sound, a thin, reedy note, is amplified in the resonators, cavities in the neck and head. It then moves to the mouth where it is formed and placed and so directed to the listeners.

In this book I am introducing you to the basics of breathing. Once these are mastered various teachers favour different methods. Our first objective is to inhale quietly and quickly and to exhale slowly and economically. I encourage my own students to begin their breathing exercises lying on the floor: in that way unnecessary tension is reduced to a minimum.

(a) Lie on your back on the floor with your arms to your sides. Slide your feet towards your seat so that your knees are raised. Start by establishing that you are relaxed in this position.

(b) Open your mouth slightly as if you are going to say 'her'. Breathe in through your mouth. This breath is rapid but not rushed. Make it a silent inhalation. Now slowly and easily breathe out through your mouth until you feel the breath is almost spent. Pause a moment and then repeat the process.

(c) Repeat exercise (b) standing.

(d) You can combine this exercise with walking. Stand still and inhale through your mouth, your lips in the 'her' position. Begin your walking as you slowly exhale. Spread the exhalation over ten paces (start with less if you experience a difficulty). Repeat the process a number of times. On subsequent occasions extend the number of paces during which exhalation takes place but don't force this. All breathing should be easy. Gradually you will find that the inhalations will deepen and the exhalation will become slower and more controlled.

(e) Exercise (b) may be combined with speech when the exhalation is economic. Lie down on your back; raise your knees; breathe in through your mouth whilst your lips are in the 'her' position; now try saying a brief rhythmic line on the exhalation: 'Nasturtium, daisy, tulip, rose'.

(f) After some practice at this you may add further flower names, keeping to the rhythmic pattern. Either choose your own or use these:

> Nasturtium, daisy, tulip rose,
> Dandelion, buttercup, willowherb, moss.

(g) Change this to a walking exercise. Stand alert and ready; inhale; begin to walk on the first word; when you have finished the text stand still. Repeat the process.

(h) Later you can use limericks or examples of rhyming tags to practise controlled exhalation. Here are half a dozen to use. Remember that there must be no strain:
　　(i) You're the king of the castle
　　　　And I'm his knavish rascal.

(ii) Build a church
     With the tallest steeple;
     Fill it with priest
     And lots of people.
(iii) The cow is of a peculiar ilk;
     One end is moo, the other end milk.
(iv) Mary, Mary, quite contrary,
     How does your garden grow?
     With pretty bells and cockle shells
     And little maids all in a row.
 (v) There was an old lady of Ryde
     Who ate stolen green apples and died;
     The apples fermented
     Inside the lamented
     And made cider inside her inside.
(vi) There was a young man of Japan
     Who wrote verses that never would scan;
     When they said, 'But the thing
     Doesn't go with a swing,'
     He said 'No! but I like to get as many words into the last line as I
     possibly can.'

The breathing exercises I have outlined above are basic and suitable for beginners of any age. From twelve years old young performers may be taught the technique of rib swing. The lower couple of ribs on either side of the rib cage are not fixed but are capable of swinging outwards with the effect that room is made for the lungs to take a greater capacity of breath:

(i) Ensure your stance is suitable and your shoulders are relaxed. As you inhale, easily and silently, raise your arms until they are at shoulder level. As you slowly exhale, lower your arms. This exercise encourages the swing of the ribs, outwards on the inhalation and downwards on the exhalation. Repeat three or four times.
(j) Repeat exercise (i) making the exhalation more slowly. Over a period of some weeks increase the length of this. Tension and strain must be avoided.
(k) Repeat the above exercise but now omit the physical action of raising your arms. Instead, place your finger tips lightly on your lower ribs and feel the outward swing as you inhale.
(l) Lie on the floor with your knees raised. Feel the small of your back against the floor. Place your fingertips on your lower ribs. Inhale and then exhale slowly. Now place your hands lightly against the side of your rib cage. Feel the rising and falling from this position as you breathe.

9.2.5 Projection

You are now ready to combine some more vocal exercises with your outgoing breath:

(a) Lie on the floor with your knees raised and your arms to your sides; feel the small of your back spread on the floor. Inhale through your open mouth. Direct the sound 'her' gently to the ceiling. Allow this to continue easily.
(b) Repeat the exercise using 'hay' and 'hoo' as the phonated sounds.
(c) Repeat but this time using a scale of five notes on the phonated sounds.
(d) Repeat the exercise in a standing position; check your stance before you begin.
(e) Practice the foregoing exercise whilst walking in the open air. The effect of uninhibited sound is liberating. If you get the opportunity to work in a spacious hall, try the exercise whilst walking across the diagonal of the floor.

Earlier I mentioned that sound is built up in the resonators. Humming helps to achieve this build up:

(f) Sit on a chair; relax your shoulders; inhale; hum on an 'm' sound whilst mentally counting to five.

Let us think about the quality of this humming sound. It is made with your lips, therefore these must be exercised:

(g) Pass your tongue over your lips; then create a 'brrr' sound.
(h) Silently push your lips as far forward as they will go; imitate a goldfish blowing bubbles or a rabbit feeding; curl your upper lip upwards and your lower lip downwards.
(i) Aiming to detach your lips from your teeth, repeat the humming; notice the change in the quality of the sound which should ring around the room.
(j) When you hum the air should be exhaled through your nose. Check that this is happening by placing your hand, palm downwards, just underneath your nose. Repeat the humming and notice the current of air on your hand. Feel, too, as you hum a tingling at the bridge of your nose.

Now we are ready to build up sound and to send it through space:

(k) Lie on your back, legs straight, arms to your side. Inhale, then hum, directing the sound to the ceiling.
(l) Repeat the previous exercise but add to it the vowel sound 'ah', merging as smoothly as possible the glide from the humming to the vowel. We may represent this in print as 'm . . ah . . .' As you prepare to inhale shape your lips in the 'hah' position; this will help to make your inhalation silent. Know that sound is travelling to the directed area.

(m) There are four other forward vowels which you may substitute in the previous exercise:

m . . . oo . . .

m . . . ay . . .

m . . . er . . .

m . . . oh . . .

(n) Take one of the sound combinations of the previous exercise and practice this on a rising scale of five notes.

(o) You may repeat the exercises in a variety of postures. Try exercises (l) and (m) standing, sending the sound from one corner of the room to another. A large hall is invaluable for this exercise, but you can effectively use a domestic room.

(p) Try these exercises whilst walking across the floor. Stand still and inhale; walk ten steps across the room on the phonation; pause; inhale and repeat the exercise several times.

(q) Repeat exercises (m) finishing with a humming sound: e.g. 'm . . . oo . . . m . . .'. This may be done whilst sitting, walking or lying down. Repeat the sounds on varying patterns of notes such as a rising five note scale, falling five note scale, rising and falling arpeggios (doh, me, soh, doh') and on octaves (doh, doh').

After you have worked for several weeks on these projection exercises you will notice three improvements: firstly, projection will increase, and without strain you will be able to speak in a hall sending the sound the length of the room; secondly, tone quality will improve through a balanced use of your resonators; thirdly, the basis for vocal flexibility is being laid, although you must not assume that flexibility of sound automatically transfers to flexibility of speech for you have yet to discover the bridge from one to the other.

9.2.6 Vocal flexibility

We have all heard speakers whose voices are monotonous. If we analyse what is happening we find that the tone is often heavy and the speaker tends to restrict the range of notes used. Additionally the unfortunate person may suffer from a pattern of speaking which is repetitious, using pauses of the same length. From this we can learn a number of positive points: speech must be light and rhythmical; it should have a musical quality; there must be an interesting range of inflections, and all appropriate means to allow the audience to comprehend the subject matter may be employed.

In these first exercises we will think about the pattern of speech and the stresses needed on certain words in order to emphasize and clarify:

(a) Let us take a sentence, 'I live in the large brick house at the top of the hill'. Imagine that a person is coming to visit you: how do they know where to find you?: 'I live in the large brick house at the TOP of the hill'. Now we shall repeat the statement. This time some unwanted cement powder has arrived, unsuitable for repairing your house. On the telephone you explain: 'I live in the large BRICK house at the top of the hill'. The postman has mistakenly left a parcel for you at another brick building, a rather small bungalow. How will you explain where you live?

(b) See how many meanings you can convey using the sample sentence of the previous exercise. Don't make this an exercise in which you apply mechanical stresses; have clearly in mind the point you want to sort out; think about your listener.

(c) Take another sentence and use this in the same way: 'The jet plane made an emergency landing at our local airfield last Saturday'.

(d) Compose several sentences which will form a basis for elementary work in flexibility.

We must be aware, especially in speaking certain kinds of lyric poetry, that sound and sense must be held in a just balance. Some candidates fail to recognize in their speaking the musical quality of sounds:

(e) What can you discern about this musical quality in the following snippet?

> Her mother died when she was young
> Which gave her cause to make great moan;
> Her father married the worst woman
> That ever lived in Christendom.

Firstly, emphasis is created by the use of alliterations: 'Make great Moan' and 'Worst Woman'. Here sound obviously helps to convey the sense. There is an emotional response to the idea of the young orphan expressed in the first line: 'died' and 'young' are two important words. We may lend this line pathos by thinking of the sounds in those two words which we wish to colour; for instance the D at either end of 'DieD' for some would express a sense of finality. The girl's relationship to her stepmother can be expressed by colouring lines 3 and 4. How would you do that? Make sure that when you consider the sound quality of words you also consider the sense and the integrity of the piece. Don't, however, be afraid to let your voice convey a wide range of expressive speaking in these exercises. You can adjust this when performing.

(f) Look at the following excerpts; use your voice in as flexible a manner as appropriate to highlight the sound qualities:

(i) The day in his hotness,
The strife in the palm,
The night in her silence,
The stars in their calm.

(ii) The East is bright
With morning light
And darkness it is fled;
The merry horn
Wakes up the morn
To leave his idle bed.

(iii)   to set budding more,
And still more, later flowers for the bees,
Until they think warm days will never cease,
For Summer has o'erbrimmed their clammy cells.

(iv) The seas are quiet when the winds give o'er;
So calm are we when passions are no more.

(v) For many days we rode together
Yet met we neither friend nor foe;
Hotter and clearer grew the weather,
Speedily did the East wind blow.

(vi) O clap your hands all ye people;
Shout unto God with a voice of triumph.
God is gone up with a shout,
The Lord with the sound of the trumpet.

(g) It is instructive to 'speak' a few sentences using a nonsense language of vowel sounds, gasps and clicks. This helps you to gain a wider range of expression. You can profitably record your attempts at this, judging to what extent you have communicated the gist of your meaning:

   (i) Persuade a friend over the telephone to come out with you tonight;
   (ii) Try to sell unwanted goods to a shopper;
   (iii) Apologize for the damage your exploding gas stove has done to a neighbour's flat;
   (iv) Beg people to give old clothes to your jumble sale;
   (v) Order the huntsmen and their hounds to leave your garden;
   (vi) Hold a conversation with a friend in this nonsense language.

(h) Here are several open-ended sentences: 'No I will never do that! Why are you asking me to do this with you? Suppose we are found out! Hush! I thought I heard a noise just them. Be quiet and listen, will you.' Apply these words to the following situations:

   (i) An old lag responding to a temptation to rob a jeweller's shop;
   (ii) A woman who is being persuaded to leave home;

(iii) A response to a scheme for cheating in an examination.
(i) Now try inventing some dialogue of your own and a variety of situations in which it could be used. If you have a friend with whom you can speak the dialogue, so much the better.

9.2.7 Articulation

A further area for regular practice is diction. Your organs of speech which undertake your articulation are the lips, the jaw, the teeth, the teeth ridge, the hard palate, the soft palate and your tongue. Consonants are formed by two of your speech organs coming into contact and partly impeding your exhalation; the precision with which they do this determines the clarity of your speech:

(a) Exercises (g) and (h) in Section 9.2.5 are suitable as lip exercises.
(b) In speech your jaw must be relaxed. Stroke your hands down the sides of your face and jaw, allowing the latter to drop open.

Your tongue is an important organ in the speech process. It needs to be lively and possibly needs strengthening. These exercises will help you to strengthen your tongue:

(c) Move your tongue vigorously from one side of your mouth to the other.
(d) Put out your tongue; curl it up to your nose and down to your chin.
(e) Making an 'l' sound, 'vacuum' as many areas of your mouth as you can reach.
(f) For some sounds the tongue contacts the teeth ridge. Practice a strongly made 't' and 'd' sound.
(g) Practise the following rhythmically:

> tah, tah, tah/tah, tah, tah/tah, tah, tah/tah . . .

Use 'doh' and 'law' in the same way.

The hard palate does not require exercise. It is important, however, that the soft palate should work vigorously as this prevents nasal, depressed speech:

(h) Yawn, keeping your mouth closed throughout, and feel the soft palate arch upwards.
(i) Look in a mirror. Drop your jaw; breathe in through your mouth and out through your nose, keeping your mouth open throughout. Watch the action of your soft palate.
(j) Chant alternations of: 'ah, ng, ah, ng, ah, ng . . .' Feel the movement of your soft palate.

Having exercised the speech organs we shall now use them in some articulation practice, taking groups of consonants which are sometimes made imprecisely.

Remember that after exercising a particular sound you must then appropriately moderate it in continuous speech.

We shall begin with the six plosive sounds. These consist of the unvoiced 'p', 't', 'k' and the voiced 'b', 'd', 'g':

(k)   Hold your hand in front of your mouth. In turn make each of the unvoiced consonants. Feel the explosion of air which hits your hand.

(l)   Without undue exaggeration speak these sentences which contain each of the unvoiced plosives:
    (i)   Peter has Passed his Preliminary examination.
    (ii) Tommy is Taking his aunt's caT To the veT.
    (iii) 'Caw!' Croaked the Crow as the dusK deepened.

(m) Use the 'palm' exercise for the three voiced plosives, 'b', 'd', 'g'. Then make up your own sentences in which each plosive occurs a couple of times.

Fricatives easily become 'dusty' and when these are blurred words are not clear. Fricatives are 'th', 'f', 'v', 's', 'z', 'sh', 'zh' and 'r'. The two speech organs forming these sounds articulate and as air passes between them friction occurs.

(n)   Try each of the fricatives as an isolated sound. Check the correct formation of each with your teacher.

(o)   Exercise the fricatives in the following sentences:
    (i)   THen we shall leave THis THrilling scene and return to THe THraldom of ordinary life;
    (ii)   Fired with enthusiasm, Fred turned on the hose;
    (iii) I remember those Vibrant Voices; they liVe in my memory;
    (iv)   Shape the S Softly as it Sings through the Space;
    (v)   Zoom your lenS on that Zebra;
    (vi)   Are you Sure this SHerry is SpaniSH?;
    (vii) Drake had got the meaSure of the aZure main;
    (viii) MaRy, MaRy, quite contRaRy.

In exercises (l), (m) and (o), although you will want to concentrate on the particular sound you are studying, eventually this must be spoken without undue emphasis; for that reason it is best to practice sentences in which the sound occurs only a couple of times.

9.2.8   General exercise for the performer

Most of the exercises I have suggested to date in this chapter have a specific application; they have an effect on the parts of your body employed in the speech process. In addition to these exercises I recommend that you go in for some other physical exercise which tones up your body. It really doesn't matter what it is, so long as you enjoy doing it. Think of the range of exercise possible. Not only are there the well-tried forms such as walking (many pianists claim that on a day in which they don't go for a walk, their fingers won't run and it is true, too, that our respiratory system and speech organs work less efficiently without exercise), running and jogging; but there are also such activities as dancing, skate boarding, cycling and swimming. In fact any kind of exercise which raises your respiratory rate is suitable. If you discover in doing the exercise you get any kind of discomfort, especially in your chest, then it is important to see your doctor and ask his advice about exercise which would suit you. Don't do too much too soon. A twenty-minute walk four or five times a week is enough to start with. Then work up to longer and more intensive forms of exercise; vary these as well.

9.3 THEORY AND PRACTICE

When you look in a syllabus you will often see that an examination contains a question or discussion time and that one of the topics for discussion is technique, sometimes expressed as 'theory'. Different topics are discussed at different grades. This implies, and is sometimes stated, that the technique the examiner asks about, will be expected to be demonstrated in the candidate's performance. 'Technical knowledge is useless unless it is practical,' states the LAMDA syllabus, and that is a wise maxim. In this section of the chapter I want to look at the technical discussion, the discussion on those areas covered by the preceding exercises in this chapter, and see how the various boards relate this to experience.

(a) The Associated Board

In the early grades of the Solo Speech examination discussion centres on the meaning of the pieces spoken. From grade 4 the candidate is expected to be able to discuss the interpretation of the pieces performed. Thus the focus is on content and interpretation rather than 'theory'.

(b) Guildhall School

In the early grades of the Speech and Drama examinations the candidate must know the range of works of the authors of his chosen pieces. From grade 4 topics such as 'the means of achieving emphasis and modulation; the use of inflection ...' are considered. At this stage the examiner looks for an interestingly modulated voice which can sort out and present the meaning of the pieces. In grade 4A the art of relaxation, posture and the use of the speech organs is discussed clearly indicating the expectations of the examiner about the candidate's performance. Grade 5 introduces the speaking of blank verse as the theory subject, and there is limited opportunity to demonstrate this by selecting one of a couple of Shakespeare excerpts from the listed pieces. Grade 6 introduces the speaking of sonnets and a choice of several is given for performance; to this is added breathing and breath control, obviously an important technical element in the art of sonnet speaking. Grade 6A introduces the subject of resonance. Grade 7 brings in the more general topic of the art of speaking verse, and an excellently chosen wide-ranging list of poetry gives ample opportunity for candidates to demonstrate their ability.

(c) LAMDA

Technical aspects are not broached until grade 6 in the Speaking of Verse and Prose examinations. Discussions begin, fundamentally, with the process of breathing and speaking and the candidate's correct use of this process should be evident in their work. At grade 8 vocal variety is discussed and, logically, by this grade the candidate should be giving signs of vocal range. At the bronze level the candidate must understand the process of resonance and projection, which again will be demonstrated throughout the performance.

(d) London College of Music

From grade 1 candidates are asked theory questions. The first two grades are concerned with the classification of vowel and consonantal sounds. It is noteworthy that in the Guildhall School scheme these are not tackled until grade 6. At grade 3 knowledge of such technical aspects as phrasing, pause, accentuation and inflection is required, and at grade 4 the candidate is expected to know about the diaphragmatic and intercostal method of breathing. It is debatable whether children taking this grade can effectively use this technique in performance. A knowledge of 'incorrect' methods of breathing is required at grade 5 and although candidates may occasionally be inept at the technique of breathing, this is obviously an area in which theory parts from practice. Tone colour, pauses and compound inflections are the areas of knowledge relating to vocal technique, whilst physical appearance is covered by considerations of gesture and facial expression. Much of the material of the earlier grades is recapitulated at grade 6, which is useful as this allows candidates an opportunity to consider the range of technical expertise which has been acquired. Resonance and voice production, strangely separated from the breathing process, figure at grades 7 and 8. One of the London College examiners has stressed that the atmosphere of a piece is of greater importance than 'speech technique', which makes one wonder why candidates are questioned on this from the first grade in such detail.

(e) Mountview Performance Grades

Questions on theory and technique do not have a place in this series of grade examinations. However, the introduction to the syllabus points out that there should be 'an increase in technique' as the higher grades are reached but the nature of this is not spelled out.

(f) Poetry Society

In the Society's examinations in Spoken Poetry no mention is made of technical expertise although examiners look for competence in the use of one's speech mechanism and a technical proficiency is expected at the stage of the adult gold medal. Grade candidates, in their speaking of two contrasting poems, are given the opportunity, states the syllabus, 'to show the range of their expressive ability', a phrase which in itself expresses the expectation that some technical powers will be at work.

The examinations in Poetic Form are set so that the candidate can illustrate a knowledge and appreciation of the structure and style of the poems chosen: again, this seems to presuppose a theoretical knowledge which is applied to particular examples.

(g) New Era

During the discussion at grade 4 in the Speech and Drama examinations the focus in on phrasing. This clearly relates to the interpretation of the candidate's chosen pieces. In the junior medal examination the candidate discusses, again in the context of talking about the chosen pieces, the use of the pause. At grade 5 the candidate has an opportunity to discuss facial expression and gesture and a liberal choice of drama is allowed in which there is opportunity for demonstration. Expressive speech is also listed. In grade 6 breath control is the subject for discussion, and this leads naturally to the development of the speech process in the intermediate medal in which resonance and tone colour figure. In a slightly detached way projection and modulation are discussed in the next two stages. In spite of this minor criticism, the New Era welds the theoretical knowledge to performance in a most commendable fashion. The technical content to be understood consists of fundamentals presented to candidates in a logical and practical sequence.

(h) Trinity College

In the Speech and Drama examinations theoretical knowledge is needed from grade 2. In this the candidate is asked about the relationship of the pause to phrasing, a very early stage at which to consider interpretation in such detail. Details of vowel and consonant formation must be known at grades 3 and 4 and, relating to personal technique, the candidate is required to know about emphasis, inflection, the neutral vowel and the use of the articulative organs. Classificatory knowledge continues at grade 6 in which the candidate deals with monoph-thongs and the component parts of diphthongs and triphthongs, all of which relate but distantly to the candidate's performance. Grade 6 introduces questions on breathing for speech production, obviously an important area, and on the interpretation of the selected pieces and of the characterization given. Here the questioning is most purposeful, relating directly to performance. At the next grade the candidate is asked about rhythm, metre and the speaking of blank verse: the listed pieces allow the candidate to select work illustrating these. At grade 8 questions are on fundamental and wide ranging subjects, securely linked to the pieces, considering aspects of voice production, dramatic interpretation and verse speaking.

In this survey of the links between theoretical knowledge and performance I have not considered diplomas. At this level the candidate is expected to be an expert in the areas of theory and practice, and whilst one would expect the demonstration in performance of a fully assimilated technique, the candidate's theoretical knowledge, in order to inform a range of work, will be greater than is shown within the confines of the recital.

9.4 THE BACKGROUND TO THE CANDIDATE'S TRAINING

When I am examining I sometimes meet a candidate whose work is geared solely to the examination syllabus. He or she may have progressed from one grade to the next, but have no experience of performing beyond that of the examination recital. Such a candidate gives a starved performance – and needs to be nourished! How is this to be achieved?

9.4.1 Repertoire

One simple way would be to extend the repertoire. Instead of working solely on your examination pieces choose others from the lists or of your own choice, and work these to performance level. This at least means that you have the benefit of a range of pieces. Another ploy is to choose alternative pieces by the authors of your selection to work on. Thus you may be presenting several paragraphs from Robert Louis Stevenson's *Travels with a Donkey in the Cevennes* and in contrast with this Roger McGough's poem 'Sad Aunt Madge', a poem seemingly written in the informal register of everyday speech. As alternatives to the Stevenson you may try other genres in order to compare them with his travelogue; there are such writings as his letters, collected by Sir Sidney Colvin, his popular novel *The Strange Case of Dr Jekyll and Mr Hyde* with its horrifying descriptions of a man's changing nature, and his essays in *Men and Books*. By this means you begin to gain a three-dimensional impression of the writer and his work and to think of him in terms more informed than simply as the author of the examination selection. Similarly with McGough. One of his interests is the changing shape and mood of poems and this is most evident in his love lyric 'A Lot of Water has Flown under your Bridge', a far cry from the tone of the poem I mentioned above. There is too his 'Square Dance' set to an appropriate rhythm, telling the story of the warriors in Flanders' fields. These poems make a contrasting trio.

9.4.2 Anthologies

The pieces on which you have worked may be built into anthologies. You might want to group several writers of the same period, such as the metaphysical poets of the sixteenth and seventeenth centuries, making your selection from the works of Robert Southwell, John Donne, George Herbert and Richard Crashaw. As well as the poems, you may look at other works which amplify our appreciation of these writers and include selections from them. There are the sermons John Donne preached when he was Dean of St Paul's Cathedral in London, and Herbert's book *The Priest to the Temple* about a country parson's life and his biographies of several of his contemporaries, the best known of which is his life of Isaac Walton. Not so well known are the diaries and letters of Southwell. Look at writings in the light of the poets' lives and see how they grow from their experiences. You could weave a commentary through your recital drawing the listener's attention to these links.

Another approach to building an anthology is to base it on a theme. Some themes have grown stale. Try new ones! Have writers produced enough about space yet for this to be a viable theme? Hospitals are the setting of many poems by contemporary poets: what kind of theme is suggested there? Methods of communication are changing rapidly. Once love-letters were written in verse and letter writing, whether it was a word of praise or a complaint, was an art in Victorian times. Can you explore the world of modern communications – the computer, the telex, the telephone and the brief form in a recital? Maybe you could contrast this with more leisurely ways of communication. Again, be wide ranging in your selection.

When you are gathering material, why not copy each piece on to a separate sheet and keep them in a ring binder or series of document files? You could then arrange the material as seems most appropriate to you, creating a progression and gaining satisfactory contrasts in mood, rhythm, register and density of sound. You will find further advice about the compilation of anthologies throughout Chapter 2 and in Chapter 7 (7.4.3).

'But when I've compiled a recital anthology, what do I do with it?' One of the most straightforward methods of preserving it is to commit it to tape. This must be done with some expertise, for the encroachments of unwanted sound and a microphone incorrectly used can stand between your speaking and the receiver's ears: so the help of a technician, amateur or professional, will be invaluable. When the tape is to your satisfaction, look for some kind of outlet. You want people to hear it and to talk honestly to you about their response to the anthology. Start at school. Can it be played to an interested group in the lunch break or after hours? Will an English or a drama teacher use the tape in a lesson? Will it form the basis of an assembly? Various institutions in your home locality, too, may welcome it. Many hospitals have an internal broadcasting system relaying material to the wards for patients to hear through their headphones. Is your tape suitable material? Contact the head of broadcasting at your nearest large hospital. The public library is another possible outlet: you may be able to arrange with the librarian, for example, to have your tape played at a certain time over several days in the children's library. A copy of it could be donated to the record library and you may find that the librarian is able to refund the cost of the materials. Local circumstances differ and when you make enquiries I am sure you will discover situations in your home area in which your tape may be used and appreciated.

A development of the taped anthology is to make a collection of suitable slides to accompany the recorded pieces. Thus I have spoken some of the poems of John Keats and illustrated them with images of the lush pastoral landscape of the Winchester water meadows, for Keats spent a while in the city shortly before his death and it was in these fields that he wrote his 'Ode to Autumn'. For those of you with video facilities it is possible to make brief programmes of ten to fifteen minutes in length incorporating words and images. This is more complex and you have to remember that your principal concern is with the spoken interpretation of the poetry.

Use opportunities that occur to perform either one of your individual pieces or one of your anthologies. A festival is an obvious time to present work to an audience and an adjudicator, although you have to remember that an adjudicator's approach is not the same as the examiner's and that the mark scale tends to be higher in festivals than in examinations. School broadcasts, entertainments for the house-bound such as disabled children or elderly people, informal religious services and celebrations, all offer you the chance to speak some of the selections of verse and prose you have worked on. If you regularly attend a church there is usually the opportunity to become a reader at services, and although your text is often limited to the Bible this is a further chance for preparation and presentation.

9.4.3 Working with other performers

One of the drawbacks of many series of examinations is that solo performance is the norm. In order to gain wider experience you need to perform from time to time with a group of people. In Chapter 7 I have written of various kinds of group examination and this is one situation in which you can work with others. There are also non-examination opportunities. School plays can give you the experience of ensemble work. Many local amateur dramatic societies also require the services of young people. Churches, too, often stage plays at Christmas and Eastertide. You will find that a list of organizations is usually kept at the public library and it is merely a matter of asking for this to discover the secretaries of the various groups. Many evening institutes offer classes in drama which sometimes branch out to give public performances. Classes may also be held in the ancillary areas of public speaking and improvisation. Again your library will have the prospectus.

9.4.4 The appreciation of drama

As well as extending your range of performance you must also widen your appreciation and allow this to shape your work. At diploma level I sometimes find that candidates know *about* literature but they have not been confronted by drama itself. A candidate may, in the course of the discussion, mention Christopher Marlowe's contribution to blank verse, another will be fascinated by his espionage activities and his death in a tavern brawl, another will have learnt a list of his play titles. I find all this unsatisfactory. Time is being spent in the wrong way. If you are required to know about Marlowe's writing, then by all means know what his principal plays are, know when he flourished, try to see him against the background of other writers of the period, but above all read a representative play and a few poems. Only in that way can the literature speak to you and you will be able to discuss with the examiner your personal response to the playwright's output. This is infinitely more worthwhile than the list of rote-learnt 'facts' which I usually have thrust at me. If an opportunity presents itself to see one of the plays, such as *The Tragedy of Doctor Faustus* which is revived with some frequency, especially by college drama groups, then so much the better. Do however think about the production and ask yourself, or better still discuss with others, such questions as: 'Is the director faithful to Marlowe's intentions? Is this a play about religious belief or about the psychology of power? If the director sets the play in a period other than the Elizabethan, does the interpretation give us a clearer perspective of the central issues? What kind of a relationship exists between Mephistopheles and Faustus and is this shown in the performance?' If plays by Marlowe and the other key dramatists such as Jonson, Congreve, Goldsmith, Sheridan, Ibsen, Chekov and Shaw are not frequently performed in your nearest theatre, then get in touch with your nearest university, polytechnic or college and ask to be kept informed of their dramatic productions. Further sources of play production are radio and television. Of course, the group nature of the theatrical experience is missing here but nevertheless you are confronted with both text and interpretation. Get into the habit of reading reviews in local and national newspapers and balance the reviewer's opinions against your own. This is a valuable way of coming into contact with informed opinion. Trace a series of reviews of a play which you have seen either live or on television through a selection of papers and journals which your library will stock. Compare the responses of the various writers to the play.

As well as studying drama and theatre I'm sure keen candidates will also get into the habit of reading poetry, reading about the poets and their intentions, and listening to poetry spoken by recitalists in the flesh and on the radio. Those living in London are fortunate to be near the Poetry Society at Earls Court which holds many recitals and talks. Provincial arts centres, too, provide opportunity to take part in readings as well as to listen to work.

By making reading and appreciation an essential part of your training you will sharpen your critical faculties. Make sure that you are able to put into words what you have discovered about literature. The time set aside for discussion and questions will then be a fruitful time and you will delight the examiner, for too few candidates have a discerning understanding of the works listed in a board's syllabus.

9.5 RESOURCES

9.5.1 Bibliographical details of works mentioned in the text

Donne, J. (ed. E. M. Simpson) (1963) *Sermons on the Psalms and Gospels*, University of California Press, Berkeley.

Gardner, H. (1957) *The Metaphysical Poets*, Penguin Books, Harmondsworth (contains poems by, amongst others, Southwell, Donne, Herbert and Crashaw; biographical details).

Henri, A., McGough, R. and Patten, B. (1967) *The Mersey Sound*, Penguin Books, Harmondsworth.

Herbert, G. (ed. J. N. Wall) (1981) *The Priest to the Temple*, SPCK, London.

Herbert, G. (ed. W. H. Auden) (1985) *Poems and Prose*, Penguin Books, Harmondsworth.

Male, D. A. (1985) *A Master Guide to 'Doctor Faustus'*, Macmillan, London and Basingstoke.

Marlowe, C. (ed. J. D. Jump) (1968) *Doctor Faustus*, Methuen, London.

Southwell, R. (ed. A. B. Grossart) (1872) *Letters*, Greenwood Press, London.

Stevenson, R. L. (ed. S. Colvin) (1911) *Letters*, Greenwood Press, London.

Stevenson, R. L. (1984) *Travels with a Donkey in the Cevennes*, Dent, London.

Stevenson, R. L. (1978) *Dr Jekyll and Mr Hyde*, Collins, London.

Stevenson, R. L. (1925) *Men and Books*, T Nelson, London.

9.5.2 Books on exercise

Carruthers, M. and Murray, A. (1976) *F/40: Fitness on 40 Minutes a Week*, Futura, London.

Hewitt, J. (1967) *Yoga and You*, Tandem, London.

Hewitt, J. (1980) *Isometrics: the Short Cut to Fitness*, Thorsons, Wellingborough.

Laban, R. (1963) *Modern Educational Dance*, MacDonald and Evans, London.

Pisk, (1975) *The Actor and His Body*, Harrap, London.

9.5.3 Technical aspects of voice and speech

(a) Printed Books

Berry, C. (1973) *Voice and the Actor*, Harrap, London.

Berry, C. (1975) *Your Voice – and How to Use it Successfully*, Harrap, London.

Burniston, C. and Bell, J. (1972) *Into the Life of Things*, English Speaking Board, Southport.

Colson, G. (1963) *Voice Production and Speech*, Pitman, London.

Colson, G. (1967) *Speech Practice*, Pitman, London.

Morrison, M. (1977) *Clear Speech*, Pitman, London.

Parkin, K. (1962) *Ideal Voice and Speech Training*, Samuel French, London.

Turner, J. C. (1977) *Voice and Speech in the Theatre*, Pitman, London.

(b) Audio cassette

Godfrey, B. *Keep fit for Voice*, Barbara Godfrey, 17 Clifton Hill, London NW8 0QE.

9.5.4 Reviews of theatre in newspapers and periodicals

Most newspapers contain reviews of plays in performance. The following is a selection of papers whose reviewers offer stimulating and informed comment: *Amateur Stage, Daily Telegraph, Drama, Financial Times*, the *Guardian, Illustrated London News*, the *Independent*, the *Listener*, the *Observer, Punch*, the *Stage, Sunday Telegraph, Sunday Times, The Times*.

9.5.5 Institutions holding part-time and short courses in practical theatre and drama studies

(a) Evening classes

City Literary Institute, Stukeley Street, London WC2B 5LJ. Morley College,

Westminster Bridge Road, London SE1 7HT. These two well-known institutions offer work of an advanced standard. Many evening institutes hold classes throughout the United Kingdom in practical speech and drama; most of these are well suited for beginners. Details can be obtained from your public library or from the local education office. Dramatic literature may also be studied at evening classes organized by the Workers Educational Association. Consult your public library or the telephone directory for the nearest branch. These tend to be located in larger towns. Study sessions in the evenings and at weekends are also organized by the extra-mural department of most universities. Contact your nearest university. Although rarely of a practical nature many courses are often linked to specific plays in performance.

(b) Short courses

The British Theatre Association holds short courses, many of which are residential, in London and at selected centres throughout the United Kingdom. Details are available from: the Education Secretary, British Theatre Association, Cranbourne Mansions, Cranbourne Street, London WC2.

The Association for Cultural Exchange organizes courses based on theatre visits in London and at the Edinburgh Festival. Residence is offered. Details from: ACE Study Tours, Babraham, Cambridge CB2 4AP.

The University of Edinburgh Extra-Mural Department also holds a one-week course in drama during the Festival. Details from: the Summer Schools Secretary, Department of Extra-Mural Studies, 11 Buccleuch Place, Edinburgh EH8 9JT.

The Extra-Mural Department of the University of Birmingham organizes an annual study course at Stratford-upon-Avon at which theatre visits play an important part. Details from: the Extra-Mural Department, Mason Croft, Church Street, Stratford upon Avon, Warwickshire CV37 6HP.

10

The examination performance

10.1 THE PARTICIPANTS IN THE EXAMINATION

10.1.1 The candidate

The examination in solo performance poses especial challenges to the candidate for in this one is alone in a strange room paired by an examiner who is unknown. Additionally there is a concentration of attention on the candidate's response to this situation. It is for this reason that the bulk of this chapter concentrates on the solo performer at the examination.

The length of the examination may be as brief as five minutes for a junior grade, or as long as an hour for the diploma, but it is a time that belongs to the candidate; he or she has paid the fee and thereby the examiner's attention is theirs for a while. Some candidates rush through their pieces feeling that it would be wrong to keep the examiner waiting. Don't do that: the time is yours in which to present your work. It is important to think of examiners as members of audiences and to make sure that you successfully communicate with them.

'My difficulty is that I get rather nervous during the practical examination,' students have told me. This difficulty is by no means peculiar to yourself and there would be something wrong if you were not nervous. Nerves tune you to give a dynamic performance. It is only if nerves get out of hand that they become a problem. For this there are several remedies. The first is to use every means of discovering confidence in yourself. One help to confidence is to know your pieces thoroughly, then you can let go and concentrate on the meanings and emotions expressed in them. Secondly, use breathing exercises to help your body gain a quiet rhythm just before the examination. Thirdly, channel all of your concentration into your pieces; let them live through you and enjoy allowing this to happen, for a sense of exhilaration comes when you are truly in tune with your work. Don't think about the effect you are having on your audience; of importance is the effect your pieces are having on you. Some candidates have an unfortunate habit of getting between their work and the audience – they draw attention to themselves. On one occasion I was examining a recital at which an audience was present. The candidate had only just begun when she stopped her performance and asked for a glass of water. This made her own needs of more importance than those of the poetry and instinctively one felt a barrier was caused which prevented full communication.

10.1.2 The examiner

The other person playing a role in this two-way interaction is the examiner. I've often thought of myself, as I pause for a moment between candidates, as a person who is waiting to be entertained. Other examiners use different expressions to describe this sense of expectancy: 'My job is to be a careful listener,' says one and another remarks that he looks forward to be interested by the candidate. These attitudes reflect the readiness of the examiner to respond to your performance. The examiner is also an adviser: he or she has to write a report stating how they see your work at the present time. The report, if it is balanced, will reflect the aspects of your performance one would wish to commend and where there is room for development. Most examiners have to write some notes during the performance, and a number of examiners have lengthy reports to compile which entail writing even whilst the candidate is performing. This practice is not ideal, but do rest assured that the examiner, through much practice, has become used to dividing attention between writing and the performance. He or she is aware of you, and that means visually as well as vocally. However, most examiners try to keep their writing to a minimum during the actual recital. The examiner is also an evaluator: they have been asked by the board they represent to award marks. These marks are as much a guide as the comments, and advice on 'reading' them is given later.

Different examiners vary in their understanding of their role. All should be welcoming. One will show this by a smile and a 'Good Morning!' when you come into the room and another will open the door and greet you whilst you are still outside the room, taking you in with him. Some boards have asked their examiners to adopt certain positions which can vary from an enthusiastic friendliness to a formal detachment, so the examiner's response to you will vary, but don't be put off for you really are welcome. After all, the examiner has usually made a long journey in order to meet you and to give personal attention to your performance. Remember that you are both going to share for a few minutes your common enjoyment of literature and drama.

It is worth pointing out at this juncture that at diploma examinations there are usually two or three examiners present. A diploma, of course, is a more challenging test than a grade examination and the presence of an extra person highlights that. The examiners will usually assess your work independently and when you have left the room they will compare their individual assessments, ultimately deciding on a joint mark which they feel accurately represents the standard of your performance. If questions are asked, they will normally divide these between themselves; in your answers you should reply to all of the examiners.

As I intimated above, different board expect their examiners to maintain different relationships with their candidates, and to conclude this section I give a summary of these expectations. You must, however, remember that each examiner is an individual and that primarily each will be him or herself, although adapting as far as possible to the requirements of their board. The Associated Board looks to the examiner to bring out the potential of the candidate; they must want the examinee to perform well; the examiner is a person who is 'with the candidate'. The New Era advised that the examiner must create an informal atmosphere, being friendly, encouraging and positive. The board makes the same point as I have: the examiner is a member of an audience who must respond to the work, giving feed-back to the candidate. The Guildhall School states that the examiner must be attentive to the candidate but not engage in unnecessary conversation: he or she is an observer giving an outsider's opinion of the performance. LAMDA looks to the examiner to be encouraging, friendly and enthusiastic, making, through discussion, a joint exploration of the candidate's pieces. The London College expects the examiner to be formal, efficient and unobtrusive: personal remarks or opinions about the work are not to be expressed. Mountview advises that the examiner is to be open to the candidate, enthusiastic and flexible in their approach to each individual. The Poetry Society sees the examiner as a person who wants the candidate to achieve their best and sets out to win their confidence. At the Royal Academy there is a panel of three examiners, which makes the situation more formal than in other examinations, although they are keen to put the candidate at ease. Trinity takes the view that the relationship of the examiner to the candidate is a formal one: the examiner is friendly but unfamiliar. These expectations of the various boards are helpful to candidates as they reflect the spirit in which the examination will be conducted; to be forewarned on this point is to be forearmed, and knowing in advance the atmosphere will help to give you confidence.

10.2 A TYPICAL SPEECH AND DRAMA EXAMINATION

10.2.1 Before the examination

I am going now to lead you through the solo speech and drama examination process step by step. Many of the points I shall make are small ones but they do help to ensure that you present yourself to advantage, and mastery of the sum total of these details can add up to an assured candidate giving a confident performance.

Let us begin a few days before the examination. By this time all of your real work will be complete: you have carefully planned your programme and rehearsed it; reading has been undertaken and you have regularly exercised your speech organs. At this stage in the adventure I think it is wise to recheck your knowledge of the words of the pieces you will perform. To be absolutely certain of these is imperative if your performance is to have the assurance that is necessary to gain a good mark. You should also ensure that you have a copy of your pieces for the examiner. Some candidates bring several books to the examination whilst others present each piece neatly written or typed on a sheet of paper. These are then put into a folder labelled with the candidate's name.

One word of advice is necessary here. If you make a copy of a poem do make sure it is in the format as it appears in print. Occasionally I am handed a hand-written poem arranged as continuous prose. This is useless as the form of the poem is important.

A couple of days before the examination it is a good plan to go through the process with your teacher. By this I mean the whole process: you will open the door, come into the room, present the text of your pieces and so on. You will perform the pieces to your teacher as well as presenting any ancillary elements in the examination such as improvisation or sight reading. It will be helpful to you if your teacher makes notes as you perform in the way that most examiners do, as candidates occasionally find this apparent lack of attention creates a barrier to their communication. An important element in this mock examination is the discussion or question time. I often find that students have not verbalized what they instinctively or subconsciously know, and are sometimes hard pressed to put knowledge into words during the examination. This pre-play is most helpful in sharpening up the verbalization process. I must not mislead any readers: I am certainly not advocating learning by rote definitions or information. The mock examination will finish with collecting up the books and wishing the examiner 'Good Day!' before leaving the room. 'Good Day!' is easier to use than 'Good Morning!' or 'Good Afternoon!': in a nervous state some candidates can't remember what time of day it is!

Let us think about your preparation of yourself immediately prior to the examination. Do try to get several early nights before your important day for this is a help with ease and relaxation. Avoid revising or rehearsing late into the night before the examination – that is counter productive.

What are you going to wear to the examination? We have already made some considerations about this in dealing with the selection of pieces in Chapters 5 and 6. Here I would like you to bear in mind a couple of new points. In order to be a good performer you need to be a confident performer and many people gain some of their confidence from their dress. If your recital demands your best suit or your dinner jacket and this gives you confidence, well and good. But if you are to perform active dramatic pieces, then this formality is unlikely to be suitable and you must dress according to the demands of the pieces. Similarly women candidates sometimes arrive at the examination room in a restricting kind of dress and high-heeled shoes. This may be unsuitable for performance.

Everybody needs to be well groomed. This means that you and your clothes must be clean. The face of any performer is of paramount importance. Some candidates, both men and women, present themselves with hair that partly covers their faces and especially their eyes. It is important that hair frames your face but does not hide it. Your eyes are your contact with your listener who also wants to see unhindered changes of expression on your face. It is important to remember this if, for one of your dramatic pieces, you wear a hat: make sure that it is well back on your head so that your face is neither obscured nor in the shadow of the brim.

Before you leave home make sure that you have with you your entry form, your pieces, notes and materials for a talk if one is to be given, any articles of token costume you may require, a change of shoes if needed and a handkerchief. Some people need to check that they have their spectacles with them. In the excitement I have known some, or even all, of these to be forgotten.

Set out for the examination in plenty of time. Nothing is worse than being caught in a traffic hold-up or on a train which is obviously late and knowing that you are going to have a rush at the last minute. Most boards stipulate that you should arrive fifteen minutes before the scheduled time and this is as much for your benefit as the examiner's. As you sit in the waiting room you may use the time to recall your relaxation as I explained in Section 9.2.1 and to steady yourself with some quiet breathing exercises.

10.2.2 In the examination room

The attendant will tell you when it is time to go into the examination room. As you walk in it is vital that you do so with confidence. From now on you are the person in charge of the situation and any decisions that are made must be yours. When I entered for one of my diploma examinations, although I had stage experience behind me, I found difficulty in feeling this confidence until one of my teachers gave me some good advice. 'As you open the examination room door,' she said, 'imagine that this door leads on to the theatre stage. The play has begun. Your audience is watching you. Now become one of the confident characters you are to play for the next half hour.' That worked!

Your first job is to sum up the possibilities of the examination room in relation to your performance: I am assuming that you are going to perform a poem, a prose excerpt and a dramatic piece. It is reasonably easy to make the initial decision on where you are going to perform your prose work. Ensure that you are in a good light – you would not, for example, perform with your back to a window – and you will bear in mind advice about leaving a 'no man's land' between yourself and the examiner so that there is a space through which you may project. Judge, too, whether you ought to change your position for the poem you are to speak; a slightly different background and posture will help to give variety to your recital. You will need, also, to sum up rapidly the possibilities of the room for your dramatic excerpt: this may involve you moving tables and chairs. Don't hesitate to change these around either before your recital starts, if the dramatic 'set' will not get in the way of the other pieces, or immediately before your dramatic excerpt. Simply tell the examiner, 'I would like to move a couple of things'. He or she will understand.

The examiner will be busy with a few administrative details, sometimes entering your name on an attendance sheet and probably wanting to make a note of your pieces. When the examiner is ready you will be asked to begin your performance. You may be told if there is going to be a break between each piece. If not, assume that you will work straight through your recital, creating a suitable pause between each item.

As a model let us look at Michael who has just taken his grade 6 examination. The introductory preliminaries over, he sat to one side of the room, and looked at the examiner. She was tall and thin with the slightly northern voice which had greeted him in a brief, friendly way when he came in. Having satisfied his curiosity about her, he looked around the room. It was large and rectangular and the examiner had her back to the bay window. He would, of course, perform towards her, but Michael realized that he would have to give especial concentration to his pieces as he could see people passing across the lawn outside. He decided not to disturb the examiner whilst she was writing but simply to place a chair, ready for his prose piece, at stage right centre and then he retired to his previous seat at the side.

'We will begin, please,' said the examiner, making Michael feel at home by this indication that she, too, was a part of the task in hand. Unhurriedly Michael walked to the centre of the performance area. 'The theme of my recital,' he announced, 'is "Fading Memories" and the first of these, my own choice, is a recollection of the boyhood of Dylan Thomas written by Daniel Jones.'

As he had planned he sat on the chair easily, thinking back to the past, the small house Thomas had lived in at Cwmdonkin Drive in Swansea. Reflectively, quietly, he began his piece:

> Five, Cwmdonkin Drive, and Warmley, the two houses were very different in atmosphere. At Dylan's we had a gas fire that spluttered, an asthmatic sheep that coughed in the field opposite, and always a few owls hooting in the wood . . .

Some of the sentiments Michael directed towards the examiner, and, although she was writing rapidly on his report, he knew that she looked up quickly from time to time in order to savour his performance. His piece drew to an end with its amusing climax. Michael delayed on this for a moment, knowing that immediately afterwards he must change the atmospheric gear in order to make a reality of the shadow world painted by Walter de la Mare. Getting up from the chair he stood beside it and, quite naturally, rested one hand on the traverse bar of its back. That change of posture was enough to break from a Welsh boyhood and arrive in a land of dreams and fantasy. ' "All that's Past" by Walter de la Mare,' and so he spoke the poem, lingering on its dreams which were 'tales told in dim Eden'. Quietly he spoke the last couplet with its reiterated sibilant suggesting the drowsiness of an era:

> . . . Silence and sleep like fields
> Of amaranth lie.

Again he knew that he must pause in this mystery he had created.

Then it was time to clear the stage for his dramatic piece. He stood at the front of the acting area and announced his final excerpt: 'From *A Midsummer Night's Dream*. Bottom, with his ass's head, and Titania are lying asleep at the front of the stage. Oberon, whom I play, decides it is time to end the mockery of their romance'. He felt that there was no need to explain about the role of Puck to whom he spoke, for his remarks to him would soon make the sprite's part in the episode clear. Walking to the rear of the performance area he assumed the character of the whimsical king. Turning, he saw in the distance the advancing figure and hailed him: 'Welcome good Robin. See'st thou this sweet sight'. Here was the cue to take the imagined Puck, or 'Robin', to the centre of the stage as together they looked at the incongruous pair of lovers sleeping. From instructions to Puck, through to the magic spell, Michael worked his way to the final endearing line of the piece, a line in which, tenderly, he could stoop to the sleeping Titania: 'Now my Titania, wake you, my sweet Queen'. For a moment Michael held the stage picture and then got up from his knees.

'Thank you very much.' The examiner's words were spoken in an impersonal voice. There was no hint of either approbation or criticism, it was merely an acknowledgement that the recital had finished. Michael returned quietly to his seat at the side of the room.

I hope you see from this particular candidate that you must be assured in your stage management and in your presentation. Of course, Michael's examination was not finished – a number of other items had to be covered. The first of these was the sight reading test. In Chapter 8 we thought about ways of preparing for this. Now let us watch the test in operation. Michael took the copy of the text from the examiner and sat down to consider it. Practice had helped to make his response to the text automatic. The reading was an extract from *Animal Farm* by George Orwell. As Michael scanned the piece he gained an impression of the content and he quickly sensed that the tone was satirical and overlaid with irony. A couple of sentences of dialogue – harsh words of command – gave an opportunity to introduce a variation of tone into the narrative. He knew that it was up to the examiner to ask him to begin. She was using the time to make some remarks on Michael's report and, without looking up, she asked him to start reading. Michael returned to the performance area, announced the title and, without hurry, went through his reading. Occasionally, especially when he wanted to emphasize points, or when he felt the dramatic activity of the narration warranted it, he looked at the examiner. Sometimes she was writing, at others listening intently to the piece. Towards the end of the excerpt, even though Michael guessed the examiner had listened to the piece many times, he made sure that he slowed the reading and gave a purposeful falling inflection to the final sentence. Again the examiner thanked the candidate and asked Michael to sit down.

The next stage of this particular examination consisted of a discussion and some theoretical questions. For the discussion the candidate was expected to know about the play from which he had performed an excerpt, the role he had undertaken, an appropriate costume for the character he had portrayed, as well as knowing about the author of the play. He was also expected to have studied literature of the period 1560–1660, concentrating on Shakespeare and two other writers selected by the candidate from a list given. Michael had chosen John Donne and Christopher Marlowe. You will notice that Michael had been wise to select a piece from a play by Shakespeare as, having to discuss that playwright's work, his area of study gained integrity. Marlowe was a contrasting playwright to Shakespeare and Michael's form at school had travelled to Stratford to see a production of his cruel farce, *The Jew of Malta*, so it was again wise to integrate this experience into his study. Furthermore Michael was expected to know about the authors of his prose and verse selections.

It soon became evident to Michael that the examiner, in her questions on literature, was attempting to discover where his interests lay and his responses to the works he had studied. Let us eavesdrop on the questioning. 'You have played the part of Oberon. Why do you think that Shakespeare introduces the romance of Oberon and Titania into *A Midsummer Night's Dream*?' Michael felt that the examiner wanted to ensure that he had a knowledge of the play generally. He pointed out that there were a number of romances shown in the play: that of Pyramus and Thisbe; that of the two pairs of runaway lovers; and that of Titania and Oberon. Each couple met with frustrations and difficulties and when they had surmounted these their affection for their respective partners was secured. The love of Titania and Oberon, on its fairy level, was one of these layers of romance and served as a foil to the others as well as a comment on them. The examiner went on to ask whether Shakespeare's plays were similar to Marlowe's. Michael thought of *Edward II*: obviously both men wrote history plays and they both wrote comedies; however, he realized from his visit to *The Jew of Malta* that this was blacker and more vindictive than Shakespeare's comedies. It was time to ask a question about Walter de la Mare. 'What have you noticed about the atmosphere of this writer's poetry?' Michael thought of several other poems he had read which made a mysterious uncertainty of people and places. Michael was surprised that there were no further questions on his literary studies for he was enjoying the encounter. Instead the examiner turned to technical points. The areas on which questions would be asked were listed in the syllabus and Michael had come to terms with these. 'In the prose description how did you achieve a contrast between the homes of Dylan Thomas and Daniel Jones' asked the examiner. Michael thought back to his prose recital and spoke of stress on relevant words, of changes of tone to convey the atmosphere of the two houses and the use of a pause in order to give a selected word prominence. Then the examiner asked Michael how he formed a 't' sound: a little puzzled by the query he explained about the articulation of his tongue tip with his hard palate and the resulting burst of air. The examiner appeared to be satisfied with the answer as she gathered up Michael's texts, returned them to him and thanked him for attending. Politely Michael in turn said, 'Thank you. Good day!' to the examiner and left the room. Like any candidate his thoughts were in a whirl and he felt it was impossible to guess how he had coped. His parents were in the waiting room and wisely they did not ask many questions about the experience; instead they took their son out to an enjoyable lunch.

10.2.3 The examiner in action

For a while attention has been on Michael but we must now change our viewpoint and look at the examiner, for many wrong suppositions exist about the way in which an examiner works and it is helpful to follow closely an examiner and her thoughts during the time that the candidate is in the room.

As Michael entered Mrs Hall was struck with his purposefulness. She was also conscious of the fact that she had only twenty minutes in which to examine this candidate, so there was no time to waste. Notes on the report sheet would have to be made during the candidate's performance and also whilst he was scanning his sight reading. In the course of her ten years as an examiner Mrs Hall had met something like two thousand candidates and therefore she had established in her head a clear notional standard for grade 6. Soon after Michael began she became aware that his tongue tip was not articulating strongly with the alveolar ridge, a fault which caused 't' sounds especially to disappear, and she made a mental note to ask him about this. Otherwise she approved of the prose piece: the performance sounded new and spontaneous; from the description he spoke she was able to picture the suburban streets of Swansea and she was impressed by the way in which Michael coloured through modulation Daniel Jones's writing. His lively interpretation merited more than a pass mark for that piece. The poetry speaking was not so competent. Certainly Michael managed to convey the mysterious grey atmosphere of de la Mare's world but the shape of the poem was sometimes lost as the candidate obviously found some difficulty in maintaining the linear rhythm. Even so, with its atmosphere, freshness and musical quality she felt that at this grade the poem would still merit a pass mark. The role of Oberon was excellently performed. Michael had summed up the dignity of the character, his plans for Titania were shared successfully with both Puck and the audience, his movement and gestures gave an indication of the costume he envisaged for the part, by his eye contact he created the reality of the sleeping partners, and his face instinctively registered his reaction to the hideousness of Bottom's 'transmorgrification'. Mrs Hall found that for much of the time she just sat back, entertained by Michael's acting. As the candidate looked at his sight reading Mrs Hall quickly jotted down some interim marks. Each piece carried a possible 20 marks, two-thirds of which (i.e. 13.33) was the pass mark. At this stage she thought that 16 should be awarded for the prose, 15 for the poem and 18 for the dramatic piece. Posture, gesture and movement as an entity carried 15 marks, as did each of voice production and enunciation. In his dramatic movement Michael was excellent and his posture during the other two pieces was very satisfactory and so Mrs Hall was able to award 14 for this. In producing his voice there was no difficulty with breathing and Michael used his resonators to good effect: 13 would be a just mark here. However, enunciation was not on occasions clear and Mrs Hall took the mark for this down to nine.

As she listened to his sight reading Mrs Hall realized that Michael was able to present the tone of the satiric writing as well as the content, an important part of the test. It was most fluent and the dialogue was kept within the bounds suggested by the rest of the reading. Furthermore the pace Michael had chosen suited the writing admirably. This was a commendable attempt and of a possible 15 marks she awarded 13.

Michael's knowledge of literature was impressive. He had profited from the work of his private teacher and of his English master at school with the result that he understood how literature worked. Mrs Hall realized that sadly she had only four minutes to spend on the questions and so she had to aim them at salient and embracive areas. Her question about the relationship of Oberon and Titania was indeed, as Michael had suspected, aimed at testing his knowledge of the play as a whole and she was delighted that Michael had taken the question further, seeing the relationship in terms of themes and structure. On the spur of the moment in order to eliminate a false divide between questions on the set pieces and those on Elizabethan and Jacobean literature, she ran questions on both areas together but kept in mind for mark purposes a clear differentiation. On coming to the theory she asked a question based on Michael's weak formation of unvoiced plosives, and then more positively she ploughed another theory question back into the area of the pieces by asking about emphasis. Mrs Hall was obviously a firm believer in relating theory to practice. Questions on pieces and literature were answered in a most satisfactory way and for each section she awarded 9 marks out of a possible 10. The theory questions gained 8 marks of a possible 10.

As well as jotting down tentative marks, by the time the examination was coming to a close Mrs Hall had also arrived at an overall 'impression mark'. First of all she considered in which category she should place Michael. Her experience told her here was work meriting a First Class Certificate. Honours was reserved for really exceptional candidates and she felt that until he had overcome his articulatory difficulty he could not be placed in that category. Her impression mark was confirmed by her analytical mark of 123 out of a possible 150. This mark was entered on the report sheet together with brief remarks under a number of headings. The sheet was not given to the candidate immediately but a few days later passed on to Michael by the local secretary for the board, a common practice. However, LAMDA examiners give the candidate a brief written report, together with the marks, immediately after the examination. A little later in the chapter we will look at Michael's report when we consider how this document should be 'read'.

10.3 COMMON FAULTS OF CANDIDATES DURING EXAMINATIONS

Michael was a competent candidate. Not all candidates match up to his standard and I would like to mention a few things that happen in the examination room which are not conducive to high marks. My first point is rather personal, I'm afraid, and is concerned with the appearance of the candidate. Both men and women, boys and girls, should make sure that their shoes, their clothes and their hair styles suit the performance they are about to give. Formal poems such as sonnets should certainly not be spoken in informal gear such as track suits or torn jeans. Similarly one can be dressed too formally for the performance, such as the small girls I have examined in the Irish Republic who present themselves in their first communion dresses. I find it disconcerting, too, when a dramatic piece is performed in bare feet – unless of course they should be bare – for in doing this you remove authority from the character: a young man paddling about the floor in his socks is not the Prince of Denmark and never will be.

'Where shall I stand?' is a question the examiner ought not to be asked immediately before the performance. That decision is up to the candidate and I have on a number of instances earlier given advice about this. Some candidates select an area immediately in front of the examiner's table in which to perform. This is particularly unfortunate if a dramatic selection is to be given. You need a divide in order to give yourself and the scene you are creating credibility and the examiner needs this distancing in order to see your performance properly. I have met candidates, too, who have imagined that the examiner is one of the characters against whom they are performing. This is wrong. The examiner is a member of a distanced audience and you must not think of him or her as sitting within the performance area. Sometimes candidates have rehearsed in a limited space and are then confronted with a large examination room. Unused to the luxury of space they rush about within the area wearing themselves out and forgetting that recital work ought to be presented on a limited scale.

Our memories are not impervious to forgetfulness. Some candidates feel that if they require a prompt they are sure to have failed their examination. Not at all! Many a professional actor needs a word of help. The problem for some is that they are not sure what to do if they forget their lines. 'Oh dear! I knew that last night!!' is not an aupicious interruption of an example of lyrical verse. Simply say quietly and firmly to the examiner, 'Prompt please,' and you will be provided with this or handed your copy of the text to look at if that would be more helpful. It is important that you get yourself onto an even keel immediately. Direct all of your concentration on to the piece. There is no point in creating a fresh hiatus because you are worried about the previous one!

When you arrive at the discussion or questions try to be friendly and open with the examiner. If you don't know a piece of factual information say so. Listen carefully to the examiner – often the remarks are a guide to the area you should be exploring. Try to indicate, especially in discussions, areas you would like to talk about. Sometimes an examiner suggests alternative ways of performing a piece and asks for the candidate's response to these. A candidate may become very defensive about the performance, whereas the examiner is looking for a person who is open to a number of interpretations and can discuss these intelligently. Don't be antagonistic to the examiner. Rest assured – he or she wants you to pass, sometimes more than the candidate does, I suspect! Avoid, too, repeating the questions. This can sound rude and it is time-consuming; in the short while available for a discussion you might as well use the time creatively in order to earn marks. On asking direct questions on theory, I have found some young candidates learn answers and definitions by rote. There is no value in this. You need to understand about technique and apply that to your performance so avoid the pat definition, especially if you don't know what it means.

10.4 MARKING THE CANDIDATE

10.4.1 Some misassumptions

The ways in which the examiner evaluates the work being presented are not always understood. The first bogey I would lay is that the examiner is confronting candidates with a desire to 'catch them out'! Nothing could be further from the truth. We have seen in this chapter that the examiner is for the candidate and makes evaluations in a postive light.

Another idea is that the examiner has some preconceived expectations about presentation. One of these is that one is looking for a voice which consciously, or self-consciously, reproduces beautiful vowel sounds. I have examined candidates who had obviously spent much of their rehearsal time in acquiring a highly artificial 'performance voice'. This resulted in unnatural and therefore un-interesting work and it was only when the candidates reached the sight reading, using their own unpolished but lively voices for this, that they revealed their vocal range and I gained an inkling of their vitality. The examiner is expecting you to bring life, interpretation, selectivity and clarity to your work; and certainly does not welcome an artificiality which robs your voice of these qualities.

A further imagined preconception of the examiner is that there are conventional and unchanging ways of performing one's pieces on stage. The surmise is that for poetry you must always stand and that you adopt a 'poetry-speaking stance' with your feet at 'ten-to-two', your back rigid and your arms held out a little way from your sides. All of this is nonsense. In this attitude tension is prevalent and it no more 'aids breathing', the reason often given for adopting the stance, than any other highly unnatural posture would do. Adopt whatever posture best serves the recital of your selection: this boils down to using your own judgment. Discernment is an important, credit-worthy element in awarding marks for interpretation.

A further misconception, and one that I've touched on earlier, is a misunderstanding of the term 'knowledge of literature'. Not all the blame lies on the candidate, for examining boards appear to be in doubt about *why* a knowledge of literature is desirable and what it should consist of. Far too many candidates plump for a potted biography of a few writers and hope that this will see them through. Meeting a writer's work, with the guidance of your teacher, is important and it is from this that one's appreciation of literature stems.

I know that there are misassumptions, too, about marking. When we were eavesdropping on Mrs Hall we saw that she arrived at an impression mark first of all and then broke that mark down into its components with the help of some running analytical marks. Don't worry about minor slips during the examination: the examiner is more interested in your overall performance.

10.4.2 Sample reports

I would like now to look at a couple of reports and see if we can 'read between the lines'. The report Michael received (see p. 201) was a detailed one and allowed the examiner to make a comment on each constituent of the examination.

Michael and his teacher were able to see from this in which genre Michael's strength lay – obviously his high mark for the dramatic selection highlighted his ability here. Marks for the pieces, together with the comments, also reveal an area on which he would have to work, the preservation of poetic form. This would be most important if he were to advance to a higher grade and speak a sonnet in this. The report also shows that there is an articulatory fault on which Michael must work; this he was aware of and so the criticism has a positive outcome. With a report as detailed as this it can be difficult for the candidate to distinguish the wood from the trees: I have underlined in my remarks some of the pointers the examiner has given the candidate.

Some reports, such as those of LAMDA and the Poetry Society are not subdivided. This has the advantage of allowing the examiner to select his

Piece	Possible marks	Marks gained	Remarks
Piece 1: Jones	20	16	I enjoyed your reflective approach to this work. You set a suitable narrative pace and yet allowed enough flexibility for us to feel that you were reaching into the past. Satisfactory posture.
Piece 2: de la Mare	20	15	Be careful to maintain and present the shape of your poem. Atmosphere successfully conveyed.
Piece 3: Shakespeare	20	18	Thoroughly entertaining. I feel you summed up the character of Oberon in this performance. Sensible stage management with an imaginative use of the available space.
Sight Reading	15	13	Highly fluent. A most competent reader: meaning clear; excellent audience contact.
Questions: pieces	10	9	An informed approach to the work and a genuine appreciation of the quality of the writing.
Questions: theory	10	8	Satisfactory answers on 'emphasis' and on formation of aspirate plosives.
Questions: literature	10	8	You have obviously enjoyed studying Marlowe's work. You avoid compartmentalizing Marlowe and Shakespeare and can appreciate their commonality and contrasts.
Voice Production	15	13	A projected voice. Tone quality to be commended.
Enunciation	15	9	Minor difficulties with several lingua-dental consonants.
Posture, gesture, movement	15	14	Pleasing informality during Piece 1. Movement and gesture used with expertise to capture the character and thoughts of Oberon in Piece 3.
Pass Certificate	100		
First Class Certificate	115		
Honours Certificate	130		Marks gained: **123**

You have gathered a wide range of material on your theme.

The excerpt from Black Beauty was rather long. Why not divide this into two and intersperse with other pieces? You brought genuine excitement to the verses from 'The Horses on the Camargue'.

I would have enjoyed your recital more if you had not read so much of it. Other than in the Roy Campbell piece there was a lack of performance quality. Texts are a help to you; they must not become a barrier.

A pleasing, clear voice.

Pass	65		
Credit	75		
Honours	85		
Distinction	90	Marks gained:	70

priorities, deciding what to mention in order to help the candidate to advance. Let us look at a typical Poetry Society report. The candidate, a ten-year-old girl has presented a Poetry and Prose Anthology at the junior advanced certificate level. It is permitted to use notes and texts in the examination although, as can be seen from the examiner's remarks, these can be a pitfall. Monica has chosen the theme of 'Horses' for her seven-minute anthology.

The examiner's time is limited by the number of candidates to be seen in a day and so only a few remarks can be made about the work presented; therefore the examiner here chose the points which seemed most important in helping the candidate make progress. In Monica's report (see p. 202) there is a balance of praise and criticism, finishing on a complimentary note. When she reads this she should ask, 'What is the examiner really saying to me?' The remark about *Black Beauty* is a minor hint on programme building. The important advice is in the next paragraph; what the examiner is saying is: 'Monica, for three-quarters of the time you were speaking the excellent material you have gathered, you stuck your head in your texts and gave yourself no chance at all to make contact with me. I suspect you have not done nearly enough preparatory work. You must think of your recital as a performance and present the work interestingly, entertainingly and with artistry to me.' The examiner may only write on the report what he *knows* to be the case. It is a fair guess that the selection from 'The Horses on the Camargue' was alive because Monica has learned the piece to speak at a festival a few days earlier. You may well ask, 'Why was Monica given a pass mark?' and again the answer to that is in the report. Although Monica was buried in her texts for much of the time, her voice was still clear and flexible. The prepartory work of compiling the anthology had been undertaken with care and the programming, apart from the intrusive wedge of the novel, was an imaginative compilation. On presentation the event fell down.

10.4.3 The examiner's advice

From these two specimen reports I hope you gain an idea of the need to sort out the critical advice so that you benefit from it. I would like to mention a number of other remarks examiners have to make with some frequency. Sometimes the advice is given: 'Select your pieces with care,' or it may be put in negative terms. This hints at a number of contingencies. It may mean that the pieces were not suited to your age. Occasionally adults perform pieces written for young children, and when I have queried this I have been told that the candidate is interested in giving recitals to children; that, however, is not the point of the examination. Candidates are expected to choose pieces commensurate with their age. To that end you will discover that most syllabuses contain, in the lists for junior grades, a couple of selections suitable for mature entrants.

Sometimes the remark refers to the gender of the speaker. A poem may be a lyric spoken by a female 'I' which, on the lips of a male speaker, sounds affected. Perhaps, instead, the examiner is suggesting that the chosen pieces are at variance with the vocal range or quality of the speaker's voice. These are all points to bear in mind when that brief remark appears on a report.

Another comment which is often penned is, 'This piece (or this recital) lacked spontaneity'. Again, there may be more than one application. The examiner may suspect that the candidate has been over-influenced by his teacher, and there are some teachers who provide a notional model of the way in which a given poem should be spoken and impose this on candidates. Or the cause of this lack of immediacy may be that the candidate has worked for too long on too limited a range of work: this can easily have a deadening effect on the pieces. It may also mean that the candidate lacks imagination: his or her own mind is closed to the poet's message and so the recital is nothing more than an inert repetition of words. To discover which of these is the cause would involve the examiner in the kind of probing it would be indecorous to undertake. He or she has simply to make the statement and leave the candidate and teacher to deduce the implications. Sometimes much the same statement is made by the examiner but using just the marks rather than comments: a candidate is given low marks for the pieces but gains higher marks for those elements in the examination which depend as much on native wit as on training.

A point examiners often have to make at diploma level is that the candidate lacks knowledge and discernment and possibly the entrant wonders in what area to be better briefed. 'All areas!' is the answer, for this charge is often levelled at the unsuccessful candidate who has not realized the wide-ranging demands of the diploma. This is the kind of person who suffers from knowing 'about' literature rather than having studied literary works and deduced principles of performance from this study. It is also the kind of person who compartmentalizes knowledge so that, having learnt that there are writers who use an epigrammatic style, does not realize the necessity to bring this knowledge to bear on mannered writing such as the plays of Oscar Wilde. For the candidate who is prepared to read literary works, study, and perform in a variety of media, the preparation for a diploma can be a challenge that is fun to surmount but unless one is prepared to undertake much work that simple statement, 'The candidate lacks knowledge,' can highlight an attitude which requires reorientation.

10.5 'UNSUCCESSFUL'

Almost everybody suffers the occasional setback and the day arrives when the post brings a report telling the candidate that in the examination he or she has been unsuccessful. How do you cope with this? Obviously you are disappointed for no one enjoys failing a challenge you have spent time and money on. An automatic response is to imagine that the examiner has in some way singled you out unfavourably: but examiners find failing a candidate dispiriting. The first thing to do is to look carefully at the report in which the marks and comments of the examiner will each tell you where your strengths and weaknesses lie. Note your strong points: these will not only cheer you up but will form a basis on which to build. List the weaknesses the examiner notes: some remarks are specific, such as, 'The candidate has not given the listener the argument put forward in this sonnet', or 'The candidate was unable to answer with accuracy questions on breathing'. These with practice and study you can rectify. Then note the general weaknesses. It may be the examiner has mentioned your lack of vocal range or writes of the paucity of your background knowledge to the Shakespeare selection. If the comment is in the nature of the former remark, much more patience and practice is needed before you retake the examination, and you must be prepared for this. If you do not wish to devote time and energy to gaining a technical mastery of this subject, you must make a decided break with speech and drama, for nothing will come of half-hearted dabbling. If the comment suggests that you are uninformed, then many of the books I have mentioned in the Resources section of each chapter will help you. Here again you need to discuss your study programme with your teacher. It may be that, on a regular basis, you need to summarize your expanding knowledge by writing a brief essay for your teacher to comment on even if you are not taking a written paper in the examination; the exercise is simply to help you clarify a subject which is often complicated and has many by-ways.

In the report, usually hidden in the mark, is an indication of the amount of time the examiner is suggesting you should spend on your studies before embarking on the examination again. A short-fall of five or six marks indicates that, whilst your work is not up to standard at the time of taking the examination, you can with reasonable speed, say about six months, expect to have raised your standards satisfactorily. A short-fall of ten marks or more means that a considerable amount of work is to be undertaken before you can successfully accomplish a retake. Only your teacher can properly advise you on the length of time this will take. It would not be within the examiner's remit to suggest that you take up another interest: sometimes, however, the mark suggests that this really is his advice and this, too, is worth talking over with your teacher. There is no point in continuing with a subject in which you show little aptitude or interest and another activity would probably offer you more fulfilment and enjoyment. There is, too, a possibility that your place is not in the examination room but with a theatre group, amateur or professional, back-stage or on-stage. In which case at least some of the skills and knowledge you have acquired will continue to serve you. So, in the light of your result, don't hesitate to change course if you feel that is proper.

10.6 TO THE SUCCESSFUL

What of those who pass? Your certificate or your diploma shows that at a certain time the representative of an examination board judged your work to be of a praiseworthy standard. However, if you stand still, you retreat. In order to maintain and raise that standard, involvement in drama is needed. Whether you teach, write about the drama, or direct, there is still a need to express yourself through performance regularly. In that way you keep alive your skill in communicating with your audience ideas, situations and characters which lie outside yourself.

10.7 OTHER EXAMINATIONS

The examination format I have described in this chapter relates to a solo performance in speech and drama examined by a representative of one of the private boards. I have selected this experience because it confronts the candidate with those difficulties I mentioned at the outset. Other solo examinations, such as public speaking, are less formal and the examiner tends to guide the candidate through the process.

Many of the matters I have raised here about solo performance also relate to duo and small group performance, for the candidates in these examinations are required to give an assured presentation in strange surroundings, although many candidates discover that in these, because they are acting with at least one friend, the strangeness of the experience is not so evident and inhibiting. What I have written here about preparation and personal presentation, the examiner's expectations and response, the use of the space available, discussion, reading the report and standards, are all pertinent to people entering for duo and small group examinations.

Candidates performing in the GCSE Theatre Arts and Oral Communication examinations do so in the familiar surroundings of their own school with their work marked by their teacher examiner. There is therefore little difference between the performance day and an everyday rehearsal, which removes much of the strain from the examination, although there is a danger that the event may lack 'occasion' and the sharpened performances arising from this.

Candidates who have opted for the acting skill in the A-Level Theatre Studies also enjoy the security of working at their home base, but they are visited by an examiner who views their work and holds a discussion with the candidates. Some of the material in this chapter, especially the sections relating to performance and the discussion, are of relevance to these students. Full reports are not supplied for the examinations conducted by the public bodies described in this and the preceding paragraph.

10.8 RESOURCES

10.8.1 For further study

Stirrup, A. (1978) *What do Examiners Want?* Education Supplies, Australia (obtainable from Samuel French, 52 Fitzroy Street, London W1P 6JR).

Pickering, K. *Speak the Speech*, Sound News Studios, 18 Blenheim Road, London W4 1ES (a series of six cassettes on which examiners from a variety of boards may be heard speaking about specific examinations).

11

An appraisal of speech and drama examinations

11.1 READERSHIP

The preceding chapters of this book have been written with students in mind. This chapter is different in as much as it is addressed to teachers and examiners, although I hope that diploma candidates will have gained that breadth of vision which will make the chapter relevant to them.

11.2 THE GROWTH OF THE PRIVATE EXAMINATION SYSTEM IN SPEECH AND DRAMA

In the last century the Royal Academy of Music began a system of examining external candidates in addition to the students who had followed taught courses in musical subjects at the Academy, awarding them grade certificates and diplomas. Examining spread from London to the provinces where numerous out-of-town centres were set up, visited by Academy examiners. Similar developments had taken place at the Royal College of Music and in 1889 these two London institutions combined to hold a nationwide series of examinations, an arrangement which continues to this day under the aegis of the Associated Board of the Royal Schools of Music. By the 1920s the Royal Academy, in addition to its music courses, ran a three-year course for intending teachers of speech and drama and it was only to be expected that, following the precedent set by the musical subjects, this too would be offered not only as an internal course but also as an external examination. There was a pleasing cohesiveness about the system. Professors who taught at the Academy, and there maintained standards, examined both the internal and external candidates, applying the same standards: the award of the external diploma was backed by the integrity of the teaching body.

In the course of time several other institutions which taught speech and drama also established external examinations, and in the early days of these a similar integrity was maintained. At the time of writing there are only three bodies, the Guildhall School, LAMDA and Mountview which offer both courses in speech and drama and also examinations which may be taken externally. In the case of the Guildhall School there is no evidence of an interaction of philosophy and standards shared between the teaching and the examining flanks of the institution; in the case of LAMDA dialogue ensues between the two sections and some in-service training is undertaken by the teaching staff; Mountview, a new examining body, offers an integrity of approach with a principal examiner also teaching on the courses. Other bodies, such as the London College of Music, have for many years offered examinations in speech and drama without the background resources of a teaching department in these areas to authenticate the awards. Some examination boards such as the New Era have an autonomous existence. Thus in the private sector of speech and drama examinations considerable variety of establishment and principle prevails.

11.3 SOME DIFFICULTIES IN THE PRIVATE SYSTEM

11.3.1 Standards

The state of affairs outlined above has several drawbacks. Firstly there is no agreed philosophy on the nature of the subject examined: 'What comprises the essence of speech and drama for this board? How, then, do we recognize the essential goodness exhibited within this? How do we make it credit-worthy?' Commonly agreed standards cannot prevail. As each board works independently of any other, fluctuations in standards are exacerbated. It has to be said that in practice this is not as unsatisfactory as it might be, and teachers can quote instances of their students entering for parallel grade examinations or diplomas of different boards and gaining much the same mark at each. The integral discipline of speech and drama helps to ensure that certain qualities within a candidate's work are recognized by examiners of different boards, and the ensuing parity of marks reflects a common awareness: most examiners are looking for a truthful interpretation of a text in which the mind and body of the candidate are brought into effective play in undertaking that interpretation.

11.3.2 What is drama?

The divorce between examining and teaching and the lack of agreement about the nature of drama leads to a second difficulty. In a survey I conducted, reported in *Speech and Drama* (Spring, 1986), about the admission requirements of the principal stage schools in the United Kingdom, a number of these claimed that they preferred applicants to have no training prior to entering the institution. Tutors spoke of the limited outlook, outmoded styles of performance, and lack of instinctive response to situations and text from which students suffered when they had been raised in a one-to-one private teaching situation. The demands of a series of examinations in drama appear not to bear a relationship to the demands stage school makes on a young person. Has the stage school an isolated notion of drama which is at variance from the examining board's isolated notion of drama? Are either aware of the drama that is happening in secondary education or in the theatre or even in everyday life?

11.3.3 Satisfying a demand

Thirdly, a large number of examining bodies have, as their catchment area, the pupils of a limited and contracting number of teachers. These teachers fall into two groups: there are those who undertake all of their teaching privately, working from a home base; and there are those who teach, usually on a part-time basis, in independent schools. A few state schools enter their pupils for the private sector examinations but compared with the total numbers in this sector the proportion is minute. Boards must, of necessity, supply teachers with the kinds of examinations they demand; if the revamped examinations of a particular board are not appreciated by teachers, then there are other boards to which the teacher is prepared to transfer candidates. Satisfying customer demand is an important determining factor in the construction of examinations. Is the customer in a position to appreciate developments in educational thought and changing views of drama? I must tread warily here, for I have a great respect for the sterling teaching given by many private practitioners. However, it is easy as a private teacher to become isolated and to be unaware of changes taking place in the theatre, in stage school and in education generally. For many teachers high marks in examinations are necessary if they are to maintain and expand their practice: parents can be over-easily impressed with high percentages. These factors can obviously militate against the raising of standards and encourage a resistance to changes in examinations. There is a danger that one kind of drama exists within the private sector, another kind which is examined by the public bodies, and a third kind which finds expression on the stage. Luckily some teachers have opportunities to break out of these constrictions as they undertake a number of stage engagements or television work, or they hold part-time appointments in stage schools and so gain the opportunity to meet new ideas about drama and their educational implications. Even so, it has to be admitted that for many there are few opportunities to gain a wider vision. There is a danger that if private examining boards become totally reliant on customer demand, only limited notions of drama will be reflected in their syllabuses.

11.4 ADVANCES IN THE EXAMINATION SYSTEM

There are signs, however, that some examining boards are becoming increasingly aware of the disadvantages that I have outlined and are making efforts to open the subject out, examining new areas of work, encouraging candidates to perform in groups and allowing more than the examiner-audience to watch the work. Let me single out several heartening examples.

11.4.1 Playing to an audience

Some boards have broken down the secrecy which surrounds examinations by allowing an audience to attend candidates' performances. Thus the candidate has more than a busy examiner to communicate with and in this is being given the opportunity to create a theatrical experience. Work at A-level may be witnessed by bona fide students. Recitals for the Poetry Society's gold medal are always held in public, and candidates attempting the George Rochford Porter award, described in Chapter 2, may opt for an audience to be present. Mountview, too, allows examinations to take place publicly and the constitutents of their performance grades, with their stress on dramatic presentation and mime, make an excellent vehicle by means of which young performers may challenge an audience.

11.4.2 Group drama examinations

Boards have become aware, too, of how isolated a candidate's work in performance can be, especially if neither the candidate nor the teacher appreciates the need to engage in some kind of group activity, and in consequence they are offering a number of examinations in which group performance is involved. These have been described in detail in Chapter 7. Sufficient to say here that the worthwhileness of these examinations depends on the opportunity to make them as theatre-based as possible and to allow a degree of informality in any subsequent discussion and evaluation. It is good, for example, that the Mountview holds group examinations in a studio offering the facility of stage lighting and the opportunity to make up, both of which help candidates to work within a creative atmosphere. Boards, mindful of the cost of time, are not always willing to allow the examiner the opportunity to hold a detailed discussion with the candidates on their presentations and this detracts from the worth of the examination. LAMDA is to be commended in as much as after the group mime examination the examiner gives the performers a verbal evaluation of the work presented. This allows for a more detailed approach and an exchange of ideas.

11.4.3 New possibilities

Who are speech and drama examinations really aimed at? Responses would differ. Some would claim that only children with examination potential should enter;

others would argue that drama is so tied in with the play and learning processes of children that it is a subject for which all children should have the opportunity to enter, and that if our notions of what is acceptable do not correspond with the kind of material children are naturally capable of presenting, then our sights are wrongly set.

What of the child who in some way does not correspond to the norm? He may be 'abnormally' gifted or intelligent, in which case his uniqueness would not be seen as a bar to candidature at a drama examination; but what if he is physically disabled, or dyslexic, or epileptic, or deaf? Ought these difficulties to be an automatic barrier to taking part in a drama examination? A development I would mention attempts to posit an answer. At its examinations in Spoken Poetry, Prose Reading, Original Poetry and the Group Programme the Poetry Society has instituted an introductory grade which is seen as a starting point for 'those who need to build future confidence'. There are various reasons why confidence should be boosted and the teacher must support the candidate and declare why he or she is applying to take the introductory certificate. This arrangement allows a young person who struggles against the odds in many walks of life to take a speech and drama examination without the risk of rejection. The work is accepted within the candidate's capabilities. This is a quiet, unspectacular development within the examination system but it is a highly significant challenge to our notions of 'success' engendered by it.

11.5 SPEECH AND DRAMA EXAMINATIONS IN THE STATE SECTOR

There is no lengthy history of speech and drama examinations in the state sector of education. Only over the past twenty years have they become established, and at the time of writing candidates are able to enter for the GCSE in Oral Communication as part of their English studies, the GCSE in Theatre Arts and, at a higher level, the A-level in Theatre Studies.

Although there is no stipulated course in Oral Communication, regional boards offer suggestions on which a syllabus may be based. These tend to encompass role play, improvisation, simulations, informal and formal talks and readings of various kinds. With this range of work available it is a pity that the examination test for some boards is funnelled down to a brief talk followed by a discussion. Hopefully a more inspired examination reflecting the spread of the work of the two previous years will eventually ensue.

Both the GCSE Theatre Arts and the A-level in Theatre Studies, as their titles imply, are theatre-based examinations. The GCSE allows options to be selected from a range of interrelated work. A welcome inclusion is the opportunity for candidates to visit live entertainments in their manifold forms and to keep an analytical logbook of these. Too often young students channel all of their energy into performance and forget that there is a need, too, to watch and evaluate. There is a substantial study element in drama at A-level, and the practical work, individually, in pairs and in groups, tends to arise tangentially out of the studies. In an attempt to prevent work becoming narrow the Associated Examining Board diverts the choice of students to works beyond the set texts when they select their practical pieces, so that an integrity of study and practice is difficult to maintain. This seems short-sighted, for practical work often illuminates study and helps theatrical history and literary texts to become living realities.

It is surprising that, at a time when improvisation, role play and simulation games are accepted as the essence of drama in the secondary school, these two examinations should be directed trenchantly towards the stage. Are there not times when work for examination purposes should be informed by non-literary and non-theatrical dramatic elements? Perhaps this question may eventually prompt the establishment to a new kind of examination in which performance is not bound to a conventional notion of theatre but is a joint sharing by candidates and examiner of a theme or a problem experimentally explored through the practice of drama.

A noteworthy social change brought about by the GCSE in Oral Communication and Theatre Arts is the break with the tradition that an examination in an aspect of speech education is an elitist preoccupation. Nowadays all children, however lacking they may appear to be in aptitude, may enter for these two examinations. If the assessments were only of individuals this would present few problems but in both examinations candidates are viewed as members of a group. This obviously can introduce tensions into preparatory classroom work and eventually lead to difficulties during the examination. To give an example: in assessing Oral Communication I have found my task complicated when several candidates in a group have set out to diminish the contribution of one of their peers during the test. Such behaviour can too easily throw a candidate off-keel.

11.6 EXAMINERS

The role of the examiner is at present in a state of flux. The more formal private boards would contest that remark: as always the examiner evaluates; he or she is a distanced visitor whom the candidates don't know personally and must remain as such; there is, if the board has provided one, a set of criteria which may be applied to the work presented by the candidates; examiners too, have personal notions of the standards of the board for which they work. Other private boards see the examiner in more human terms and these are the boards which favour a lessening of formality. I remarked in the previous chapter that representatives of the Poetry Society and of the Associated Board saw the examiner as a person who won the confidence of the candidate, wanting each to give of their best. There is an obvious divide between this view of the examiner's role and that held by the

Guildhall School and the London College of Music of a person saying little and carefully maintaining a distance between the candidate and the evaluator.

Examiners contribute much to the successful image of an examining body. On some boards their opinions and advice shape the examinations which are offered; other boards have little converse with their examiners on matters of policy.

What kind of people become examiners? On several boards the examiners are representatives of the teachers who enter candidates for examinations: they are chosen from successful teachers. On one board, a conservative and elderly collection of people for the most part, the local representatives, many of whom have an external diploma of the institution and who have organized the local examinations in their home area for years, are invited to the board as a mark of esteem. There are disadvantages in such a practice as the board becomes staffed by people of narrow experience. In contrast the Poetry Society selects examiners from a wide range of suitable people and on the board are teachers whose sphere of work ranges from the primary school to adult education, actors, poets and broadcasters; the training that each has received, too, is wide-ranging, encompassing university, stage school, speech therapy and experience in the theatre and broadcasting. Examiners usually serve an apprenticeship, tailing several established examiners and, after watching them at work, examining for several sessions in conjunction with them. Some boards hold an annual meeting of examiners in which procedural problems are sorted out: however, in these meetings there is scant opportunity to discuss matters of fundamental importance or to increase the examiner's awareness of the teaching and practice of drama. Some boards argue that there is no need for inservice development: some examiners are in employment connected with a branch of dramatic activity, often teaching, and, it is claimed, any further training would be supererogatory. A refreshing change from this attitude is that of LAMDA: here training days for examiners on such subjects as the Alexander technique, mime, and Shakespeare in performance have been held, staffed by tutors from the stage department. Examiners on many boards are members of the Society of Teachers of Speech and Drama which, through its annual residential courses, day conferences and regional meetings enables its members to work with other professionals, as well as to reconsider from time to time the place of drama in today's educational system. Allowing for this kind of continuing education there is still a need for some boards to consider the desirability of closely focused developmental sessions. After all, examiners hold a highly responsible position.

In the state system the role of the examiner is somewhat different. At GCSE level a teacher examiner, one of the staff of the school, is appointed to be in charge of the examining of the subject he or she represents. Other teachers may assist. His or her task is shaped by a visiting assessor who arranges several agreement trials at which local teacher examiners meet in order to come to terms with the marking standards expected by the GCSE regional boards. An elaborate and reasonably successful system of moderation is undertaken. Thus, teachers are examining candidates whom they themselves have taught and the notion of the examining stranger is challenged. This arrangement applies to both Theatre Arts and Oral Communication.

At A-level visiting examiners are used. In assessing theatre skills their task is a traditional one. When the group project is assessed, the course tutor advises the visiting examiner on the areas of work for which each of the group has been responsible, and the tutor grades, for the benefit of the examiner, the way in which candidates have met their respective responsibilities. The majority of the personnel examining in A-level are themselves tutors in tertiary education and often teaching the Theatre Studies course, although they do not examine their own students.

In the state system a further notion is challenged. No longer are examiners expected to hold superior qualifications or to have wider experience than teachers and tutors whose students they evaluate. Indeed, as we have seen, at GCSE level the examiner is evaluating his or her own students. The extent to which this is dictated by financial expediency could be debated.

11.7 ADVICE TO CLIENTS

Each board has a responsibility to the teachers who enter candidates and this is discharged in various ways. The most widely disseminated method of contact with teachers is the syllabus. Some boards make this more than a formal statement of their requirements; advice is given to both teachers and candidates. The Associated Board slips an insertion into the syllabus for this purpose, LAMDA gives helpful notes on the marking system, and the Poetry Society gives both a philosophical statement and detailed advice on each of its examinations. The regional GCSE boards publish booklets for teachers on the Theatre Arts course, and the Associated Examining Board offers a most helpful booklet on the Theatre Studies course and examination. These are additional to the syllabuses.

Several syllabuses contain bibliographies and of special value are those compiled by Trinity College and the Guildhall School. The latter also publishes a series of pamphlets varyingly helpful to the candidate, written by members of the examining board.

Some boards, amongst which may be mentioned LAMDA, the London College and the Poetry Society, also hold one-day conferences for teachers from time to time at which practical advice is given and at which teachers are informed of future developments. Suggestions made by teachers at these sometimes influence the availability of examinations. For instance, the request for the Poetry Society to reinstate an examination in the speaking of Shakespearean blank verse has resulted in a trial return of this examination.

11.8 ACCREDITATION

The various private examining bodies work with complete autonomy. Amongst them there is no agreed parity of standard, no agreement on the kind of person who should be an examiner, no agreed policy on the criteria for evaluation, no common consideration of what is the *raison d'être* of the various boards. Nor is there an exclusivity in the right to examine. Anyone can set up an examining board in speech and drama and issue certificates and diplomas. What then is the currency – certificates and diplomas – of the various boards worth? In order to award a drama degree a college of higher education has to allow its staff, facilities, courses and students to be scrutinized by various panels of experts set up by the Council for National Academic Awards. A drama school, if its courses are to be acceptable to the theatrical profession, must be scrutinized by the National Council for Drama Training. No similar safeguard of standard and integrity exists amongst the private awarding bodies. Are candidates being short changed? In an attempt to get boards to think seriously about this lack of accountability I spoke with administrators about the possibility of the scrutiny of examinations by either an external body or by a confederacy of representatives of the institutions. All of the officials stated that such an external guard would be unwelcome and the system unworkable, and several bodies pointed out that an accountability already existed – to their clients. That clients referred more often to teachers than to candidates was illuminating, for it is they who guide the majority of candidates to a particular board, aware of the different strengths and weaknesses of each. The difference of outlook of the various boards is a factor which is evidently appreciated, rather than criticized, by teachers and there is a fear that an umbrella regulator would introduce an unwanted blandness to the examinations under offer.

A validation process exists for examinations in the state system. These are carefully considered by panels set up by the Secondary Examinations Council. The areas considered at the panel meetings on which I have served have included the content of examinations, the marking system, and the range and cohesiveness of both the course and the examination. In addition to the SEC, county drama advisers (a post occasionally, and not totally successfully, subsumed within that of the English adviser) have a watching brief on the drama teaching within their authority, and they are also responsible for organizing, sometimes through liaison with teachers' centres and colleges which undertake initial teacher training, inservice and short courses. Thus teachers in state education, and we have seen that many combine this role with that of an examiner, have regular opportunities in the vicinity of their work to pursue through courses and workshops a continuing education. Although not formally part of the accreditation system this is an important element in ensuring that the teaching and examining within drama course is of a creditable standard.

11.9 THE FUTURE

Drama is used in a growing number of contexts. We see it employed in language teaching, in training for management, in hospital and day centres as psychodrama and drama therapy, as a method of teaching, as a means of expanding forms of theatre such as street entertainment, agitprop, dance and music theatre, and in the combination of textual and non-literary trends exemplified in a company such as the Mediaeval Players. Examination boards must become more aware of the breadth of work accomplished under the title 'Speech and Drama' and respond to current need by examining and evaluating a wider range of activity. Occasionally it would be good to see a board become part of the drama vanguard promoting new and exciting forms of examination which give something to both the theatre and the community.

Perhaps this widening vision and a desire to lead could be achieved by a closer liaison of the private and public examination bodies. Each holds different views of the drama process: if only each sector took cognizance of the other the pair would discover ways in which their work is complementary. A dialogue is not an impossibility!

Liaison between boards is only a beginning. At present a plethora of polarized views of drama is held. For some it consists of a learning process in which an end product is of no interest; others see drama as a way of making a new creative statement free from the trammels of text or scenario; for some drama is an onslaught on right-wing sensibilities, a cruel activity which shocks; and, of course, for some drama is the representation of preformulated ideas and words. Various umbrella organizations mushroom, under whose shade numerous drama and theatre organizations group themselves; unfortunately this is the sheltering of the like-minded, a comforting huddle in which prejudices can be reinforced. Genuine dialogue amongst people of divergent views is desperately needed so that practitioners may gain a total prospect of the range of views and activities which constitute this strangely unwieldy entity called 'speech and drama'. Only then can we begin to share an understanding of the worth of drama's constituent parts and from the basis of this integrated concept project a means of evaluation. We can come out of the corners we so zealously guard, casting aside the weight of moribund tradition and reified opinion, so that performance may be opened to a wider range of people and conditions than we dare consider possible at the moment.

Index